Autocracy and Health Governance in Russia

Vlad Kravtsov

Autocracy and Health Governance in Russia

palgrave
macmillan

Vlad Kravtsov
Department of Political Science and Law
Spring Hill College
Mobile, AL, USA

ISBN 978-3-031-05788-5   ISBN 978-3-031-05789-2 (eBook)
https://doi.org/10.1007/978-3-031-05789-2

© The Editor(s) (if applicable) and The Author(s), under exclusive license to Springer Nature Switzerland AG 2022

This work is subject to copyright. All rights are solely and exclusively licensed by the Publisher, whether the whole or part of the material is concerned, specifically the rights of translation, reprinting, reuse of illustrations, recitation, broadcasting, reproduction on microfilms or in any other physical way, and transmission or information storage and retrieval, electronic adaptation, computer software, or by similar or dissimilar methodology now known or hereafter developed.

The use of general descriptive names, registered names, trademarks, service marks, etc. in this publication does not imply, even in the absence of a specific statement, that such names are exempt from the relevant protective laws and regulations and therefore free for general use.

The publisher, the authors, and the editors are safe to assume that the advice and information in this book are believed to be true and accurate at the date of publication. Neither the publisher nor the authors or the editors give a warranty, expressed or implied, with respect to the material contained herein or for any errors or omissions that may have been made. The publisher remains neutral with regard to jurisdictional claims in published maps and institutional affiliations.

This Palgrave Macmillan imprint is published by the registered company Springer Nature Switzerland AG

The registered company address is: Gewerbestrasse 11, 6330 Cham, Switzerland

Preface

That effective health governance is crucial to social betterment is acknowledged by Vladimir Putin. Still, to date, Russia has failed to reach the point when any meaningful breakthrough in the health sector is undeniable. Most success stories are borderline fake, and it is getting difficult for the regime to conceal its disastrous response to the coronavirus epidemic that hit Russia disproportionally hard. Why and how does it happen? This investigation reveals that the Russian personalistic regime lacks an institutional setup that could compel elites to refrain from pursuing self-interest and, instead, serve in society's interest as a whole. The enduring patterns of behavior are best described as a system of personalized exchanges or bargains between the ruler and the ruled, including populace, key political actors, and governance intermediaries alike. Such an institutional setup has far-reaching consequences for the quality of governance. Ultimately, personalistic regimes cannot develop a rational system of incentives that would stimulate principals, elites, state administrators, and societal intermediaries to work impartially for the population's welfare. This arrangement is detrimental to health governance but is likely to persist as long as actors' plans are consistent with each other.

The book promotes learning and debates across three strands of literature and appeals to advanced undergraduates, academics, and public health practitioners. For comparativists, the manuscript highlights specific mechanisms and practices through which authoritarian, personalistic regimes govern health. This investigation could serve as the basis for a new research program on varying ways in which different types of nondemocratic regimes generate governance practices in health. It is my hope that this research orientation will structure new debates. For students of global health studies, the book fills the often lamented gap about the lack of political explanations for health governance in authoritarian regimes. The scholars of health governance will be intrigued by my analysis of why and how personalistic and authoritarian regimes fail to attain collective (social) goals, promote social justice, and work for health equity. For Russianists, the book offers detailed empirical descriptions and in-depth analyses of a wide array of health governance episodes. Also, the book provides an analytical framework of bad governance rooted in the rational institutionalist tradition and connected to competence-control theory. Let's not forget about the non-academic world of readers. Policy entrepreneurs need this perspective to understand the underlying political determinants of health, redress their strategies accordingly, and deploy their advocacy tactics more effectively. Writing this book, I also tried to give a general readership interested in how Russia works a sense of the mindset of the key political players and the regime-induced constraints under which elites operate.

Portions of the resented research appeared in a variety of academic settings, mostly during several panel sessions at the Annual Conventions of the International Studies Association, International Studies Association-South, and Alabama Political Studies Association. I would like to thank Roger A. Coate, Alex Ruble, Simon Rushton, Owain D. Williams, Nicholas David Thomas, Jaclyn Bunch, and Pamela Zeiser for their insightful comments regarding my earlier ideas that found their way into this manuscript. In addition, I thank Dr. Lisa Hager and Harold Dorton for the course releases in Spring 2021 and Spring 2022 that allowed me to spend more time on writing and research. Most of all, I thank Michelle McDevitt.

This book is for Alexey Navalny, the Berlin Patient, who sacrificed his health and freedom, hoping to make Russia a better place.

Mobile, USA   Vlad Kravtsov

Contents

1	**Personalistic Regimes and the Processes of Governance**	1
	Introduction	1
	Russia's Electoral Authoritarianism Under Personalist Rule: Essential Features	5
	Governance in Putin's Russia: Optimizing Responses and Undesirable Outcomes	12
	The President Promises: Providing Public Goods in the Electoral Autocracy	14
	Bureaucrats Endure: Maintaining Patronage vs. Improving Performance	16
	Intermediaries Retreat: The Weakness of Oversight and Organizational Atrophy	20
	Elites Adapt: Over-Compliance and Gaming Strategies	23
	Summary: Sustaining the Negative Equilibrium	26
	Research Approach	28
	Next Steps	31
	References	33
2	**Providing Goods: Health Mandates and Authoritarian Performance**	41
	Introduction	41
	Personalistic Legitimacy: Plenteous Promises and Faulty Mandates	43

	Decommodification of Medicines: Benevolent But Not Efficient	49
	Substituting Imports: Far-Flung Changes with Few Benefits	53
	Spending Priorities: Resources for Mega-Projects, Austerity for All	60
	Benevolent President: Providing Particularized Goods	67
	Conclusion	71
	References	72
3	**Managing Actors: Faulty Controls and Flawed Performance**	79
	Introduction	79
	Faulty Controls: Patronage, Mandates, and Networks	81
	Bureaucrats Endure: Deficits of Quality and Excesses of Loyalty	88
	Creating Privileges: Powerful Firms, Poor Services	93
	Officials on Autopilot: HIV/AIDS Crisis as a Nonpriority	100
	Conclusion	108
	References	109
4	**Constructing the Oversight: Organizational Atrophy and Particularized Exchanges**	115
	Introduction	115
	Police Patrols: The Pathologies of Internal Oversight	118
	Fire Alarms: The Weakness of External Oversight	126
	Oversight and Quasi-State Organizations: All-Russian Popular Front	130
	Oversight and Professional Organizations: National Medical Chamber	136
	Oversight and Nongovernmental Organizations: Repression and Tolerance	140
	Conclusion	144
	References	146
5	**Securitizing the Epidemic: Ideological Adaptations and Illiberal Meanings**	153
	Introduction	153
	Elites Adapt: Illiberal Meanings and Corporate Vulnerability	156
	FSKN: HIV/AIDS as a Case of Narcoagression	166

Minzdrav: Securitization as a Gaming Strategy	170
ROC: Securitization for Rechurching	175
Were Alternative Responses Feasible?	180
Conclusion	183
References	184

6 Conclusions, Implications, and Dashed Hopes — 189
Introduction — 189
Is (Moderately) Optimistic Assessment Warranted? — 192
Additional Perspectives on Bad Governance — 197
   Kleptocracy and Governance in Russia — 198
   Neoliberalism and Russian Health — 201
   Implications for the Securitization Debate — 206
   Looking for a Bigger Picture — 208
Conclusion: Will it Get Better? — 211
References — 215

Bibliography — 221

Index — 253

CHAPTER 1

Personalistic Regimes and the Processes of Governance

All institutions are subordinated to the main task -- confidential communication and interaction of the supreme ruler with citizens. Various branches of government converge on the leader's personality; [they are] considered a value not in and of themselves, but only to the extent that they provide a connection with him. Besides, informal communication methods operate around formal structures and elite groups.
   —Vladislav Surkov, 'Dolgoe gosudarstvo Putina,' Nezavisimaya Gazeta, 2 November 2019.

It seems to be simple: just do your duty, do your job efficiently and have a direct connection with people... But at the same time, this is the most difficult thing because the ultimate success depends on whether or not there is trust in the government... Depending on whether there is trust, the support from people either emerges or lacks. And if there is no support, then there is no result.
   —Vladimir Putin, an exclusive interview to Irada Zeinalova, NTV, June 23, 2019.

INTRODUCTION

Many people worry about the quality of and access to healthcare, and the blatant disregard of people's health needs could be politically costly. Not surprisingly, for nearly two decades, Russian authorities spent much effort and considerable sums of money to improve health administration.

© The Author(s), under exclusive license to Springer Nature Switzerland AG 2022
V. Kravtsov, *Autocracy and Health Governance in Russia*, https://doi.org/10.1007/978-3-031-05789-2_1

Vladimir Putin compared himself to "a slave in a galley" and St. Francis, who "daily hoed" the area that the Lord had allotted to him, and he consistently evoked these two self-seeking images to indicate his commitment to advance people's interests. Putin's entourage, including the State Duma's speaker Vyacheslav Volodin, portrayed Russia's president as a triumphant champion of national welfare but conveniently skated over the fact that social problems in the country persisted or, in some instances, worsened. On the eve of the Putin regime's bi-decadal anniversary, the health balance sheet is indubitably not in the Kremlin's favor. Put broadly, Putin's rule ushered massive problems, including health inequalities, and exacerbated general degradation of health quality and management. The flurry of health reforms and dense regulatory activity of 2012–2020 failed to bring positive health outcomes and wrecked good governance, perhaps beyond repair. Regardless of the Russian government's efforts, most success stories are borderline fake. Disillusioned with the Kremlin's ability to govern effectively, the leading Russian experts in healthcare management recommended terminating any further reforms in the health sector (Shishkin et al. 2018). Importantly, perpetual problems with health governance implicate not so much individual administrators' competence as a root of the problem as the regime in general. The question is, how did it come to this?

In post-communist Russia, arguments in favor of nondemocratic mechanisms of development find many proponents. For instance, Andranik Migranyan, a notorious opinion leader, has argued for the need for the iron fist in all political action and governance (Migranyan 2004; see his foundational interview published as early as 1989). Still, no matter how well autocratically inclined politicians and opinion leaders rationalize and justify the advantages of authoritarian rule (Jones 2019), the myth of authoritarian effectiveness has been rightfully debunked (Rodrick 2010; Yasuda 2017; Thomson 2019; Huang 2020; Pan 2020) and the misplaced belief in state autonomy as a necessary condition for modernization demolished (Geddes 1994). By definition, authoritarian regimes rest on political insiders' privileged access to power and institutions, and thus not only do autocracies stymie a broad distribution of power in society, but they tend to impoverish people as well (Acemoglu and Robinson 2019). It is safe to assume that autocrats are not very good at providing public goods and services (Lake and Baum 2001), but we still do not know much about the distinctive ways in which nondemocracies beget inefficient governance systems and how and why they fail to effectuate mechanisms of solving crises of governance at home. The finding that "[p]olicy changes are the easiest to agree to in personalist dictatorships" (Ezrow and Frantz 2011: 115)—as intuitively accurate it may be—still does not shed enough light on the quality and mechanics of authoritarian governance.

This book answers a call to move beyond analyzing how different nondemocratic regimes "maintain or lose power to a consideration of how they make policy" (Taylor 2014: 226). In particular, this chapter relates the main characteristics of governance in Russia to the core features of the Russian variant of authoritarianism, defined as electoral authoritarianism under personalistic rule. Reformulating North's (1990) insights, the noun "governance" describes the set of tools through which principals and agents deliver fundamental goods and services as delimited by the endogenous, optimizing responses of key political actors to their institutional setting (political regime). Because not all authoritarian regimes are made similar, the big question is how, why, and with what consequences distinct types of nondemocratic regimes, which are recognizably different from each other, generate and shape observable social practices in health. New debates could be structured around this program (e.g., Yildirim et al. 2022 make a similar call for the study of military regimes, although they prematurely note that the effect of regime type on policy agendas is overstated).

The central argument for understanding bad governance in Russia is that in many post-communist states health administration is bound to personalistic authoritarianism. The features that inhere in a personalistic rule circumscribe the effectiveness of all governance action in the country. The adjectives "good" or "effective" describe the extent to which the state plays the role of wealth maximizer for society and "state officials are true civil servants, working for the public good in a fair way, rather than pursuing primarily personal or elite interests" (Taylor 2011: 4). This book is the first attempt to systematically investigate the underlying authoritarian mechanisms that damage health administration and fail at improving health outcomes. It adds value to health politics literature by laying bare personalism's hidden workings that trigger Russia's poor state of health and exposing challenges global and local health entrepreneurs face. Today, we hear plenty about the Kremlin's hostility to its political opponents, but we often overlook how it hurts ordinary people, who deserve more than they receive. This book will take readers through the story of how Putin's personalism strives to survive while it impedes competence, efficiency, and justice in Russia's health sector.

An essential lesson is that multiple shortcomings of the enacted health policies and the failure to correct the faulty course of action are sequelae of personalistic regimes, not rare errors individual regulators make. Personalistic regimes endanger health, and we need to understand how their health governance mechanisms function. I contend that the failure is by design; because personalistic regimes rely on personalized exchanges or bargains instead of impersonal rules and permanent organizations, all actors put self-interest ahead of patients' needs. The described arrangement is detrimental to health governance but is likely to persist as long as actors' plans are consistent with each other, and thus far no exogenous shocks (such as macroeconomic shifts, external economic sanctions, or the unexpected and unprecedented spread of COVID-19) has been able to change that.

Health governance will continue to be deeply flawed as long as the control of the state remains in the hands of few; bad governance practices, the so-called "spoliation," are the logical outcome of the regime's institutional design. In the long term, personalistic rule will undermine state capacity and lead to the significant under-provision of health goods and services below the reasonable level. It is safe to assert that Russia has evolved to become less a contractual (i.e., a state that provides public goods and services) than a predatory (a coercive and extractive state that promotes the particularized interests of dominant groups within the state) state (on definitions consult Evans 1995: 12; Vahabi 2016, 2020). On balance, the regime's ability to deliver tangible, not faked, breakthroughs is limited.

This chapter proceeds as follows. First, I highlight the regime's primary features that make Russia institutionally different from other authoritarian regimes. Second, through an examination of personalized contracts and optimizing responses—with their roots in self-interested behavior fostered by the regime—I present my main argument: how and why personalistic regimes impede good governance. The third section discusses my research approach, while the last one outlines the main themes for the rest of the book, chapter by chapter.

Russia's Electoral Authoritarianism Under Personalist Rule: Essential Features

All authoritarian regimes concentrate power, severely limit access to politics—defined as an institutionalized struggle for power—and maximize economic and cultural levers of power.

Russia is authoritarian, but not all authoritarian regimes are made similar. The literature proposed different ways of classifying nondemocratic rule (Wintrobe 1998: 7–15; Haber 2008: 694). As Linz and Stepan remind us, "Typologies rise or fall according to their analytic usefulness to researchers" (Linz and Stepan 1996: 39), and the proposed research program will perforce have to justify how and why it breaks down the broad analytical category of "authoritarian regime" into its specific variants. Authoritarian regimes differ in the ways they legitimize themselves and how they concentrate, maximize, and transfer political power (on the insightful discussion of the typology and the underlying variables, see Ezrow and Frantz 2011: 8–23; Gandhi 2008: 1–39). Autocracies could be institutionalized via political parties (Magaloni 2006: 32–41; Stromseth et al. 2017) and professional military and security apparatus (Cook 2007; Svolik 2012: 123–161; Kandil 2016; Gürsoy 2017; Klein and Vidal Luna 2017); they can rest on traditionalistic (Linz 2000: 144–151) and neopatrimonial (Bratton and van de Walle 1997: 61–96) foundations; and they even can belong to a variety of "gray zone" or hybrid regimes with different degrees of political pluralism which Lucan Way labels "democracy by default" (Way 2015). This section describes the contours of the personalistic regime in Russia.

The literature diverged in characterizing the Russian regime as tyranny (Snyder 2018), hybrid (Taylor 2014), bureaucratic-authoritarian, or simply hyperpresidential system (Gel'man and Starodubtsev 2016). This investigation describes the Russian regime as electoral authoritarianism under personalistic rule (for the categorical definitions and measurements, see Geddes et al. 2018: 11, 79–80). In general, personalistic regimes center around one individual, who, unlike leaders in a party-state regime, is not beholden to the permanent organization; unlike monarchs, does not enjoy an abstract, divine or traditional source of authority; and, unlike leaders elsewhere, cannot rely on ethnic groups, religious communities, and kinship-based structures. Although earlier literature, following Max Weber, designated such regimes as "sultanistic" (Linz and Stephan 1996: 44–45, 51–54; Chehabi and Linz 1998), personalism is the term of choice. Additional terms—such as caudillismo, caciquismo, and oligarchic democracy (Linz 2000: 143–144)—capture characteristics of similar but not identical regimes. The remainder of this section discusses how Russia's autocracy is institutionalized, and the section that follows elaborates the governance implications of Russia's political regime.

All authoritarian regimes use coercion, but personalistic regimes are peculiar: they rely on imitated and hollowed-out electoral procedures while deploying the vast repertoire of strategies of electoral control to convince non-elites in their claim to power based on their ability to defeat the regime's opponents (Levitsky and Way 2010; Schedler 2013; Seeberg 2014: 1270; Golosov 2016). Personalistic rulers cannot simply abolish elections because a decisive victory over their opponents signals elites that the leader remains in charge (for the itemized discussion of why formally contested elections are indispensable in authoritarian systems, see Hale 2015: 67–69, 71–72). Although the risks posed by competitive elections decrease once the first few electoral cycles are over (Bernhard et al. 2020), convoking or allowing competition, even heavily manipulated and staged ones, continue to entail risks for the regime's stability. Excessive electoral fraud might trigger popular uprisings, elite defection, and topple individual autocrats (as it happened during the wave of "color revolutions" in Eurasia in the early 2000s, see Way 2008). Although rulers do not forswear coercion against non-supporters, they prefer targeted repressions to massive violence.

Therefore, rulers must attract and keep genuine supporters, elites and non-elites alike, to reduce uncertainty over outcomes and avoid democratization. It stands to reason that rulers are likely to seek attractive inducements to sustain their power. The foundational studies point in this direction: To achieve popularity among ordinary people, autocrats, first and foremost, need to shore up their legitimacy by performing well in governing the society (Geddes 1994: 132), while macroeconomic success allows rulers to dole out more particularized benefits for their supporters (Geddes 1994: 139). After all, few people would prefer authoritarian rule on ideational grounds without expecting any material benefits in return. Overall, the excellent news for dictators is that instrumental values and performance-based appeals trump the intrinsic attractiveness of liberal values (Foa 2018).

Although the inherent weaknesses of formal constraints are typical for many post-soviet countries in Eurasia (Hale 2015: 76–80), removing executive term limits is crucial for the survival of personalistic regimes

(Oseiet al. 2020; Hartmann 2022). In 2012, Putin ran for two additional (also extended to six-years) terms, and in 2020, he moved to become a president-for-life. Because non-elites with negative views of the economic situation oppose breaking term limits (Chaisty and Whitefield 2019), rulers continue to offer material inducements as a non-coercive strategy of creating compliance. However, the step-by-step removal of temporal limits on their power also ablates formal rules and non-elite punishments, which could otherwise compel rulers to act as previously promised. Simply, as Russia's personalistic regime evolves, the ruler's commitments to constituency-serving behavior are progressively less credible.

Further, personalistic regimes are best characterized by the lack of permanent impersonal organizations. Permanent organizations provide nondemocratic regimes with a strong institutional structure; they crystallize the dominant coalition's internal relationships and make the regime stable and predictable. However, being distinct forms of natural states, personalistic regimes limit the ability of organizations to form perpetually and acquire independent power. Instead, basic natural states build a social organization on personal relationships (North et al. 2009: 2, 21) and, consequently, undermine the role impersonal rules and procedures play in the political system. The atrophy of perpetual organizations (for the empirical overview, see Taylor 2018: 54–60) and impersonal rules at the core of personalistic autocracies turn these regimes into particularized nexuses of contracts between rulers and constituents, rulers and elites. It surely does not help that "Putin doesn't believe in self-regulating institutions, because he thinks that without manual steering he would lose control of the country, which could lead to conflict, even civil war, that other great powers would exploit" (Taylor 2018: 76).

In Russia, a powerful political machine, United Russia (*Edinaya Rossiya*), has been essential for maintaining Putin's personalistic regime (Remington 2008; Reuter and Remington 2009; White 2011; Aburamoto 2019; Saikkonen 2021): it permeates all regional legislatures and provides loyal elites with some sense of cohesion and institutionalized access to spoils. In essence, United Russia coordinates patronal networks across a vast country, and that is why the party is essential for the survival of Putin's personalistic regime. However, United Russia is a weak dominant party, and it looks more like Kazakhstan's Nur Otan than the communist party of China. United Russia's popular appeal and ability to dominate elections heavily depend on Putin's popularity among the masses, while its internal cohesion stems from its proximity to the ruler and perceived ability to provide protection and access to valuable activities and resources. Main functionaries owe the privilege of their social, economic, and political positions to Putin's favors. Consistent with Smith's (2005) argument, United Russia benefited from the opposition's weakness and the ruler's willingness to make rents to its members, and these initial conditions also prevented the party from becoming a strong and impersonal organization. Arguably, between 2005 and 2008, United Russia attempted to institutionalize itself as the central locus of authority and initialize broad policy debates within three main factions. However, such an attempt proved to be ill-fated, as it became apparent once Putin returned to the highest office after a short hiatus as a prime minister.

The most noteworthy implication for governance is that United Russia cannot sanction the ruler and impose restraints on his power. Instead, as Isaacs and Whitmore (2014) note, United Russia is a personalized organization, which is "not endowed with the agency to perform the archetypal duties typified by dominant parties in other authoritarian states." Weak institutionalization reinforces the point that the ruler, not bound to the internal rules and sanctions of the dominant party organization, does not have to honor his commitments to the public (Reuter and Remington 2009; Gehlbach and Keefer 2011), while United Russia itself is "more a target of intensive lobbying than a source of unified and consistent policy direction for the country" (Remington 2008: 960). It surely would be a mistake to view Putin as an agent of the dominant party and United Russia as his principal.

While the foregoing point is widely understood, persistent is the claim that Putin is a mere agent of the *siloviki* (members of the domestic security community) in general and the Federal Security Service in particular (Satter 2016; Belton 2020; Fel'shtinskii and Popov 2021). Because of the popularity of this view, it deserves further elaboration. *The siloviki* have been in the center of academic interest for nearly two decades (Kryshtanovskaya and White 2003; Rivera and Rivera 2006; Soldatov and Borogan 2011). There is no need to deny that Russian *siloviki* or individuals with power ministry ties have been massively present in the federal and regional elite and in government since the early years of Putin's presidency (Kryshtanovskaya and White 2003) and have helped sustain Russian authoritarianism. They helped governors to control their provinces (Yakovlev and Aisin 2019), penetrated and militarized business elites, instilled the fear of repressions (Gel'man 2020a, b), and put the street protest under control (Petrov and Rochlitz 2019). Notably,

Putin was a career KGB officer for over a decade and briefly directed the Federal Security Service (FSB) under Boris Yeltsin administration in 1998–1999; and he consistently enlisted the individuals who since chose the same career path to key governance positions (Belton 2020). Arguably, the *siloviki* helped Putin develop an image of the national savior in the wake of terrorist attacks in the Moscow suburbs (Satter 2016) and thus contributed to his popularity.

However, Rivera and Rivera (2018: 221) find that "the militocracy framework rests on a rather thin, and in some cases flawed, body of empirical research." It is essential to keep in mind that the prominent members of *the siloviki* group owe their career take-offs to Putin's favors he doles out on the individual basis, not to the coercive institutions themselves. Despite the ability of key individuals with the secret police background to make big decisions and control the entire sectors of the economy (such as Sergey Ivanov, Igor Sechin, and Sergey Chemezov; see Blank 2008), the *siloviki* as a group of corporate actors were not the institutional backbone of Russia's authoritarian regime (Renz 2006; Taylor 2017) and were not in complete control over the government. Unlike their counterparts in the regimes institutionalized along military lines, such as Egypt or Myanmar, the *siloviki* play only an instrumental role in Putin's system. Although autocratic control over the public in the context of the rapidly deteriorating economic conditions requires the support of the specialists in coercion, the regime employs a multitude of measures, including reorganizations and agency terminations, to ensure control over its repressive apparatus (Petrov and Rochlitz 2019). Considering other cases (see, for instance, Svolik 2012: 123–161), we can predict that once the regime's reliance on repression becomes necessary, *siloviki*'s political dominance will materialize. Still, this scenario does not belong to the foreseeable future because of the *siloviki*'s internal fragmentation, institutional conflicts, and rivalries (Taylor 2017). All this hinders *siloviki*'s prospects of becoming the regime's weight-bearing institution before the end of Putin's natural lifespan.

Finally, authoritarian regimes could revolve around comprehensive ideologies, which could unite domestic elites and promote self-enforcing moral constraints. Although the percentage of nondemocracies with an official ideology, mandatory for all citizens, is low (Guriev and Treisman 2019: 110), ideology-like frameworks endure in many places. They generate norms and make meanings intended to create non-material sources of compliance among non-elites and nurture grassroots sensibilities favorable to the regime. In this respect, the Russian story seems confusing at first. Toward the final years of the Soviet Union, communist ideology, although mandatory, no longer resembled a coherent set of ideas structuring political action and governance, while genuine believers, elite and non-elite alike, were treated with suspicion and open disdain by their peers (Yurchak 2006). Since the early years of Russia's democratic transition, ideas and ideology were less important than the interests of key political players (Hanson 2010). Scholars often view ideological incompleteness as a systemic feature of personalism (Robinson 2020). Unlike tacit contracts and personalized exchanges, it has little purchase in ensuring the individual elites' consent and obedience, while genuine ideological commitments that impinge on personalized exchanges and bargains could destabilize the regime. Yet, makeshift ideological frameworks are replete in Putin's Russia, and they are valuable for the ruler and his subordinates.

No matter how convoluted and contradictory, ideological discourses in Russia built on Putin's illiberal and confrontational sensibilities that he had initially revealed during his first and second presidential terms. Early on, Vladislav Surkov (in office, 1999–2011), misleadingly credited with being "the hidden author of Putinism" (Pomerantsev 2014), proposed three ideological pillars (such as statism, developmentalism, and great-power imagery), commonly known as "the sovereign democracy" doctrine. As evident from Putin's patter at the 2020 meeting of the Valdai discussion club, the main points of the doctrine linger in his political outlook and reveal his idiosyncratic views (Taylor 2018: 40; Putin 2020). Later on, Putin embarked on another ideological soul-searching. Experiencing massive legitimacy deficits, exemplified by the massive protests, which erupted during the winter of 2011–2012, the regime seems to have settled on an awkward ideological construct, "spiritual-moral values" (note that Russian inelegant word *skrepy* mean "clamps," not values). Although these two ideological stances seem substantively different, they represent the regime's illiberal leaning and supply average Russians with "an appealing framework for making sense of the world" (Laruelle 2020: 116). Further, aggressively peddled illiberal discourses also seek to convince non-elites that the liberal opposition, with its stress on individual rights and open self-expression, is less desirable than Putin's leadership. In turn, elites reproduce these ideological attributes in numerous public utterances and incorporate them in governance practices to create facts on the ground, validating Putin's self-serving ideological posturing and thereby protecting their contracts with the ruler. In other words, although electoral authoritarianism is not institutionalized around clearly recognizable programmatic ideologies, illiberal and anti-Western leanings are prominent in Putin's Russia, and they are valuable for the ruler and his elites as manipulative means of maintaining political power.

Rulers often find it in their best interest to construct ideological frameworks in order to complement material inducements and redirect attention from poor performance. As astute observers of Russian politics note, no ideological mobilization is likely to prop up the regime's legitimacy for a prolonged period of time absent material gains. It is telling that even amid ideological mobilization during the invasion of Ukraine in the Spring of 2022, Putin found it in his best interest to promise further infrastructural upgrades. In this sense, the Kremlin's illiberal posturing is functionally similar to other personalistic regimes' efforts to construct an appealing ideological narrative (as it happened, for example, in John Magufuli's Tanzania, see Paget 2020; Talleh Nkobou and Ainslie 2021). Still, at the end of the day, without positive inducements, propaganda efforts are less attractive for non-elites (Blackburn and Petersson 2021), and it is likely to expect the regime's increased reliance on aggressive and arbitrary enforcement of laws designed to uphold conservative or traditional (read: illiberal) values. In turn, elites readily adopt conservative attitudes to protect their contracts with the ruler and justify their domination over society. Understandably, the Kremlin's success in the pursuit of conservatism created the imagery of a widespread moral panic, which centered around the notion that the rotten Western values could compromise Russia's survival and erode its identity. This moral panic is convenient for the ruler's political objectives of staying in power and is encouraged by the regime. Average citizens, whose actions seem to challenge the regime's sensibilities—they range from offending religious feelings and promoting alternative lifestyles to posting nude photos with Orthodox cathedrals in the background—are singled out and often prosecuted on criminal charges.

In a nutshell, the main features of Russian personalism are as follows. First, the regime hinges on the persona of the leader but not on some durable political institutions or organizations to which politicians and state officials are accountable. The strongman must maintain a broad and genuine popular appeal by projecting an image of a competent and committed administrator and providing material inducements to non-elites. When the delivery of economic benefits and social services falls flat, the ruler surrenders to spin strategies, which conceal the regime's poor performance. Second, none of the officially sanctioned organizational forms such as the dominant political party (United Russia), coercive apparatus (the *siloviki*), and formal political institutions (the State Duma) should be taken at face value because these forms do not propose binding rules and do not generate obstacles for the ruler. Instead, the regime relies on tacit contracts (a reciprocal exchange of special favors and the promise of protection in the hierarchy of power in return for loyalty and subservience on behalf of state officials, private actors, and noncommercial organizations) as the primary method of political control that ensures the regime's stability. Third, instead of imposing a single comprehensive ideology, the regime fabricates a variety of makeshift ideological frameworks as "sovereign democracy" and a newly found discourse of "traditional values," which rulers develop to bolster their legitimacy and elites tap into in order to signal their fealty and value. Although electoral authoritarianism is not institutionalized ideologically, rulers often find it in their best interests to use ideological frameworks, complementing material inducements and redirecting attention from poor performance.

In essence, personalism is a constitutive institution that generates the rules of the game and orders tacit contracts between actors. These rules are neither impersonal nor ensconced in perpetual organizations. In Russia, the enduring patterns of behavior among relevant political actors are ensconced in calculations of cost and benefits and, to a lesser degree, in a variety of intangible and hard to interpret intra-elite norms and conventions, including symbolic obeisance and anticipatory obedience. The following section reveals complicated relationships between the principal and the agents, and it also discusses how Russia's authoritarian setup shapes governance practices.

Governance in Putin's Russia: Optimizing Responses and Undesirable Outcomes

My analysis of how the Kremlin governs Russia builds on the vast literature on indirect governance, and it also sheds light on the complexity of principal-agent or governor-intermediary relations in the context of electoral authoritarianism under personalistic rule. This section goes over four sets of governance situations. The first subsection discusses relationships between the ruler and the people, wherein the former communicates the promises of social betterment and offers particularized material inducements. As Russia's personalistic regime evolves, the principal's commitment to constituency-serving behavior, necessary for improving health outcomes, becomes less credible. In the meanwhile, shallow performance rhetoric intensifies, and tolerance to faked stories of success grows. The second subsection highlights the relations between the ruler and elites, both bureaucratic and business, in charge of policy implementation. Putin's patronal obligation is to provide access to valuable activities and resources; fulfilling this obligation undermines impersonal controls over agents, and any strictly merit-based incentive schemes to maintain Weberian bureaucracy are hindered. At the same time, narrow mandates and manual steering restrict bureaucratic autonomy, which is necessary for agents' ability to pursue substantive goals competently. The third set of relations is between the principal and intermediaries or meso-level regulators entrusted with monitoring activities. The practices of monitoring, initially credible, suffer from hierarchical management, organizational personalization, and self-censorship. Instead of granting intermediaries an autonomy to pull fire alarms on bad implementation practices, the principal constructs and rewards responsiveness to his political goals. Fourthly and finally, I discuss the elite's vassal-like over-compliance with the principal's demands and the ensuing correlation of goals between the ruler and the elite. As the latter adapts to the principal's ideas and values, it fails to push the principal back and maintain the professional ethos and the sense of true public mission.

The pages that follow explore how Russia's regime brings to life an array of optimizing responses that jointly impede the quality of governance within the multi-level architecture that connects major participants in health affairs to the regime's principals. The system of optimizing responses is a product of an electoral regime under personalistic rule. In essence, the institutional setup of Russia's personalistic regime prompts an equilibrium among self-interested actors involved in the process of governance, while principals and their agents jointly make prospects of significant improvements for an average Russian less real.

The President Promises: Providing Public Goods in the Electoral Autocracy

That Russian personalistic regime legitimizes itself through elections, albeit neither free nor fair, has profound implications. In the context of electoral authoritarianism under personalistic rule, the leader's performance-based approval is essential for surviving in power without resorting to costly coercion. Because personalistic systems derive legitimacy from contested—although heavily manipulated—elections, the rulers must appear competent and effective to the electorate.

The question is how to minimize potential alienation caused by increasing electoral manipulations and placating those who might question the utility of a low political turnover, which leaves the country in the same individual's hands for an extended period of time. Material inducement is a non-coercive strategy designed to generate a high level of public support; it is desirable for a leader who wants to harvest public acclaim and legitimize administrative domination over elections. When rational-legal or procedural legitimacy is lacking, promises of benefits establish a personalistic linkage to votes (Levitsky and Loxton 2013: 110) and thus cements tacit contracts between the ruler and the people. Insightful observers of Russian affairs understand this point well as they describe the domestic social contract in terms of trading political and civil rights for the prospects of economic growth and social order and offering loyalty and political faithfulness in exchange for stability and social protection (see, for instance, Auzan 2005).

Still, the implicit contract between the ruler and average Russians is fleeting. First, the main reason is that personalistic leaders prioritize political survival and control of elites over substantive goals like improving population health. The competence-control theory understands the diremption between political and substantive goals reasonably well, but it implies that the balance between them is possible (Abbott et al. 2020: 16). Putin's social promises are submitted to the logic of his survival, while considerations of people's welfare are secondary. Personalistic rulers must appear to work in the interest of people's welfare but, failing to maximize it, might find it in their best interest to fake progress and manipulate information. This outcome is consistent with Daniel Treisman's conceptualization of Russia's regime as an informational autocracy, wherein its leaders "rather than killing and imprisoning thousands to inspire fear, …attempt to convince citizens that they are competent and benevolent leaders" (Treisman 2018: 14; see also Guriev and Treisman 2019, 2020). That Russia became an "informational autocracy" based on lies about social betterment and ramped up electoral fraud is hard to deny after the events of 2020 (Electoral fraud becomes highly sophisticated and difficult to expose, consult Shpil'kin 2021).

Second, although dictators understand the value of improving welfare, their commitment to social betterment is not credible without formal constitutional or partisan constraints. As personalistic leaders remove constitutional term limits, announce the decision to rule for the rest of their natural lifespan, and ramp up electoral fraud, they de facto remove "rules and punishments that make it impossible to act otherwise than previously committed" (Levi 1989: 61). Consequently, the leader with commitment deficits is likely to tolerate the numerous gaming strategies that high-powered state bureaucrats and governance intermediaries routinely deploy. It is astonishing how the principal's promises go hand in hand with the propensity of his subordinates to misrepresent policy outcomes, hide wasted resources, misinform the public, and conceal protests against healthcare mismanagement.

The third and final problem is that delivering particularistic benefits to constituents could be costly, but governing health for the benefit of all is even more so. It follows that the ruler will try to minimize the costs needed for implementing health policies while maximizing revenue and prioritizing spending on the specialists in violence, crucial for the quelling of potential protests. Dmitry Medvedev, responding to concerned citizens in regard to the diminished standards of living in the country, even coined a callous maxim: "There is just no money, but you hold fast." As empirical chapters demonstrate, attractive health initiatives intended to secure Putin's popularity (such as decommodification of medicines and import-substitution of medical supplies) were also dictated by the need to save revenue. Ignoring the primary function of prices as signal mechanisms in the post-socialist economy, Putin wants agents to cap prices on medicines and expects private suppliers to participate in public tenders against their economic interests.

Although the overall high tax burden on the economy grew (including the dramatic increases in the payroll tax, confiscation-like pension reform, and proposals to tax bank deposits), the Kremlin introduced cuts in the federal health budget, even amid the ongoing epidemic of COVID-19. This austerity is a road to a predatory state that extracts "as much revenue as they can from the population" (Levi 1989: 3) but jettisons patients' needs and sheds social ends. In Putin's system, the priority of political survival combined with protecting revenue and slashing the health budget will continue to belie the prospects of good health governance.

On balance, while political results for the regime's stability look satisfying, outcomes for health governance are not. Much as Putin is satisfied with imitating the improvement of citizens' welfare and public health, so are his subordinates and societal intermediaries. Yet, substantive failures, of which Putin is cognizant, to date failed to precipitate a national crisis in his legitimacy. Ordinary patients might be happy to settle for a few goods and passable services and accept the elites' shameless self-promotion without outrage. That federal TV is in control of loyalists and propagandists—and the older generation of Russians still is not very discerning when it comes to information literacy—does not help spread the incriminating information and precludes synchronized understanding of the scope of the problem. Further, while poor outcomes of health governance might result in declining electoral performance, loyalty can be bought by making popular decisions in other policy arenas. In the long term, with the dissipation of tangible material inducements for non-elites and the diminishing rents for the dominant coalition, the Kremlin is likely to face the erosion of compliance and might prioritize coercive strategies.

Bureaucrats Endure: Maintaining Patronage vs. Improving Performance

Principals have powerful incentives to increase bureaucratic competence, at least in the areas crucial for economic performance and revenue extraction (Geddes 1994: 139). There is no need to deny the effectiveness of such technocrats as Alexey Kudrin, Elvira Nabiullina, and Mikhail Mishustin during their tenure in the Ministry of Finance, the Central Bank, and the Federal Taxation Service, respectively. Mishustin, for instance, was credited for ramping up the collection of taxes (Krivoshapko 2020). Still, the regime's success in implementing the fiscal reform during the early years of Putin's presidency does not tell us much about how the principal manages the bureaucracy.

As principal-agent theory has it, the principals could not increase performance efficiency without constructing appropriate incentives for agents. An optimal incentive scheme is difficult to achieve, but an impersonal system of rewards for competence (such as merit-based recruitments and promotion) and punishments for ineptitude is a bare minimum to maintain Weberian bureaucracy (Fukuyama 2013: 348). As this subsection shows, the principal might not find it in his best interest to systematically reward his subordinates for competence or punish them for ineptness and failures. Although the Kremlin retains an option of rigid controls over elites, state agents, and intermediaries, the regime is careful not to erode the underlying system of informal obligations.

Previous investigations lend credence to that conclusion. Stanislav Markus (2015: 97–102) notes that Putin and Medvedev consistently threatened to cut down the number of state staff, thereby trying to subjugate the multiplying bureaucracies. The principals did not implement rational-legal and impersonal mechanisms of control over agents, but they used tools of control that allowed them to fire any state official or political office holder for the "loss of trust." Such a bespoke arrangement is politically expedient as it allows an autocrat to wield arbitrary power. As it seems, nobody could be secure in Putin's system: rampant are the legal prosecutions of the domestic elite (Sergey Storchak, Vyacheslav Gaizer, Andrey Belyaninov, Alexey Ulyukaev, Mikhail Abyzov, and Ivan Belozertsev, to name a few high-profile cases). However, these arrests result from non-transparent intra-elite grudges and are often triggered by the desire to redistribute economic assets, stop the appointed officials from preventing shady business deals, and weaken patrons of informal networks (Gaaze 2015, 2017; Stanovaya 2019). For personalistic rulers, punishing mediocre performers, careerists, and rent-seekers—despite their public scolding of brazen (*"oborzevshie"*) state officials—is hardly an option since top bureaucrats might decide to hold back their loyalty and thus create fissures the regime's genuine opponents might exploit during upcoming electoral cycles.

The very nature of personalistic rule hinders the impartial system of rewards and punishments: a personalistic dictator has to maintain a single power pyramid based on a system of personalized bargains and reciprocal obligations (Hale 2015: 20). Lest his subordinates defect or disobey (a situation all too possible in case of systemic uncertainty which characterizes electoral autocracies, see Egorov and Sonin 2011; Bernhard et al. 2020), Putin must satisfy their self-interest, including rent-seeking behavior. At its core, it is privileged access to valuable activities and resources that induce elite's compliance. Once the principal treats agents as clients, their relationship becomes codepedent, and the ruler's ability to effectively manage—reward and punish for the right reasons—his administrators diminishes. Impersonal punishments, necessary for keeping the runaway bureaucratic apparatus in check, make little sense given that actors, once excluded from the dominant coalition, are likely to search for alternative patrons.

In general, incentivizing and rewarding agents' competence and independence across the board is treacherous. Doing so could improve the chance of attaining substantive goals, but encouraging independence could undermine Putin's political goals. For personalistic rulers, incompetence is not an anathema. As Jon Elster (2018: 280) insightfully put it: "...because they [principals, rulers – V.K.] tended not to like the successes of their own agents, they sometimes deliberately chose less competent underlings. When these mostly average individuals were imbued with an inordinate desire for glory, they could not succeed by the route of competence. Instead, they used their equally inordinate power to remove or resist competence in others." The inverse is true, too: consistent with the standard competence-control trade-off view, from the ruler's vantage point, actors' assertiveness, independence, and effectiveness could undermine the principal's controls.

Another essential dimension of maintaining the ruler's power over actors is the so-called manual control—top-down dictation of actions "in which the mechanics of every process were to be tightly controlled by the Kremlin's men" (Belton 2020: 304; Treisman 2018: 16–18). It is one of the ubiquitous practices in personalistic administration that is well-understood. Documentary evidence suggests that manual control (or manual steering) and micromanagement are common to multiple layers of authority, ranging from the regime's principals to the Ministry of Health. Instead of maintaining the system of general mandates, Putin often interferes on behalf of individuals who appeal to the ruler to decide outcomes and obtain his agreement to change the terms of mandates in their favor. For citizens who could directly address the president at the high-profile TV broadcast Direct Line (*Pryamaya Liniya*) and ask him to ensure the delivery of social services at the local level or remedy their individual situation, manual steering is a good thing. That presidential involvement does not always help is another matter; the negative follow-up stories rarely get national coverage and, for that reason, do not obnubilate the autocratic image of being concerned for others.

More often than not, manual control is about creating privileges. It inheres in Russian personalism since the regime's weak institutionalization is devoid of other, ideological or partisan, methods of control over domestic elites. Although it is hardly helpful to promote competence and improve performance, manual control is essential to the system of personalistic rule because it satisfies Putin's clients' self-interest and thereby induces compliance and loyalty to the regime in general and Putin personally. As a result, the commanding heights of governance are squarely in the hands of Putin's close associates, while some interests and positions become very well entrenched. But for the general audiences, the Kremlin tends to justify this approach referencing the need to generate a system of incentives for a fistful of private actors and state-owned enterprises to accumulate profits and invest heavily in domestic industries, thereby increasing the state capacity. While the actual damage generated by this governance approach is hard to measure, the negative externalities are apparent (see, for instance, Detkova et al. 2018).

Still, as explained in the previous subsection, Putin's claim to rule necessitates the delivery of goods and services to average Russians. To deal with the conundrum, Putin's administration designed an elaborate system of bureaucratic mandates and performance-based indicators. Because Putin's promises of social betterment are specific and particularistic, his mandates are rarely general and straightforward in nature. For instance, his agents receive instructions to implement import substitution of pharmaceutical products and medical supplies but not provide high-quality goods and improve service delivery in the healthcare system. In practice, setting a large number of very narrow mandates and cumbersome top-down dictations undermine agents' independence and competence and, in the long run, stymie substantive goal attainment (Fukuyama 2013: 357; on the negative consequences of expansive social engineering and excessive regulatory complexity, see Scott 1998; Kling 2016). Still, it is unclear whether the failure to achieve these mandates is a necessary and sufficient condition that leads to the dismissal from employment or whether the set indicators are appropriate instruments for improving actual outcomes. This consideration makes me think about imposed metrics not as a mechanism of control over governance actors but as a commitment signal designed to bolster Putin's popularity among the masses (and key governmental officials openly acknowledge that, see Galimova 2018; Nagornykh 2018).

In summary, any personalistic ruler relies on agents, top state officials, and intermediaries, but in Russia, emerging codependence allows and incentivizes Putin's clients to pursue parochial, self-serving interests and leads to a de facto inversion of authority, wherein the regime becomes bound to some of its subordinates. Making rents and ensuring the stability of top bureaucratic jobs (the stasis of cadres in Putin's Russia is noticeable) undermines the principal's controls over the substantive goals of governance. Meanwhile, the objective of working for the public good is alarmingly and perilously compromised. In terms of improving the quality of governance, culling the individual underperformers makes little sense, too: punishing underperformers still would not alter the self-interested behavior of newcomers, beholden to the ruler and not to the formal organizations. It is a severe problem because authoritarian principals proclaim social betterment as their central goal—and many Russians take it at face value—but incentivize their agents to imitate progress and tolerate slipshod performance.

Intermediaries Retreat: The Weakness of Oversight and Organizational Atrophy

Monitoring federal and regional bureaucracies is essential to good governance. At a minimum, principals have to solve informational arthritis that emerges when they cannot directly observe the actions of state agents. Police patrols and fire alarms (McCubbins and Schwartz 1984) are two analytical concepts that describe the main strategies for exposing bureaucrats' poor performance or moral hazard and taking the first steps to correct policy implementation. The Kremlin uses both approaches, and both are equally defective in their application. Politically, "informational autocrats," including Putin, must maintain the credibility of performance rhetoric directed at non-elites. For personalistic rulers, it is essential to convey an impression that the principal does not turn a blind eye to the runaway bureaucracies. The Kremlin faces the need to develop a system of oversight lest the dissatisfaction with incompetent or self-serving bureaucracies transforms into declining public support for the regime. However, being bound by patron-client relationships, a political master also needs to protect his top subordinates and shield his strategic decisions from public scrutiny.

Turning to the core insights of the competence-control theory, it stands to reason that external monitors are effective under non-hierarchical management and with considerable autonomy in interpreting the terms of the principal's grant. Simply put, an effective oversight requires the mode of indirect governance called trusteeship. The problem for personalistic rulers is that trusteeships may invert authority: "the trustor has superior authority ex ante, but may be subject to the trustee's authority ex post" (Abbott et al. 2020: 14–15). However, the informational autocrats must remain in control and prevent the exposure of inefficiencies and policy failures. As a result, the regime designed a solution allowing for select professional associations and social actors to participate in indirect governance, but it also maintained control over them via presidential administration (which makes external "fire alarms" resemble quasi-state or parastatal institutions) and permitted external watchdogs' capacities to decline in effectiveness due to underuse, neglect, or divestment of resources.

In practice, the Kremlin constructed and maintained politically expedient mechanisms of popular accountability. The vernacular notion of "public control" (*'narodnyi kontrol'*)—actors outside the state monitor the implementation of Putin's decisions at the grassroots level without questioning his strategic directives—captures the essence of the ruler's grant of oversight. In Putin's system of governance, any independent oversight of the Cabinet-level state officials is antithetical to the principle that key elites should not undergo public scrutiny. Simultaneously, street-level bureaucrats (including ordinary doctors and their immediate superiors, hospital administrators, and regional authorities) bear the brunt of negative exposure frequently followed by incriminations and punishment. The Kremlin expects to benefit from this arrangement as long as the health monitors help Putin connect to non-elites, exploit the anti-corruption theme, and shift the blame from the regime's wrongdoings to street-level actors.

More profoundly, personalistic regimes, being a form of basic natural states, exhibit a tendency to limit the ability of individuals to form perpetually lived organizations that non-elites are likely to support. As North et al. (2009: 15) remind us, "organizations consist of specific groups of individuals pursuing a mix of common and individual goals through partly coordinated behavior." For formal organizations to achieve common goals, it is essential to maintain an independent corporate identity not reducible to its leaders. However, personalistic regimes inhibit the formation of permanently lived organizations, and this strategy helps rulers diminish the credibility of their collective demands and contain possible exposure of commitment deficits. Notably, Putin's trusted subordinates precluded the formation of a unified health surveillance organ capable of internal police patrols, while the power of small-scale entities (such as *Rospotrebnadzor*) varied dramatically depending on the specific powers and authority delegated to their heads by the principal.

In Putin's Russia, surveillance agencies and monitoring organizations, both internal and external, suffer from the undermined sense of corporate identity. Unsurprisingly, Putin's personalistic regime fosters further personalization of organized groups (for the nuanced discussion of the concept and typology, see Rahat and Kenig 2018: 117–131). Russian monitors of health, internal and external alike, underwent the process of political personalization in which the political weight of individual actors vis-à-vis the power of the organization increased over time while the centrality and power of the group declined. The regime, hypothetically, could increase intermediaries' loyalty through partial accommodation of their organizational demands. Still, offering particularized benefits and supporting narrow self-interests is more valuable and expedient for the regime as it allows crowding out the intrinsic motivation in oversight (Abbott et al. 2020: 25).

One, the All-Russian Popular Front, claimed a role of a public controller over the governmental functionaries, but the presidential administration directed its actions and purpose. The Front also functioned as a temporary place for reserve players, who had to wait for openings within the officialdom, and a potential substitute for the ruling party (Melikyan 2014; Pertsev 2015, 2020). Another one, the National Medical Chamber, aspired to improve governance practices in the country, but the privilege of using this organization for external oversight lay with the identity of its irreplaceable leader, Leonid Roshal, rather than the organization itself. Further, these two formally separate organizations suffered from overlapping memberships, which eroded their organizational identity. Understandably, there was a great deal of self-censorship among health intermediaries since exposing incriminating evidence of inequities and injustices in health governance could undermine both Putin's popularity and intermediaries' personal prospects. Needless to say, the Kremlin squeezes relentless watchdogs out of public activities by designating them as agents of foreign influence, undesirable organizations, or simply extremists. Under the threat of imprisonment, many independent journalists and political organizers from Alexey Navalny's team find it best to leave the country to avoid criminal charges.

Those who monitor health governance on Putin's terms receive particularized benefits. Consistent with the logic of personalized exchanges and bargains, the cooptation of prominent individuals and organizations in the patronal pyramid allows watchdogs to have protection, chase social prestige, hope for political mobility, and enjoy access to the state resources (Flikke 2018). For instance, members of the coopted medical associations can protect themselves from the independent media that exposes poor health services and from the *siloviki*, who increasingly criminalize common medical mistakes. Those civil society actors, who internalize the idea of social work as "the art of the possible" and strive to remain in Putin's seductive orbit, over time, become part of the state machinery but lose their autonomy to the principal and undermine their authority (e.g., Bindman et al. 2019; Ljubownikow and Crotty 2016; Olimpieva and Pachenkov 2013; Chebankova 2012).

In brief, being deeply embedded in Putin's regime, societal intermediaries cannot advance their self-interests by pulling fire alarms if doing so involves an open clash with the principal, top administrative elite, and intermediaries' handlers from the presidential administration. Notably, internal and external intermediaries are also bound to self-censorship, no matter how beneficial it might seem to expose the government's misconduct in order to improve the quality of health governance. The described weakness of the oversight system is by design: Putin's personalistic regime cannot allow permanent self-regulating organizations to emerge as an alternative locus of authority.

Elites Adapt: Over-Compliance and Gaming Strategies

Predictably, in personalistic regimes, elites, agents, intermediaries are loyal not to perpetual organizations, coherent ideologies, specific policies, or the public, but they must be faithful in allegiance to the ruler. Brian Taylor (2018: 27–28) discusses Putin's habit of demanding loyalty as a structuring principle of his rule. Arguably, Putin's loyalty to his political masters convinced the ailing president Boris Yeltsin to select Putin as his successor in 1999 (at the very least, Yeltsin openly praised Putin's loyalty in his memoirs). The habit of demanding loyalty incentivizes elites and state officials to over-comply—and vocal disagreement with Putin's strategic decisions or airing the regime's dirty laundry in public could be interpreted as stabbing him in the back—lest the principal "loses trust" and punishes them.

State officials and intermediaries, who choose to follow or anticipate the principal's wishes without questions or criticism, become Vassals.

(For an insightful typology of four ideal–typical categories of intermediaries, including Vassals, Zealots, Mandarins, and Opportunists, consult Abbott et al. 2021.) Unlike Zealots, who are faithful to the impartial and thorough implementation of specific policies and strictly observe professional ethos, Vassals would not sacrifice the ruler's self-interest for policy gains. As Vassals, elites refrain from challenging the faulty terms of the principal's mandates, interpret the ruler's directives to advance his ideological posturing at the expense of their professional responsibilities, and report doctored policy results to bolster Putin's image as a benevolent and competent ruler. Importantly, Vassals shield the Kremlin from public accountability and hide the facts of governance flubs in order to sustain "informational autocracy."

The incentives to become Vassals lie in the nature of Russia's personalistic regime. Although intermediaries might disagree with Putin's injunctions on managing health issues, an open dissent makes them worse off. Zealots and committed policy entrepreneurs lack sufficient incentives to prioritize public interest over the ruler's political objectives and, unless they adapt, find themselves sidelined. Mandarins, directing their loyalty to their organizations' fundamental rules and protocols, could not endure within the personalistic system that discounts impersonal rules and formal organizations to which political insiders could otherwise be beholden.

In the strict view, Vassals are emotionally attached to the ruler and remain faithful even at the expense of sacrificing their self-interest. In Russia, devoted Vassals—like Dmitry Medvedev, who surrendered his political capital by giving the presidency back to Putin—might be hard to come by. However, in personalistic regimes, loyalty functions as an investment that could bring elites closer to the ruler, protect their careers, and ensure access to valuable activities, resources, and privileges. It is rational for elites to signal their fealty and expect particularized material inducements and personal gains in return for subordination. Because Russia's elite depends on the ruler's favors for the privileged access to activities and resources, Vassals hugely benefit from personalized exchanges and thus choose to observe tacit contracts and mutual obligations between them and the ruler. As a growing number of individuals desire privileged access while rents dissipate, the returns on loyalty fall, and therefore loyalty must be spoken even louder and in evermore subservient ways. The centrality of loyalty in all political life generates three noteworthy consequences for the quality of governance.

First, Putin's subordinates recognize him as the only strategic decision-maker, adjust their goals to the principal's, and internalize the narrow terms of bureaucratic mandates. As competence-control theory has it, the complete correlation of substantive goals between principals and agents eliminates competence-control tradeoffs, while goal divergence incentivizes rulers to wield hard controls making agencies less competent (Abbott et al. 2020: 19, 30). Goal convergence could effectuate improvements in the quality of governance, but it could also direct governance practices in the opposite direction. Similar to Opportunists, Vassals readily "pivot to new goals, policies, procedures, or tasks when incentivized to do so" (Abbott et al. 2021: S89). All this is consistent with the general finding that "elites in personalist dictatorships tend to have policy preferences that mirror those of the dictator" (Ezrow and Frantz 2011: 114). Predictably, excessive subordination leads to poor performance (Fukuyama 2013: 359).

On the flip side, when the principal's wishes are not clear, when the boss withholds a direct command, or when bureaucratic mandates are too general, agents become paralyzed by indecision (for a vivid example how even a routine situation could create a conundrum for agents, see Taylor 2018: 134–135). It is clear that with attenuated legislative accountability and limited electoral competition, career administrators and elected local officials display little interest in working hard to improve the quality of public goods provision (Zavadskaya and Shilov 2021; Beazer and Reuter 2021). Being on autopilot does not promote independence and professionalism, as a standard account of principal-agent theory holds, but it impairs intent interagency coordination and determined execution.

Second, ideological adaptations—although antithetical to the public interest—are essential tools for reassuring Putin of subordination and loyalty. It appears that a wide range of agents, intermediaries, and societal actors adopt Putin's ideas and values. Besides predictably mirroring Putin's policy preferences, actors also create facts on the ground that reify his illiberal vision. That elites creatively interpret their formal mandates according to the ruler's ideological wishes is an adaptive, optimizing response that seeks to prevent neglect, divestment of resources, and agency termination. This optimizing response triggers mission drifts, which compromise the attainment of substantive goals. Ideological adaptations to illiberal posture also allow Putin's subordinates to exculpate their inefficiencies, while eager propagandists use ideological constructs to blame the regime's malperformance on its political opponents, whether real or invented. Adopting expedient ideologies provides a correlation of political goals between the principal and agents, but it could not increase agents' competence, let alone the sense of professional ethos and public-service mission.

Finally, other optimizing behaviors include bureaucratic gaming strategies that fabricate stories of success and validate Putin's social promises. Improving health outcomes is genuinely challenging, and the level of policy success desired by Putin is far from guaranteed. Faking performance protects state administrators' in the context when high-level bureaucrats are accountable only to their principal. Thus, to defend themselves and satisfy Putin's need to maintain the impression of his ability to deliver goods and services, Russian regulators and bureaucrats tend to imitate breakthroughs in health governance. Numerous gaming strategies, outcomes misrepresentations, misuse of resources, policy misinformation, and self-serving issue-framings ensue. If deployed skillfully, gaming strategies satisfy the regime's principals but damage public services provision to ordinary people.

The resultant consequence for the quality of governance is that bureaucrats cannot constrain the principal's proclivity toward the moral hazard. The normative ideal of good governance envisions the authority flowing from responsible and competent administrators to the principal, while bureaucracies "can play their most important role as part of a system of checks and balances" (Miller and Whitford 2016: 21). But in personalistic systems, elites, agents, and intermediaries are tamed by the rulers and adapt to their demands, and parochial goals prevail over societal gains.

Summary: Sustaining the Negative Equilibrium

Putin might find it in his best interest to improve health outcomes, but the regime's setup limits his agents' desire and ability to do so, and that attests to the institutional weakness of electoral authoritarianism under personalistic rule. In democracies, good governance is secured by strong formal institutions, a high level of transparency and political accountability of state officials, and a self-enforcing professional ethos of civil servants bound by the rule of law. But in Russia, good governance faces all too many obstacles. As the process of health governance unfolds, Putin has to strike an equipoise between promoting his elites' private interests and providing a sufficient level of public goods and services for non-elites. That the regime's principals and agents desire to preserve an institutional setup to maintain their power over society and that they seek no broad institutional change in governance practices lest they weaken their political clout is evident. The contractual and transactional core of personalistic regimes is best captured by the notion of relational authority, which is "contingent on the actions of both the ruler and ruled, is an equilibrium produced and reproduced through on-going interactions" (Lake 2009: 29).

Because Putin's choices are circumscribed, he perforce navigates between a predatory and a contractual state, a common dilemma of those personalistic regimes that shy away from relying on outright coercion. The resultant is a system of health governance in which the government strongly asserts its role as a chief guarantor of health but fails to deliver. Without denying the fact that any governance process is likely to produce some negative externalities (no society is a machine that simple repairs can fix), it should be clear that inefficient and unfair practices entrenched in personalistic authoritarianism undermine the attainment of generic policy goals in the long-term perspective.

Here comes the enduring pathology of Putin's regime. All actors who desire to participate in personalized exchanges and bargains first and foremost pursue their self-interests. When not submitted to the constituents' interests and institutional constraints, health governance practices become the objects of spoliation. In essence, elites learn to embrace bad governance in the process of interaction, in much the way political elites learn the usefulness of authoritarianism (Grigoriev and Dekalchuk 2017). While bad governance decisions are not officially sanctioned (after all, there is no official injunction to pursue narrow self-interests or make medicines less available to the people), they emerge out of the desire of relevant political actors to uphold their part in the personalistic bargain. Bad health governance and inefficient outcomes became accepted as a standard way of interaction among key political actors who remain sufficiently satisfied with achieving their self-serving goals. The persistent level of public acquiescence (except for small-scale protests among health professionals across Russian provinces) combined with the growing level of the elite's subservience is antithetical to real change, and all that compliance debilitates any realistic prospects of improving Russia's health governance. All this allows for the emergence of an equilibrium in which principals and their subordinates are likely to be satisfied with socially inefficient outcomes, even though ordinary patients and street-level bureaucrats are likely to be not.

Research Approach

The outlook presented here is a rational-institutionalist perspective. It views ministers, bureaucrats, the private sector, civil society, and medical associations as actors who strive to attain their objective, rational interests within the confines of personalism (for a valuable discussion of deploying various strands of rational-institutional explanations, see Parsons 2007: 69–74; 76–85). Although I do not aspire to present a formal model of personalism, this investigation follows the rationalist micro-foundations. It provides explicit statements about who the key political actors are, what motivates them, and how the political environment in which they interact becomes hard to change.

Abstractly put, health actors' choices are functions of their position within a personalistic regime wherein their subsequent actions follow a distinct path and generate socially undesirable consequences. If politics verily is "the art of the possible," agents must operate and govern within the system's observable rules and constraints imposed by leaders. Politics, after all, is not "the art of the impossible," as an infamous political operator and oligarch turned into a sworn Putin's foe in exile, Boris Berezovsky (1946–2013), erroneously believed. The detailed analysis of the unmistakable pressures that inhere in personalistic systems constitutes the bulk of the chapters. It is important to stress that the main actors are not engaged in the cost–benefit analysis external to personalism. This argument explains governance action vis-a-vis personalistic rule as a human-made organization with its own rules and conventions (for a helpful way of delineating explicitly institutionalist arguments in contrast to structural, ideational, or psychological arguments about institutions, see Parsons 2007: 67).

I do not adopt this perspective because other approaches, including critical theories, are less theoretically compelling in principle (alternative explanations appear in the concluding chapter). This choice emerges out of multiple observations of actors' behavior. Ideational factors might be necessary for shaping governance practices and effecting change. However, norms and ideas regarding the appropriate health governance styles cannot impinge on actors' cost–benefit calculations and do not inform their actions. Put boldly, norms, ideas, professional ethos, and the genuine desire to improve people's health security cannot reprogram and redefine main actors' interests cast in a rational, self-interested, and transactional mold. On the contrary, they slowly vanish from governance practices.

Still, why Russia? While Russia might not be a typical case in all the particularities of health governance inherent to personalistic regimes, this book urges further research on the perverse effects personalism and other types of nondemocratic regimes impose on health governance. The strength of focusing on a single country and investigating the regime's principals, specific government agencies, top state administrators, and governance intermediaries is to explore in-depth the processes that connect multiple actors (which have to operate within the confines of a particular personalistic regime) with actual health governance processes and their outcomes. A broader comparative and qualitative study could have hardly completed such an undertaking.

From an analytical perspective, it is helpful that personalism in Russia has been in the making for almost two decades (Baturo and Elkink 2016). By 2004, only several years in his first presidency, Putin found decisive success in overcoming the problem of the dispersion of political power. Political parties either submitted to his control or operated outside the legal, institutionalized arenas of struggle for power. The governors accepted the new rules of the game wherein they became accountable personally to Putin instead of their electorate. In 2020, Putin changed the Constitution he had sworn to protect and acquired the legal instruments to keep his power for life (Teague 2020). Putin had concentrated and maximized his power, but good governance did not ensue. For the most part, this book is concerned with Putin's third (2012–2018) and fourth, still ongoing (2018–2024), presidential terms. Covering the entire period of Putin's third presidential term also allows this investigation to increase the number of observations. At this point, the governance patterns are hardly changeable; problems with the state's quality and efficiency are most salient and best observable in this period of consolidated authoritarianism. The study's time frame is mostly 2012–2020, Putin's third and fourth presidential terms, which hitherto have been by and large absent from policy research due to informational constraints that inhibit arriving at a satisfying understanding of the governance process in Russia. Part of the problem is that researchers do not have adequate access to information regarding internal decision-making, which authoritarian systems are interested in concealing and even misrepresenting data for the sake of creating the pretense of successful governance. Elite members have no incentives to openly and honestly respond to inquisitive questions. But, as my research shows, these challenges are surmountable. When necessary, I briefly delve into earlier periods, as well.

Much of the information in the manuscript comes from extensive reading of the industry news and reports (published in such diverse outlets as Vademecum, Pharmatsevticheskii Vestnik, Meditsinskaya Gazeta, Medportal, and RBC, which, in my opinion, still give reliable qualitative and quantitative data on health governance over the last decade), as well as government documents (available at Kremlin.ru), published proceedings of the State Duma's health committees, the Ministry of Health documents, publicly available interviews with top health administrators, media appearances of influential individuals, and the online records and official reports of nongovernmental and quasi-governmental organizations (such as ITPC and ONF). Although these sources of information are not flawless, many of them are not yet heavily censored, unlike the hitherto independent business and political press, such as Kommersant and Vedomosti. Uncovering the evidence necessary for this investigation has been a laborious task. Nevertheless, interpreting the uncovered data provides a nuanced level of understanding of how Putin's system operates, its main actors' motivations and constraints, and why the regime cannot provide collective goods at the level that would bring positive social outcomes. Drawing attention to hitherto overlooked sources of information creates value for those specialists in Russian affairs who wish to continue to probe health governance processes even further.

Zooming in on the distinct episodes of health governance (ranging from the regime's inability to respond to the epidemic of HIV/AIDS to its inability to organize access to the essential life-saving medicines) allows us to expose a system of health governance in which all health actors claim to protect health but simultaneously fail to deliver. A close-up investigation of diverse health governance episodes has empirical merits and methodological advantages. Bringing together a diverse set of episodes of health governance is an advantage because it allows an observer to break free from the issue-specific analysis, which often involves claims that the issue area under investigation is exceptional (be that HIV/AIDS or COVID-19). Then, the policy measures under investigation are neither exceptional within the overarching system of governance nor incomparable to other health-related problems with which health administrators routinely deal.

There is a methodological advantage as well. Bringing under investigation substantively diverse instances of health governance managed by diverse sets of actors allow us to raise questions whether there is a fundamental commonality among all of them and whether the national system of health governance is cohesive in the sense that it is produced and shaped by a single generative structure. I argue that these episodes are interconnected and driven by the single underlying logic of personalistic rule. In addition, examining this empirical diversity helps evaluate my explanation's interpretative range. I contend that various episodes of governance, no matter how substantially diverse, indicate the persistence of the same practice generated by the necessity to regularly delimit choices and subjugate them to incentives and constraints of the Russian personalistic regime. These considerations drive the mode of inquiry.

Next Steps

The discussion of the episodes of health governance in the book follows the analytical arc as described in this chapter, and they appear in the relevant empirical chapters. This chapter has discussed the essential features of Russian personalistic rule that disrupt good governance and produce a scum of inefficiency the Kremlin tolerated for the last ten years. Chapter 2 exposes the regime's main practices in providing health goods to average Russians: it outlines how and why Putin's promises fall flat. Empirically, it documents perpetual drug shortages against Putin's wishes to make essential life-saving medicines accessible and affordable to all patients, traces poorly managed transition to pharmaceutical independence, and contrasts popularity-boosting mega-projects in health against the ill-conceived health care "optimization" (read: reduction) informed by the regime's revenue-maximizing concerns.

Chapter 3 reveals the primary strategies the regime uses to manage the multitude of health actors. It documents the principal's inability to punish his subordinates for incompetence and the negative externalities of manual control resulting in privileges and rents. Paradoxically, although the list of potential clients is ample, and thus Putin could replace any inept or corrupt agents, the new pool of his subordinates is likely to become sensitized to the boss's political goals and not so much responsive to the substantive goals at hand. Ultimately, no changes in top cadres, no matter how radical, will change much in the way the system operates. The chapter also investigates the Kremlin's manual management style, resulting in privileges and rents for the well-connected actors. The chapter also discusses how the ruler's disengagement from active leadership leaves core state actors without incentives to respond to public health crises.

Chapter 4 examines failures of oversight, both internal and external. It highlights the propensity of internal health surveillance organs and external actors to provide political value for the regime's principals to the detriment of impartial monitoring and oversight activities that could otherwise correct the faulty course of the Kremlin's actions. Since their inception in the early days of Putin's rule, internal health surveillance agencies struggled to maintain their bureaucratic powers and gradually settled on satisfying the Kremlin's political agenda. Meanwhile, nonstate intermediaries, coopted into the national architecture of health governance, shied away from exposing the deep-seated problems in Russia's health sector but pursued their narrow interests, ranging from protection to access to valuable resources and activities. Ultimately, intermediaries (especially in their individual capacity) decide to speak loyalty to Putin and avoid exposing poor decisions since such behavior will make them worse off.

Chapter 5 focuses on the unfolding discourses: how, why, and with what consequences relevant health actors securitize HIV/AIDS and damage the quality of the national response to the epidemic. This chapter proposes that key actors move to protect their contracts with the autocratic principal. They interpret Putin's illiberal ideological frameworks as a mandate to find and eradicate ontological threats to the country instead of eliminating public health crises. As elites settled on the discourse of HIV/AIDS as an ontological threat, they created facts on the ground for the ruler, and securitization thus became advantageous for agents to signal their fealty, seeking to justify and further his illiberal posture. Needless to say, all that had nothing to do with good health governance but, as a self-seeking gaming strategy, health securitization helped agents exonerate their underperformance.

Chapter 6 concludes the investigation. In addition to reiterating my main argument, it also attempts to take stock of the empirical assessment, comparing and contrasting pessimistic and optimistic views on the health governance outcomes in the country. The final chapter also discusses three prevalent explanatory perspectives, including the exposition of kleptocracy as the chief motivation of contemporary authoritarian regimes, the spreading neoliberal reason as the driver of failures in health provisions, the securitization approach, and the tendency to investigate the Russian case through the lens of numerous microscale strategies.

REFERENCES

Abbott, K.W., et al. 2020. Competence–Control Theory: The Challenge of Governing through Intermediaries. In *The Governor's Dilemma: Indirect Governance Beyond Principals and Agents*, ed. K.W. Abbott, et al., 3–36. Oxford: Oxford University Press.

Abbott, K.W., et al. 2021. Beyond Opportunism: Intermediary Loyalty in Regulation and Governance. *Regulation & Governance* 15 (S1): S83–S101.

Aburamoto, M. 2019. An Indispensable Party of Power? United Russia and Putin's Return to the Presidency, 2011–2014. *Russian Politics* 4 (1): 22–41.

Acemoglu, D., and J. Robinson. 2019. Rents and Economic Development: The Perspective of Why Nations Fail. *Public Choice* 181 (1): 13–28.

Auzan, A. 2005. Grazhdanskoe obshchestvo i grazhdanskaya politika. *Polit.ru*, 1 June.

Baturo, A., and J.A. Elkink. 2016. Dynamics of Regime Personalization and Patron-Client Networks in Russia, 1999–2014. *Post-Soviet Affairs* 32 (1): 75–98.

Beazer, Q.H., and O.J. Reuter. 2021. Do Authoritarian Elections Help the Poor? Evidence from Russian Cities. *The Journal of Politics* 84 (1): 437–454.

Belton, C. 2020. *Putin's People: How the KGB Took Back Russia and Then Took On the West*. New York: Farrar, Straus and Giroux.

Bernhard, M., A.B. Edgell, and S.I. Lindberg. 2020. Institutionalising Electoral Uncertainty and Authoritarian Regime Survival. *European Journal of Political Research* 59: 465–487.

Bindman, E., et al. 2019. NGOs and the Policy-making Process in Russia: The Case of Child Welfare Reform. *Governance* 32 (2): 207–222.

Blackburn, M., and B. Petersson. 2021. Parade, Plebiscite, Pandemic: Legitimation Efforts in Putin's Fourth Term. *Post-Soviet Affairs*. https://doi.org/10.1080/1060586X.2021.2020575.

Blank, S. 2008. Ivanov, Chemezov, and State Capture of the Russian Defense Sector. *Problems of Post-Communism* 55 (1): 49–60.

Bratton, M., and N. van de Walle. 1997. *Democratic Experiments in Africa: Regime Transitions in Comparative Perspective*. New York: Cambridge University Press.

Chaisty, P., and S. Whitefield. 2019. The Political Implications of Popular Support for Presidential Term Limits in Russia. *Post-Soviet Affairs* 35 (4): 323–337.

Chebankova, E. 2012. State-sponsored Civic Associations in Russia: Systemic Integration or the 'War of Position'? *East European Politics* 28 (4): 390–408.

Chehabi, H., and J. Linz. 1998. *Sultanistic Regimes*. Baltimore: Johns Hopkins University Press.

Cook, S. 2007. *Ruling But Not Governing: The Military and Political Development in Egypt, Algeria, and Turkey.* Baltimore: Johns Hopkins University Press.

Detkova, P., E. Podkolzina, and A. Tkachenko. 2018. Corruption, Centralization and Competition: Evidence from Russian Public Procurement. *International Journal of Public Administration* 41 (5–6): 414–434.

Egorov, G., and K. Sonin. 2011. Dictators and their Viziers: Endogenizing the Loyalty-Competence Trade-off. *Journal of the European Economic Association* 9 (5): 903–930.

Elster, J. 2018. The Resistible Rise of Louis Bonaparte. In *Can It Happen Here? Authoritarianism in America*, ed. C. R. Sunstein, 277–312. New York: Dey St.

Evans, P.B. 1995. *Embedded Autonomy: States and Industrial Transformation.* Princeton: Princeton University Press.

Ezrow, N., and E. Frantz. 2011. *Dictators and Dictatorships: Understanding Authoritarian Regimes and Their Leaders.* New York: The Continuum Publishing Group.

Fel'shtinskii, Yu., and V. Popov. 2021. *Ot Krasnogo Terrora k Mafioznomu Gosudarstvu: Spetssluzhby Rossii v Bor'be za Mirovoe Gospodstvo (1917–2036).* Kyiv: Nash Format.

Flikke, G. 2018. Conflicting Opportunities or Patronal Politics? Restrictive NGO Legislation in Russia 2012–2015. *Europe-Asia Studies* 70 (4): 564–590.

Foa, R.S. 2018. Modernization and Authoritarianism. *Journal of Democracy* 29 (3): 129–140.

Fukuyama, F. 2013. What is Governance? *Governance* 26 (3): 347–368.

Gaaze, K. 2015. Stsenarii posadok: chem opasno dlya Kremlya delo Gaizera. *Forbes.ru*, 23 September.

Gaaze, K. 2017. Chto oznachaet prigovor Ulyukaevu. *Carnegie.ru*, 15 December.

Galimova, N. 2018. Otsenki dlya Kremlya: zachem upravleniya Kirienko vvodyat KPI. *RBC*, 27 November.

Gandhi, J. 2008. *Political Institutions under Dictatorship.* Cambridge: Cambridge University Press.

Geddes, B. 1994. *Politician's Dilemma: Building State Capacity in Latin America.* Berkeley and Los Angeles: University of California Press.

Geddes, B., J. Wright, and E. Frantz. 2018. *How Dictatorships Work: Power, Personalization, and Collapse.* New York: Cambridge University Press.

Gehlbach, S., and P. Keefer. 2011. Investment without Democracy: Ruling-party Institutionalization and Credible Commitment in Autocracies. *Journal of Comparative Economics* 39 (2): 123–139.

Gel'man, V., and A. Starodubtsev. 2016. Opportunities and Constraints of Authoritarian Modernisation: Russian Policy Reforms in the 2000s. *Europe-Asia Studies* 68 (1): 97–117.
Gel'man, V. 2020a. The Politics of Fear: How the Russian Regime Confronts its Opponents. *Russian Social Science Review* 61 (6): 467–482.
Gel'man, V. 2020b. Porazhenie bez Srazheniya: Rossiiskaya Oppozitsiya i Predely Mobilizatsii. In *Novaya (Ne)legitimnost': Kak Prokhodilo i Chto Prineslo Rossii Perepisyvanie Konstitutsii*, ed. K. Rogov, 63–69. Moskva: Fond Liberal'naya Missiya.
Golosov, G.V. 2016. Why and How Electoral Systems Matter in Autocracies. *Australian Journal of Political Science* 51 (3): 367–385.
Grigoriev, I.S., and A.A. Dekalchuk. 2017. Collective Learning and Regime Dynamics under Uncertainty: Labour Reform and the Way to Autocracy in Russia. *Democratization* 24 (3): 481–497.
Guriev, S., and D. Treisman. 2019. Informational Autocrats. *Journal of Economic Perspectives* 33 (4): 100–127.
Guriev, S., and D. Treisman. 2020. The Popularity of Authoritarian Leaders: A Cross-National Investigation. *World Politics* 72 (4): 601–638.
Gürsoy, Y. 2017. *Between Military Rule and Democracy: Regime Consolidation in Greece, Turkey, and Beyond*. Ann Arbor: University of Michigan Press.
Haber, S. 2008. Authoritarian Government. In *The Oxford Handbook of Political Economy*, ed. D.A. Wittman and B.R. Weingast, 693–707. New York: Oxford University Press.
Hale, H.E. 2015. *Patronal Politics: Eurasian Regime Dynamics in Comparative Perspective*. New York: Cambridge University Press.
Hanson, E. 2010. *Post-Imperial Democracies: Ideology and Party Formation in Third Republic France, Weimar Germany, and Post-Soviet Russia*. New York: Cambridge University Press.
Hartmann, C. 2022. Authoritarian Origins of Term Limit Trajectories in Africa. *Democratization* 29 (1): 57–73.
Huang, X. 2020. *Social Protection under Authoritarianism: Health Politics and Policy in China*. New York: Oxford University Press.
Isaacs, R., and S. Whitmore. 2014. The Limited Agency and Life-cycles of Personalized Dominant Parties in the Post-Soviet space: The Cases of United Russia and Nur Otan. *Democratization* 21 (4): 699–721.
Jones, C.W. 2019. Adviser to The King: Experts, Rationalization, and Legitimacy. *World Politics* 71 (1): 1–43.
Kandil, H. 2016. *The Power Triangle: Military, Security, and Politics in Regime Change*. New York: Oxford University Press.
Klein, S.H., and F. Vidal Luna. 2017. *Brazil 1964–1985: The Military Regimes of Latin America in the Cold War*. New Haven: Yale University Press.

Kling, A.S. 2016. *Specialization and Trade: A Reintroduction to Economics: An Introduction*. Washington, D.C.: Cato Institute.
Krivoshapko, Yu. 2020. Dvizhenie vverkh: Sem' dostizhenii Federal'noi nalogovoi sluzhby pod rukovodstvom Mikhaila Mishustina. *Rossiiskaya Gazeta* No. 8 (8062), 16 January.
Kryshtanovskaya, O., and S. White. 2003. Putin's Militocracy. *Post-Soviet Affairs* 19 (4): 289–306.
Lake, D.A. 2009. *Hierarchy in International Relations*. Ithaca and London: Cornell University Press.
Lake, D.A., and M.A. Baum. 2001. The Invisible Hand of Democracy: Political Control and the Provision of Public Services. *Comparative Political Studies* 34 (6): 587–621.
Laruelle, M. 2020. Making Sense of Russia's Illiberalism. *Journal of Democracy* 31 (3): 115–129.
Levi, M. 1989. *Of Rule and Revenue*. Berkeley and Los Angeles: University of California Press.
Levitsky, S., and J. Loxton. 2013. Populism and Competitive Authoritarianism in the Andes. *Democratization* 20 (1): 107–136.
Levitsky, S., and L. Way. 2010. *Competitive Authoritarianism: Hybrid Regimes After the Cold War*. New York: Cambridge University Press.
Linz, J. 2000. *Totalitarian and Authoritarian Regimes*. Boulder, CO: Lynne Rienner Publishers.
Linz, J., and A. Stepan. 1996. *Problems of Democratic Transition and Consolidation: Southern Europe, South America, and Post-Communist Europe*. Baltimore: Johns Hopkins University Press.
Ljubownikow, S., and J. Crotty. 2016. Nonprofit Influence on Public Policy: Exploring Nonprofit Advocacy in Russia. *Nonprofit and Voluntary Sector Quarterly* 45 (2): 314–332.
Magaloni, B. 2006. *Voting for Autocracy. Hegemonic Party Survival and its Demise in Mexico*. New York: Cambridge University Press.
Markus, S. 2015. *Property, Predation, and Protection: Piranha Capitalism in Russia and Ukraine*. Cambridge: Cambridge University Press.
McCubbins, M.D., and T. Schwartz. 1984. Congressional Oversight Overlooked: Police Patrols versus Fire Alarms. *American Journal of Political Science* 28 (1): 165–179.
Melikyan, T. 2014. ONF god spustya: mulyazh partii ili strategicheskii proekt Kremlya? *Moskovskii Komsomolets*, 12 June.
Migranyan, A. 2004. Chto takoe putinizm? *Strategiya Rossii v XXI veke* No. 3.
Miller, G.J., and A.B. Whitford. 2016. *Above Politics: Bureaucratic Discretion and Credible Commitment*. New York: Cambridge University Press.
Nagornykh, I. 2018. Vernut' doverie narodnykh mass: Kreml' zadumalsya nad programmoi na 2019 god. *RTVi*, 13 November.

North, D.C. 1990. *Institutions, Institutional Change and Economic Performance.* Cambridge: Cambridge University Press.

North, D.C., J.J. Wallis, and B.R. Weingast. 2009. *Violence and Social Orders: A Conceptual Framework for Interpreting Recorded Human History.* New York: Cambridge University Press.

Olimpieva, I., and O. Pachenkov. 2013. Corrupt Intermediaries in Post-Socialist Russia: Mutations of Economic Institutions. *Europe-Asia Studies* 65 (7): 1364–1376.

Osei, A., et al. 2020. Presidential Term Limits and Regime Types: When Do Leaders Respect Constitutional Norms? *Africa Spectrum* 55 (3): 251–271.

Paget, D. 2020. Again, Making Tanzania Great: Magufuli's Restorationist Developmental Nationalism. *Democratization* 27 (7): 1240–1260.

Pan, J. 2020. *Welfare for Autocrats: How Social Assistance in China Cares for its Rulers.* New York: Oxford University Press.

Parsons, C. 2007. *How to Map Arguments in Political Science.* New York: Oxford University Press.

Pertsev, A. 2015. Privet iz GDR: Kak Kreml' primenit Narodnyi front. *Carnegie.ru*, 9 December.

Pertsev, A. 2020. Edinaya Rossiya pomenyaet nazvanie i obedinitsya s Narodnym frontom. *Meduza.io*, 25 February.

Petrov, N., and M. Rochlitz. 2019. Control Over the Security Services in Periods of Political Uncertainty: A Comparative Study of Russia and China. *Russian Politics* 4 (4): 546–573.

Pomerantsev, P. 2014. The Hidden Author of Putinism: How Vladislav Surkov Invented the New Russia. *The Atlantic*, 7 November.

Putin, V. 2020. Vystuplenie na final'noi sessii diskussionnogo kluba Valdai, 22 October. http://kremlin.ru/events/president/news/64261.

Rahat, G., and O. Kenig. 2018. *From Party Politics to Personalized Politics? Party Change and Political Personalization in Democracies.* New York, Oxford University Press.

Remington, T. 2008. Patronage and the Party of Power: President-Parliament Relations Under Vladimir Putin. *Europe-Asia Studies* 60 (6): 959–987.

Renz, B. 2006. Putin's Militocracy? An Alternative Interpretation of Siloviki in Contemporary Russian Politics. *Europe-Asia Studies* 58 (6): 903–924.

Reuter, O.J., and T.F. Remington. 2009. Dominant Party Regimes and the Commitment Problem: The Case of United Russia. *Comparative Political Studies* 42 (4): 501–526.

Rivera, D.W., and S.W. Rivera. 2018. The Militarization of the Russian Elite under Putin. *Problems of Post-Communism* 65 (4): 221–232.

Rivera, S.W., and D.W. Rivera. 2006. The Russian Elite under Putin: Militocratic or Bourgeois? *Post-Soviet Affairs* 22 (2): 125–144.

Robinson, N. 2020. Putin and the Incompleteness of Putinism. *Russian Politics* 5 (3): 283–300.
Rodrick, D. 2010. The Myth of Authoritarian Growth. *Project Syndicate*, 9 August.
Saikkonen, I. 2021. Coordinating the Machine: Subnational Political Context and the Effectiveness of Machine Politics. *Acta Politica* 56 (4): 658–676.
Satter, D. 2016. *The Less You Know, the Better You Sleep: Russia's Road to Terror and Dictatorship under Yeltsin and Putin*. New Haven and London: Yale University Press.
Schedler, A. 2013. *The Politics of Uncertainty: Sustaining and Subverting Electoral Authoritarianism*. New York: Oxford University Press.
Scott, J.C. 1998. *Seeing Like a State: How Certain Schemes to Improve the Human Condition Have Failed*. New Haven and London: Yale University Press.
Seeberg, M.B. 2014. State Capacity and the Paradox of Authoritarian Elections. *Democratization* 21 (7): 1265–1285.
Shishkin, S.V., et al. 2018. *Zdravookhranenie: Neobkhodimye Otvety na Vyzovy Vremeni*. Moskva: Tsentr Strategicheskikh Razrabotok.
Shpil'kin, S. 2021. Vybory po nakatannoi kolee. *Troitskii variant—Nauka*, 5 October.
Smith, B. 2005. Life of the Party: The Origins of Regime Breakdown and Persistence under Single-Party Rule. *World Politics* 57 (3): 421–451.
Snyder, T. 2018. *The Road to Unfreedom: Russia, Europe*. America. New York: Tim Duggan Books.
Soldatov, A., and I. Borogan. 2011. *The New Nobility: The Restoration of Russia's Security State and the Enduring Legacy of the KGB*. New York: Public Affairs.
Stanovaya, T. 2019. Grudges Before Politics: Arrests in Russia Are Increasingly Random. *Carnegie Moscow Center*, 5 April.
Stromseth, J.R., E.J. Malesky, and D.D. Gueorguiev, eds. 2017. *China's Governance Puzzle: Enabling Transparency and Participation in a Single-Party State*. New York: Cambridge University Press.
Svolik, M. 2012. *The Politics of Authoritarian Rule*. New York: Cambridge University Press.
Talleh Nkobou, A., and A. Ainslie. 2021. Developmental Nationalism? Political Trust and the Politics of Large-Scale Land Investment in Magufuli's Tanzania. *Journal of Eastern African Studies* 15(3): 378–399.
Taylor, B.D. 2011. *State Building in Putin's Russia: Policing and Coercion after Communism*. New York: Cambridge University Press.
Taylor, B.D. 2014. Police Reform in Russia: The Policy Process in a Hybrid Regime. *Post-Soviet Affairs* 30 (2–3): 226–255.
Taylor, B.D. 2017. The Russian Siloviki and Political Change. *Daedalus* 146 (2): 53–63.
Taylor, B.D. 2018. *The Code of Putinism*. New York: Oxford University Press.

Teague, E. 2020. Russia's Constitutional Reforms of 2020. *Russian Politics* 5 (3): 301–328.

Thomson, H. 2019. *Food and Power: Regime Type, Agricultural Policy, and Political Stability.* Cambridge and New York: Cambridge University Press.

Treisman, D. 2018. Introduction: Rethinking Putin's Political Order. In *The New Autocracy: Information, Politics, and Policy in Putin's Russia*, ed. D. Treisman, 1–28. Washington, D.C.: Brookings Institution.

Vahabi, M. 2016. A Positive Theory of the Predatory State. *Public Choice* 168 (3): 153–175.

Vahabi, M. 2020. Introduction: A Symposium on the Predatory State. *Public Choice* 182: 233–242.

Way, L. 2008. The Real Causes of the Color Revolutions. *Journal of Democracy* 19 (3): 55–69.

Way, L. 2015. *Pluralism by Default: Weak Autocrats and the Rise of Competitive Politics.* Baltimore: Johns Hopkins University Press.

White, D. 2011. Dominant Party Systems: A Framework for Conceptualizing Opposition Strategies in Russia. *Democratization* 18 (3): 655–681.

Wintrobe, R. 1998. *The Political Economy of Dictatorship.* Cambridge, UK: Cambridge University Press.

Yakovlev, A., and A. Aisin. 2019. Friends or Foes? The Effect of Governor-Siloviki Interaction on Economic Growth in Russian Regions. *Russian Politics* 4 (4): 520–545.

Yasuda, J. 2017. *On Feeding the Masses: An Anatomy of Regulatory Failure in China.* Cambridge: Cambridge University Press.

Yildirim, T. M., et al. 2022. Agenda Dynamics and Policy Priorities in Military Regimes. *International Political Science Review* 43 (3): 418–432.

Yurchak, A. 2006. *Everything Was Forever, Until It Was No More: The Last Soviet Generation.* Princeton: Princeton University Press.

Zavadskaya, M., and L. Shilov. 2021. Providing Goods and Votes? Federal Elections and the Quality of Local Governance in Russia. *Europe-Asia Studies* 73 (6): 1037–1059.

CHAPTER 2

Providing Goods: Health Mandates and Authoritarian Performance

It must be admitted that the state will not avoid participating in developing some sectors of our economy in the near future. I mean the direct participation of the state. It will not be possible, and there is no need to leave. The strategically important sectors will be under the constant attention of the state.
 —Vladimir Putin, in the first presidential address to the Federal Assembly, 8 July 2000.

I do not see any serious failures<...> All the tasks set have been achieved. All set goals have been achieved. The tasks have been completed<...> As for my personal perception, I am sure I am not ashamed of the citizens who voted for me twice, electing [me] the President of the Russian Federation. All these eight years, I plowed like a galley slave, from morning to night, and did it with full dedication.
 —Vladimir Putin, reflecting on his first two presidential terms.

INTRODUCTION

In nearly all of his numerous interviews and carefully staged press conferences, Vladimir Putin keeps promising to improve people's well-being, instructs his subordinates to work better, and boasts numerous successes. Healthcare is no exception. As the first opening quote exemplifies, on many occasions, Putin stated that tangible improvements in the health sector constitute no less than a central function of the state. The second quote that opens this chapter introduces another important theme for the ensuing pages. Putin does not hesitate to offer self-serving remarks about the quality of his governance, although these utterances are no more than exercises in self-promotion. Putin has recently been more circumspect than before (in 2019, he acknowledged that reorganization of medical care had not been efficient), but a victorious sentiment endures (see numerous praises for the Sputnik-V and other homemade coronavirus vaccines developed by the state-owned enterprises).

Never mind that Russian health experts do not identify the regime as the constitutive institution, driving inefficiencies that seem to multiply recently. Never mind that for average Russians, recurrent but low-key implementation flubs could appear less important than they really are. Knowledge of individual tragedies, though by no means trivial, almost always exposes specific but not far-flung episodes of state failure. Over time, the patients are destined to experience the full burden of the underlying pathology of Putin's governance strategies. On the verge of Putin's fifth presidential term, fewer foreign medicines are available to the patients; domestic producers are often unreliable and make inferior medical products; there are fewer hospital beds with fewer but burned-out physicians; and many routine health procedures are on indefinite hold. "The morgue is full. Calling an ambulance is pointless" is but one disturbing headline that summarizes Russia's crumbling state capacity in the deadly times of COVID (Kotlyar 2020). How did it come to this?

The main line of argument is as follows. Without denying the difficulty, intractability, or malignness of health-related issues, it is an institutional arrangement of Russia's personalistic regime that bears the onus of responsibility for bad outcomes. An autocrat declares his commitment to achieve substantive goals but is more concerned about his political survival. The competence-control theory understands the diremption between political and substantive goals fairly well, but it implies that the balance between the two is possible (Abbott et al. 2020: 16). However, Putin designs high-profile health initiatives (decommodification of medicines, import substitution policies, and national projects in health) as an authoritarian bargain with society, providing public goods in return for political support. Putin issues many bureaucratic mandates, but they are often of low quality because they, first and foremost, must support the needs of informational autocracy, not substantive policy goals. Additionally, the mandates' inherent flaw is in proscribing needful and routine spending while directing resources to the politically expedient projects in excess. Further, because Putin's agents are best conceptualized as Vassals—for the reasons explained in the preceding chapter—they prioritize meeting Putin's political needs, expectations, and desires at the expense of the quality of regulation and patients' satisfaction. As the chapter shows, an institutional arrangement incentivizes state bureaucracies to deploy gaming strategies, misrepresent policy outcomes, hide wasted resources, and misinform the public. The detailed line of reasoning is in the first section of this chapter.

Empirically, this chapter profiles four health governance episodes, each linking the ruler's core health promises and the ensuing governance process, which featured either low-key or high-profile governance flubs. The second section documents how the regulators tried to implement Putin's promise of making essential life-saving medicines accessible and affordable to all patients. The third section traces the flurry of regulations intended to make Russian patients less dependent on imported pharmaceuticals and medical devices. The fourth section turns to the Kremlin's intent on high-profile mega-projects in health accompanied by its decommitment from providing adequate resources for routine operations in the health sector. The last one discusses examples of microscale mandates Putin issues, following up on individualized promises he makes during high-profile and televised communication with average Russians.

Personalistic Legitimacy: Plenteous Promises and Faulty Mandates

The necessity to manage the fundamental uncertainty of elections incentivizes rulers to expand the provision of public goods and escalate public services' efficiency (Treisman 2011). After all, those Russians who vote for Putin and United Russia and are willing to turn a blind eye to electoral irregularities do not support Putin's regime because they genuinely prefer authoritarianism to democracy (Carnaghan 2007; Hale 2011; Kolesnikov and Volkov 2020), but because they seek material inducements and social benefits. Convincing the public of the Kremlin's competence and effectiveness—in contrast to the opposition, which had presumably failed to propose a proper social agenda and could not govern effectively—is essential for the regime's survival. And Putin repeatedly makes a point by accusing the opposition of incompetence and predatory behavior (Putin 2010, 2012, 2017).

As Jim Rosenau (2003: 280) noted, "historical criteria of legitimacy are being replaced by performance criteria, and, as a consequence, fewer and fewer patterns of habitual compliance seem to sustain the life of communities." Consistent with this general observation, significant improvements in governance practices (Martin et al. 2022; Owen and Bindman 2019; Truex 2017) and strong state capacity (Croissant and Hellmann 2017; Hanson 2017) elicit public support. For their part, autocrats seek to sustain performance-based popularity in order to stay in power, weather formally competitive elections, avoid losses in public confidence (Hale 2015: 282–291), and prevent defection among the elite (Hale and Colton 2017). The particularistic provision of public goods and services remains essential in maintaining the regime's popular appeal even in the context of under-delivery of services in general (Blackburn 2020; Han 2020; Duckett and Wang 2017; Hutcheson and Petersson 2016). In this respect, Russia is not unique: betting on performance-based legitimacy seems central to politics in other nondemocracies, too (Han 2020; Ratigan 2022). Simply put, nondemocratic rulers' primary concern is to shore up their legitimacy by effective performance (Hutcheson and Petersson 2016) and offset the inconvenience of low governmental ratings.

Relying on performance-based legitimacy tied to the provision of public goods and services was central to the entire period of Putin's tenure in politics. At the outset of his presidency, Putin humbly represented himself as a hired manager whose main task was to make the state functional and user-friendly. He portrayed himself as a technocrat with little taste for concentrating and maximizing power for its own sake. Notably, in his annual Presidential Address to the Federal Assembly in 2002, Putin formulated his mission as follows: "the direct duty of the state is to… provide the population with high-quality public services and effectively manage state property… We must make Russia a flourishing and prosperous country. To live in it comfortably and safely. So that people can work freely, [and] earn for themselves and their children without restrictions and fear" (Putin 2002). His presidential addresses and lengthy annual press conferences that followed have reiterated this essential point. Later on, Putin predictably claimed that "[i]mproving the quality and life expectancy of citizens is one of the key development goals of the country, it is around these tasks, around a person everything should revolve, everything should be built, including our national projects" (Putin 2018a).

Insightful observers of Russian affairs describe the domestic social contract between the ruler and non-elites in terms of trading political and civil rights for the prospects of economic growth and social order and offering loyalty and political faithfulness in exchange for stability and social protection (see, for instance, Auzan 2005). During his two presidential terms, Putin enjoyed the benefits of economic growth without initiating deep institutional reforms and thus seemed to have the contract with non-elites fulfilled. It stands to reason that favorable material circumstances generally enabled the regime to achieve generic policy goals. Had he stepped down in 2008, Russians would have likely remembered Putin as one of the most effective leaders in the country's history. But his decision to return to the official commanding heights despite legal and constitutional constraints caused an acute legitimacy crisis and pushed Putin on the old road of plenteous promises, but this time in unfavorable circumstances.

The crucial moment for the regime's legitimacy unfolded in the winter of 2011–2012. In the wake of protests triggered by electoral fraud, Putin signed eleven so-called "May Decrees," which supplied new health indicators to be achieved by 2018 while highlighting Putin's image as the champion of the ordinary people in contrast to the disappointed and frenzied "creative class" that took protests to the streets of Moscow. These "May Decrees," although not newfangled by any measure, were touted as evidence of Putin's continued and increased commitment to social betterment. This example is but one instance within a string of decisions that connect potential legitimacy problems to ramped-up promises of social betterment.

At the same time, the Kremlin pursued the goal of increasing compliance among non-elites by offering non-material inducements: a sense of belonging to a rising great power in exchange for people's willingness to tighten their belts (Shevtsova 2015; Grozovskii 2016). Indeed, at the onset of Putin's third presidential term, the Kremlin made use of territorial expansions, recycled cults of military glory, patriotic education, national pride, and gendered norms to shore up the regime's public approval (Novaya Gazeta 2021; Barabanov and Morar 2007; Sperling 2014). A heavily doctored version of World War II, endorsed by the masses via public performances, seemed to have become a symbolic centerpiece of the Kremlin's grand narrative. Still, although militaristic posture and illiberal sensibilities accompany the artificial image of Russia as a great power, Putin did not abandon the strategy of promising to maximize people's welfare.

By 2018, although Putin had consolidated public support by annexing Ukraine's peninsula of Crimea in 2014, his popularity slowly dwindled (Nikolskaya and Dmitriev 2020), and people's relationship with the regime looked more like acquiescence than enthusiastic support. As the seductive lure of geopolitical expansion faded, Putin began stressing the goals of modernization and development as central to his presidency with new gusto. To maintain an image of a competent and benevolent leader, he offered a new round of material inducements and reiterated his promise to make real improvements in the lives of average Russians. The executive orders, signed on the eve of his fourth term in office in May 2018, gave special prominence to health matters. Once more, he promised to overhaul the economy, spend trillions of rubles on the crumbling infrastructure and social issues, and, importantly, vowed to improve access to medicines and fix the health system's inadequacies. Further, instead of invading Ukraine in the Spring of 2021, which independent analysts considered feasible and professional propagandists desirable, at his yearly presidential address, president Putin once again started beating the old drum of targeted and particularized spending.

Putin's strategy of material inducements—as they take the form of concrete and particularistic promises to the masses—requires issuing mandates which closely reflect the president's promises but ignore critical expert input. From the standpoint of political expediency, the principal's mandates need not be well-crafted, but they have to be attractive enough for the electorate and perceived as credible. From the standpoint of competence-control theory, these mandates hardly promote genuine autonomy or bureaucratic competence. In a similar vein, by revealing Putin's nontransparent and single-handed decision-making practices, commentators point out the low quality of presidential mandates. Referencing well-informed political insiders, Gaaze (2014) indicates that the top governmental officials had little purchase in influencing Putin's strategic decisions, such as the course on import substitution of foodstuffs that, unsurprisingly, programmed the low quality of regulation and massive negative externalities.

Overall, Putin issues bureaucratic mandates that often are contradictory, unclear, lopsided, or microscale.

- Contradictory mandates instruct agents to improve access to goods and services across the vast country without spending adequate resources. Putin expects agents to improve people's access to hospitals and primary healthcare physicians in the rural areas, but he also demands the further consolidation of hospitals in the remote parts of the country and the reduction of emergency care facilities. These kinds of mandates require agents to achieve measurable indicators, brushing off patients' interests and needs.
- Some mandates are unclear, but state agents, evading roles of Zealots or policy entrepreneurs, cannot really decide what the directives' grand purposes are, except for trying to implement them to the letter of Putin's words. Agents cannot competently achieve contradictory or unclear mandates, and state officials, instead of maximizing the well-being of society, focus on lending credence to the ruler's desired image of a public-oriented leader.
- Lopsided mandates are disproportionately weighted in favor of one agency despite the necessity of inter-agency cooperation in the interest of people's welfare. Directing the government to achieve pharmaceutical independence, Putin put the Ministry of Trade and Industry (hereafter, Minpromtorg) in charge, which regulated with little concern about patients having an appropriate drug supply.
- Microscale mandates, which illustrate Putin's propensity for manual steering, are explicit and targeted directives to remedy a harmful or unwelcome situation, usually at the individual or communal level. Putin seems to like helping individuals, but his magnanimity hardly addresses a set of systemic problems. Although microscale mandates attempt to bear the image of the president's benevolence against the sagging healthcare system and regional authorities' callousness, they do not improve the enduring health governance practices.

The discussed features of Putin's mandates have a ripple effect on agents. For their part, elites are interested in protecting their careers and getting access to rents while readily fabricating stories of success that validate Putin's broadly advertised social promises. They have adapted and internalized the role of decision-takers. State officials and intermediaries, who choose to follow or anticipate the principal's wishes without questions or criticism, become Vassals (on terminology, see Abbott et al. 2021). Unlike Zealots, who seek to implement specific policies to the best of their abilities, Vassals would not sacrifice the ruler's political objectives for policy gains. Instead, they refrain from challenging the faulty terms of the principal's mandates and report doctored policy results. Importantly, Vassals bolster Putin's image as a competent national leader, shield the Kremlin from public accountability, and hide the facts of governance flubs in order to sustain "informational autocracy." These constraints prompt the ruler's subordinates to show quantifiable but hardly meaningful results in order to avoid Putin's disapproval.

In this context, faking performance is an optimizing response to the personalistic system of governance: it protects state administrators vis-a-vis the principal and "creates facts" on the ground, necessary to manipulate the submitted information about health initiatives' success in his favor (Guriev and Treisman 2019; Paneyakh 2014; Kukulin and Kurennoi 2017). It follows that regulatory density, reformist fervor, and an endless cycle of half-baked changes do not flow from the desire to serve the constituency. On the contrary, incessant in-house changes all too often generate unexpected, unintended, and undesirable consequences hurting the quality of Russian health governance.

Notably, bureaucrats often manipulate measurement processes to improve measured performance (e.g., counting repackaged pharmaceuticals as Russian-made, which leads to output distortion but meets the intended goals on paper). They frequently add, delete, and cycle new objectives and programmatic components (e.g., the national priority projects' objectives in health and their assessment methods shifted over time). Sometimes, they misrepresent numbers to imply that all patients receive the treatment (e.g., they adopt very low thresholds for initiating therapy in the HIV-positive population). They also manipulate measure selection to convey the misleading impression of significant increases in spending over time (e.g., they measure social spending in the national currency despite the ruble's free fall). Eerily reminiscent of how the dictatorial Kremlin dealt with the failing five-year plans by reshuffling and hiding the metrics in the 1930s, the current government tends to extend the national priority projects for years in order to hide disappointing outcomes (Galieva 2020). For a theoretical discussion of these gaming techniques, see Moynihan (2010).

The overall consequences flowing from the intent regulatory activity might appear confusing. If an observer is satisfied by accepting the official narrative, then a conclusion that the regime achieved some generic goals is indubitable. However, such a view skates over the ineffectiveness of agents' performance and multiple negative externalities flowing out of the principal's faulty mandates and agents' self-seeking actions. Much as Putin is satisfied with imitating the improvement of citizens' welfare and public health (Putin 2008), so are his subordinates and societal intermediaries. Increasingly apparent is that the rhetoric of performance becomes less credible, and thus promissory and performance-based legitimacy will decrease in utility, giving way to coercive strategies.

DECOMMODIFICATION OF MEDICINES: BENEVOLENT BUT NOT EFFICIENT

In Russia, a promise to tame prices on essential goods is essential for maintaining the regime's popularity, and Putin consistently signaled to the public that he monitored the situation and issued appropriate directives. Given a dark collective memory of how the instability of prices and inflation ushered political turbulence—Andrey Konchalovsky's new film *Dear Comrades* is but one artistic reminder—Putin understands the importance of ensuring access to essential goods. Controlling prices is more than an intuitively appealing idea: Putin embraces the vision of the USSR as a normative ideal, and the communist rule was legitimized more by the stability of prices and full employment than by the elusive Marxist utopia. Most recently, in July 2021, Putin instructed his subordinates to reverse the rising prices on popular foodstuffs, including sunflower oil, buckwheat, tubers, and vegetables, necessary for preparing traditional meals. By November, agents implemented this microscale mandate using several market-based mechanisms, and the prices fell, confirming Putin's benevolence (Kuz'mina and Perevoshchikova 2021). This story is an illustrative example of Putin's social promises. However, in contrast to keeping the prices of agricultural products low, medicines and medical devices are another matter.

Essentially, Putin promises that federal or regional budgets would foot the bill for some pharmaceuticals while wanting agents to cap prices on medicines and expecting private suppliers to participate in public procurement, sacrificing their profits. The principal's commands to control prices impair their functionality as a market signal; recurrent deficits and unsuccessful public tenders predictably ensue. As noted prior, Putin's subordinates recognize him as the only strategic decision-maker, adjust their goals to the principal's, and internalize the terms of bureaucratic mandates. For them, keeping prices artificially low and showing the boss their loyalty and competence is more important than keeping drugs on the pharmacies' shelves. The government took several steps to implement Putin's mandate.

Firstly, toward the end of Putin's second administration, the Russian regulator (the Ministry of Health) approved a freshly compiled list of essential life-saving medicines (ELSM), numerating which drugs must be covered by the federal or regional budgets provided to patients who qualify free of charge. On the positive side, free medicines would circumvent the problem of their availability for low-income Russians. The original intent was to include safe and effective drugs for treating the most prevalent diseases, including HIV and tuberculosis. Over the years, the number of items expanded from nearly 500 to about 700 international nonproprietary names, meaning the government had to manage several thousand trade-name products and pharmaceutical forms. However, regulators never offered a coherent explanation of how and why certain drugs made it on the list. The head of the Russian pharmaceutical manufacturers association, Viktor Dmitriev, noted that neither treatment standards nor the budgetary process could have justified the ELSM list in its current form. Overall, because of the nontransparent top-down decision-making style, there is no guarantee that patients' interests and needs could be adequately protected. The appearance of a pharmaceutical product on this list is no guarantee of patients receiving it.

Secondly, as the government wanted to keep essential medicines affordable, it unilaterally imposed price ceilings, above which no manufacturer was legally allowed to sell medicines to pharmacies and distributors. The government also constantly maneuvered and manipulated different methodologies to justify extremely low prices for public tender. This approach triggered significant complications that plagued the otherwise public-spirited obligation of Russia's authorities, and it hardly incentivized any foreign or domestic pharmaceutical firms to compete for the Russian market or remain interested in it. The ELSM list included many barely profitable drugs, and as companies began to freeze their production, many popular medicines disappeared from the public auctions and private stores alike. Worse, although the Russian currency devaluations became quite common, manufacturers were allowed to raise prices only once a year and not exceed the official inflation rates.

Some regulatory ideas to keep costs down were downright extreme. In 2014, as Minpromtorg (the Ministry of Industry and Trade) proposed defining the initial (maximum) selling price by referring to manufacturers' prices, distributors were facing genuine prospects of financial ruin

(Zvezdina 2014). Equally unreasonable was the proposal that mandated prices of the ready-to-use pharmaceutical products do not exceed the costs of their active pharmaceutical ingredients (APIs). Almost a decade after the authorities introduced the concept of the essential medicines list, regulators—in this case, the Federal Antimonopoly Service, or FAS—finally offered a sensible methodology of setting domestic prices: not higher than the lowest one in the twelve countries picked by the regulator. Still, these countries of reference had a multitude of pricing policies, taxation approaches, mechanisms of insurance reimbursement of the cost of drugs, and the Russian regulator's behavior smacked of arbitrariness (Kalinovskaya 2019).

Thirdly and finally, drug firms had to register their products, freezing price tags per official regulations. Failure to comply meant that neither retail nor wholesale distributors could sell unregistered batches of medicines. Consequently, drugstores and hospitals had to freeze all stocks of the needful medicines in their warehouses for the entire period of price negotiations. The process of registration was full of hidden hurdles. In 2015, prices on active pharmaceutical ingredients increased due to the ruble's devaluation, but companies could not re-register the new prices with the regulators. Commonly, regulators disagreed about price points and were tardy in approving the lists for the coming year, which complicated the registration process, contributing to the drugs' deficits on the shelves. Often, the regulators wanted more documents from manufacturers than specified in the regulations and failed to respect deadlines. For their part, desperate patients tried to obtain the life-saving but unregistered drugs illegally, only to face serious criminal charges, resulting in incarceration convictions.

The three aforementioned factors working together appear to account for the low efficiency of the otherwise benevolent promise to help ordinary Russians access drugs, circumventing their financial circumstances. Uncertainty and the lack of transparency never played a constructive role here: time and again, the industry and experts had to figure out the ever-changing rules of the pharmaceutical regulation. The government weakened firms' commercial motivation and undermined market mechanisms, while pharmaceutical companies failed to introduce new products to public procurement because they had little idea whether the previous year's list would be corrected, expanded, or shortened (Baranova 2013). Worse, because it was unprofitable to keep their products on the ELSM list, many health firms wanted to get off it (Deryabina and Vittel' 2016).

For instance, in 2021, Abbott, willing to lose access to public procurement, petitioned to sell its influenza vaccine, Influvac, on the private market—but the petition was denied. The permanent vanishing of many medications on the ELSM list from pharmacies and public tenders became a genuine threat to Russian patients.

It is surely appropriate to point out the low quality of Russian health regulation as the source of artificial deficits. Year after year, patients had to deal with the massive shortages of medicines, often lasting up to three months. In 2011 alone, more than $1bn worth of drugs, or roughly 200 medicines, did not hit the counters since selling available but unregistered drugs would be a crime (Markina 2011). Worse, by the end of 2019, about 900 imported drugs left the market, 25% of public procurement failed, and many patients could not purchase even basic drugs (Ryakin 2019). According to independent estimates, in the first five months of 2019, more than 28 thousand public health tenders had no bidders. The same year, the full line of essential life-saving medications was available only in seven out of 85 administrative regions of the Russian Federation, while the rest of the provinces faced shortages.

Shockingly, for an extended period in 2019, there was simply no insulin in the country (Mukhina 2019). The Saratov oblast was hit especially hard: the government had shut down the only charitable nonstate organization helping people with diabetes, referencing its subversive activity. One Duma deputy claimed that the insulin crisis was blown out of proportion by the supporters of Alexey Navalny, Putin's sharpest critic. The same year, vanished heparin, an anticoagulant prescription medicine used to treat and prevent the symptoms of blood clots. In short, the shrinking supply of many essential medications from pharmacies and failed public tenders became a genuine threat to Russian patients.

Given the importance of drug access as the regime's social promise, Putin had to explain the issue of stockouts and shortages, trying to project an image of a caring leader in command of governance minutiae. However, as his commitment becomes less credible with fewer political constraints he must respect, the disengaged or disinterested president speaks in generalities. On December 17, 2020, Putin tried to defuse the public disappointment with the lack of life-saving drugs in the country: "Yes, in some regions now <…> there are not enough medicines both in hospitals and in the pharmacy network, and free medicines are not given out. But these are not the same problems that we faced at the beginning.

This is the problem of logistics, late purchases, deliveries. In general, the industry reacted <positively>" (Izvestiya 2020).

Drug access is an integral part of well-functioning health systems; it is a "necessary component of fulfilling the right to health." In general, the increasing costs of medications, not to mention the prohibitively high prices of the patented items, undermine human security, which requires the state to rise to the occasion. However, Putin's mandate imbricates the directive to provide affordable medicines with an injunction to save revenue, much needed to butter the repressive apparatus. Overall, Putin has been obsessed with eliminating waste (see, for example, Putin 2007, 2008, 2018b). Notably, speaking at the pharmaceutical factory, Gerofarm, on November 16, 2018, Putin said: "In general, more than 380 billion rubles of budgetary funds are spent annually on drug provision in our country, and we need to clearly, clearly understand how rationally they are used and whether these expenses allow us to relieve people of the burden of spending on necessary drugs … but the main goal is to avoid overpricing." In this light of the analysis provided in the preceding chapter, cutting "waste" indicated lack of credible commitment to improving welfare rather than a genuine desire to streamline domestic expenditures.

Not surprisingly, there is little prospect of avoiding tragic losses of human life. In 2021, a ten-year-old girl, Eva Voronkova, in a direful need of foreign medicines, which the government failed to register for public tender, died in a Moscow intensive care unit. In Russia, four thousand people who suffer from cystic fibrosis lack access to qualified specialists and innovative therapies routinely available in the West. Instead of prioritizing human health, the government instructs hospitals to purchase the cheapest generics, despite their substandard quality and potential side effects. Losing profits and bumping into all too many bureaucratic obstacles, foreign manufacturers simply recall their drugs from the Russian market (Merzlikin 2019).

SUBSTITUTING IMPORTS: FAR-FLUNG CHANGES WITH FEW BENEFITS

Although the liberalization of trade, services, and products is supposed to stimulate economic growth, the keen observers of global health are not thoroughly convinced that open markets are decidedly beneficial for domestic development (Labonté and Ruckert 2019: 132–133). The dominance of foreign goods in domestic health systems could undermine human and pharmaceutical security. Instead, ramping up domestic capacity to manufacture both ready-to-use medicines and medical devices alleviates national dependence on imports, helps preempt possible shortages of internationally produced active pharmaceutical forms, and gives credence to bargaining leverage against the vendors of brand-name medications. Although working toward these objectives is commendable, developing strong pharmaceutical capacities is trying.

To President Putin, the state of the domestic pharmaceutical sector was saddening. According to the official estimates, during the first two terms of Putin's presidency, the Russian health sector entirely relied on foreign drugs and medical equipment. In 2009, domestic pharmaceuticals took only 23% of the market in monetary terms and 58% by volume. Further, by 2009 about 85% of drugs made at home relied on imported ingredients. Domestic companies that made complex medical devices and surgical instruments used foreign manufacturing equipment or plainly relied on foreign materials and components. In October 2009, Putin instructed the government to begin substituting imported drugs and medical supplies but prioritized the need for industrial development over health (Interfax 2009; Putin 2009). Putin issued a bureaucratic mandate, considering not so much the real needs of the patients or healthcare system rather than the desire to showcase the public-centered developmental initiative, part of the broader ideological trend of resurgent Russia, rising from her knees to challenge Western dominance.

Ideologically driven mandates must be particularly trying for non-ideological elites. There was a definite vacillation among top bureaucrats about the purpose of the mandate. According to Viktor Khristenko, the intention was simply to develop critical competencies in the Russian industry, which had been backward compared to the Western giants (Makarkina et al. 2014). I think that Khristenko was right; speeding up industrial competency was the only realistic advantage gained from Putin's mandate, although the quality of domestic medicines and medical devices left much to be desired. For Dmitry Medvedev, import substitution was tantamount to rapid and all-encompassing industrial and social breakthroughs. His rhetoric of modernization (see Medvedev 2009)—outright comical and compromised by his inordinate admiration of gadgets—became the signature of his presidency, 2008–2012. Sergey Chemezov, whose state corporation, Rostec, developed monopolistic appetites, started banging the drum of moral panic and claimed that multinationals would crush domestic manufacturers without state intervention. Although the industry liked the support of the state, the government caught the major private players by surprise every time it complicated or changed its arcane rules.

In addition to a heavy geopolitical undercurrent, the government interpreted import substitution as a revenue-saving strategy in the context when it had to deliver health goods and services in the wake of a 2008 financial meltdown. In the same direction points the fact that the federal law "On the Circulation of Medicines" (No. 61-FZ, adopted on April 12, 2010) did not prescribe regulating exorbitantly expensive drugs for orphan diseases. By definition, an orphan drug treats rare conditions, and there are no market-based solutions to help more than five million Russians, who suffered at the time. However, most orphan drugs had to be imported from abroad, and the government delegated responsibility to raise money for treatment to domestic charitable foundations while footing the bill for only 200 thousand patients (see Olevskii 2019).

Amid this confusion and vacillation, a joint governmental Commission on import substitution convened only a few times and soon vanished. The Ministry of Industry and Trade (hereafter, Minpromtorg) took charge of implementing Putin's mandate. A comprehensive governmental program (known as Pharma 2020) planned to increase the price share of homemade drugs in the internal market to 50% and no less than 85% in the segment of essential medicines, with no less than 200 analog or me-too medicines replacing foreign generics. To reach these goals, Moscow adopted a three-prong approach. The government (a) required localization of foreign medicines and medical devices, (b) erected barriers and complications for foreign companies to participate in public tenders, and (c) invested in research and development.

According to the Ministry of Economic Development Order No.427, issued in December 2008, pharmaceuticals originating in Russia received preferences in the procurement process (DSM 2019: 56). The government considered local goods 15% lower in price than indicated in the bidding application. Later on, the government would discuss increasing the preferential pricing up to 25%. These contract rules make sense, but, in practice, the packaging stage counted as domestic production. Happy were those Russian firms that packaged foreign pills and benefited from preferential pricing (Makarkina et al. 2014). Packaging, defined as a modification to suit local markets, should count as a localized product. Repackaging firms are vital as they prepare the product for distribution according to the specific needs of hospitals, pharmacies, and other healthcare institutions. However, this structure of governmental rewards makes domestic repackaging look like a rent-making scheme (I will return to this point in the next chapter).

Although the regulator dragged its feet for nearly nine years before establishing stricter benchmarks and appropriate incentives for the localization of medicines, many foreign firms took the initiative to localize some drugs in the country, while many Russian firms specializing in drugs and medical devices advanced technically (Batalova and Bateneva 2019; Vedomosti 2019). And that is the most the government can realistically hope to achieve. Although it is hard to ascertain whether the course on localization improved patients' access to better medicines and made them more available, some reports indicate a marginal increase in prices.

Further, that the government set out to limit foreign firms' ability to enter the national public sector was surely unwelcome from the standpoint of patients' interests. In 2015, participants of the ONF forum pulled fire alarms, fearing patients would lose access to foreign medical products that had no substitutes in the country. During the Q&A session that followed, Putin tried to convince his intermediaries that blanket bans were not in anyone's interests and would not happen. Still, the same year, the regulators issued several orders, collectively known as "odd one out" (*tretii lishnii*), thereby restricting foreign manufacturers of both pharmaceuticals and complex medical devices from participating in the public procurement in the case if two suppliers from Russia submitted their applications, too.

Offering contracts to Russian firms cost the federal budget excess spending, despite foreign companies being ready to offer competitive and, in many cases, lower prices. Worse, because Russian law does not require quality controls over the production of generics, an aggressive import substitution policy could decrease the safety and efficacy of medical products patients receive. It should not be taken as a surprise that the inferior quality of domestic products and frequent shortages incentivized public entities to evade state regulations. As hospitals found multiple loopholes in the procurement laws and requested tenders for specific foreign products and predetermined suppliers (Shubina and Rechkin 2017), the share of domestic products in the market stagnated. Since only the optionality of implementation mitigates the strictness and dysfunctionality of Russian laws, gaming the system was inevitable. Not to mention that manipulating technical specifications was sometimes downright fraudulent and oriented toward collusion and self-enrichment.

In response to snowballing evasions, the regulator adopted additional ad hoc initiatives to push foreign companies out of the national procurement system. The government made a point of itemizing medicines and medical devices barred from public tenders, and it also proposed quotas favoring domestic products. As time went by, the list of pharmaceuticals and medical devices to be excluded from competition at public tenders expanded considerably. For instance, in 2015, regulators moved on to develop an arbitrary list of 100 foreign-made medical devices and banned them from domestic markets, despite the lower quality of the domestic analogs. In 2019, the government added 14 more items to the list. On balance, the odd-man-out rule and its further amendments destabilized the pharmaceutical market and damaged competition, while it did not guarantee the requisite volume of pharmaceutical products on the domestic market (Yasakova 2021; Nikishina 2021).

Lung ventilation devices, medical equipment necessary for many health conditions, were at the center of one prominent controversy. Although health professionals wrote Medvedev a letter asking him not to move forward with these unwarranted restrictions, the former dismissed their plea as dictated by emotions, not the state interest. According to Manturov, because at least two Russian companies had been producing devices to support newborns' breathing, the ban on foreign-made lung ventilation devices for state-owned hospitals was justified (Ivanov 2015). This behavior is a good example of how agents can push their mandate to the point when its execution undermines substantive objectives of governance. It also brings to light that neither considerations of quality nor concerns for patients' access to life-saving devices were central in agents' motivation.

Putin's mandate for import substitution got a second wind in the wake of Western economic sanctions for the annexation of Crimea in 2014. Somehow, admired became the erroneous notion that insulating the country against international importers would inflict a penalty on the antagonistic West and genuinely promote domestic self-sufficiency. It is not surprising that Putin reiterated the objective to achieve total independence from the foreign manufacturers of essential drugs and medical equipment on the very first day of his third presidential term. Legislators followed Putin's implicit instructions. In 2018, legislators considered a comprehensive ban on all drugs originating from the states that joined the US-led sanctions but left the decision at Putin's discretion (Antonova 2018). After much wrangling, the State Duma deputies left further restrictions at the government's discretion (Levkovich 2018). However, realizing the limited capacity of the domestic medical industry, legislators allowed the import of pharmaceuticals not manufactured at home, albeit with confusing exceptions.

The legislative confidence in pharmaceutical sovereignty would not have been possible without victorious reports of top bureaucratic agents. Manturov's plenary speech entitled "Biomedicine: Horizon 2035" exemplified such confidence. The head of Minpromtorg tried to convince his listeners that the strategy of state investments in the pharmaceutical sector was a story of success. There were a few indeed: Russia's Generium replicated eculizumab, an international nonproprietary name for Alexion's Soliris. However, once the Accounts Chamber admitted that Pharma 2020 was the worst of all state programs, the government allowed Minpromtorg extra four years to reach its target indicators.

Although average Russians felt only a minor positive impact from the regulatory state of agitation, the state administrators who carried out the pharmaceutical strategy found it necessary to massage the numbers to demonstrate their effectiveness to the principal. Because Putin's mandate was about quantifiable criteria, state administrators spin the outcomes accordingly. In March 2019, Manturov's deputy, Sergey Tsyb, speaking at a congress of pharmaceutical industry workers, announced that the share of Russian-made products in the essential medicines list reached 86.2% (Gritsenko and Osipov 2019). There is no need to be impressed with these numbers: the ELSM list is an artificial construct and hardly attests to the pharmaceutical industry's robustness; most substituted pharmaceuticals had lost their therapeutic value and had to be replaced by the new line of drugs. Further, if counted by volume, the proportion of all home-produced drugs stayed consistently at 58%. Russian pharmaceuticals gained less than 10% of the market's share in monetary terms, although the original plan had 20% as the desired benchmark. Worse, independent experts attributed the decrease in imports to various exogenous factors, including currency fluctuations and patent expirations (see DSM 2019: 90).

Provided numbers allowed Russian politicians to claim that everything went according to the original plan, and the principal's promises materialized in full. On December 10, 2019, Putin summarized the country's progress with import substitution: "It is not that we want to replace imports at any cost, but we must understand that we need to be independent and do some basic things ourselves. Pharmacology is developing, and the pharmaceutical sector is developing, the industry is developing, we have a whole program provided with financing. And I must say that the industry is working better and better" (Putin 2019b). In reality, after more than ten years of intense regulatory activity, the results of import substitution remain mixed at best. The public absorbed the costs of the private sector's risks in a variety of ways, from footing the bill for unsuccessful pharmaceutical research and development to having to rely on less effective pharmaceutical forms and inferior medical devices of Russian origin.

There can be little doubt that the agent, *Minpromtorg*, took the nomenclature of essential and life-saving medicines as its laundry list for import substitution, despite that replicating those mostly outdated medicines would have hardly made the principal's promise of a technological breakthrough a reality. Domestic developers struggled to substitute Roche's and AstraZeneca's brand-name medicines, while the latter found it commercially reasonable to stop sales (Gritsenko and Osipov 2019). Russian companies could at best make analogs of 128 foreign medicines included on the ELSM list; and it is plausible that in the case of international economic sanctions in response to the Kremlin's aggression against Ukraine, domestic production of these drugs will ensure some basic level of pharmaceutical sovereignty. This is an alarming juncture in time to ponder the issue of domestic research and development, in which the government invested so heavily in order to materialize the principal's dream of Russia as a rising pharmaceutical powerhouse. If the pessimistic scenario for the future becomes a reality, there is no doubt that the principal and his spokespeople would retrofit the original import substitution mandate to fit the imagery of the geopolitical struggle with the choleric West.

Purchasing expensive foreign drugs and entering protracted negotiation periods could be considered harmful, but there is no disagreement that implementing import substitution threatened or complicated many lives. Recently, in October 2021, one charitable foundation, "Sunflower," founded by famous film director Timur Bekmambetov to identify and sponsor the patients with initial stages of immunodeficiency, pleaded the government to purchase foreign immunoglobulin. According to the National Institutes of Health's (NIH) website, immunoglobulins are glycoprotein molecules produced by plasma cells that aid in the immune response by recognizing and helping to destroy particular bacteria or viruses, thus being critical in treating many pathologies, including immunodeficiencies and autoimmune diseases. In Russia, the situation was nothing short of life-threatening. According to media reports, more than half of the patients who needed the drug had either been receiving it intermittently or not at all for almost two years (see Osipov and Kostarnova 2021). By 2022, only a few flacons remained in the entire country. To be sure, the shortages of immunoglobulins were entirely human-made. For years, the government imposed an extremely low price ceiling, which eroded any market incentives for foreign firms to sell them on the Russian market. At the same time, the domestic monopolist—Mikrogen, a subsidiary of Nacimbio, which will be discussed in the next chapter—could not ensure uninterrupted production of the drug. Eventually, the federal Ministry of Health agreed to raise the price ceiling, but it would take six months for the product to appear in public tenders.

Spending Priorities: Resources for Mega-Projects, Austerity for All

A great deal of speculation and disagreement persisted among Russian observers about the inner drivers of national mega-projects that funneled many resources into the national healthcare sector and their outcomes. On the one hand, domestic observers hailed national health programs as an innovative tool for implementing national development goals of utmost priority (Evropa 2007: 39–60). To be fair, the government proposed many ambitious programs and initiatives, as it made plenty of promises regarding the massive influx of money in the healthcare sector for the sake of its modernization (Kommersant 2010; Visloguzov et al. 2010). On the other hand, a tendency to look separately at spending for priority projects and the deteriorating hospital sector obfuscates a picture of how the Kremlin misrules Russian health.

This section seeks to correct such a narrow view. Because modernizing the healthcare sector is costly, the problem of saving revenue looms large. The continual concentration of resources on high-profile campaigns drained the routine operations in healthcare. My analysis also licenses the view that although the principal envisioned investments in mega-projects as a stimulus for the healthcare industry and pockets of efficiency portable to other sectors, they failed to do so. Given that the ruler lacks credible commitment, the sharp contrast between Putin's positive visualization of health outcomes and the ensuing unimpressive track record of performance makes sense.

As early as September 2005, at the dawn of Putin's second presidential term, the government launched the ambitious National Priority Project on Health (NPPH). According to the official narrative, Russian leaders designed these mega-projects as the mechanism of an intense and "smart" investment envisioned to stimulate economic development across the board and improve the availability and quality of social services. The mechanics of these programs was to concentrate budgetary and administrative resources in the select areas (including housing, healthcare, and infrastructure) and assign the implementation metrics (TASS 2019). The Kremlin designed these programs to dial-up spending on high-tech medical devices, underwrite expensive treatments for rare diseases, and construct cutting-edge medical centers (Evropa 2007: 39–60). The initial stages of the program could be considered fairly successful: in 2006–2010, the government spent a total of 607 bn rubles (approximately $20 bn), renewed about 70% of the ambulance fleet, and financed the construction of 15 federal centers featuring high medical technologies.

From the outset, as the authorities envisioned NPPs as a pocket of efficiency, they insulated these programs from bureaucratic politics and disputes. But it was a story of inefficiency, nonetheless. Even the flagship initiatives, such as the task of constructing and equipping the nationwide network of specialized clinics, which was supposed to increase the availability of high-tech medical care, were barely accomplished, and substantial financial losses ensued (Rodionova 2014). Consistent with the inner logic of personalistic contracts, massive governmental investments satisfied the Kremlin's concern to secure the support of the citizens by delivering hitherto unavailable or scarce goods and services.

The first iteration of these mega-projects in health only appeared to be "technocratic," while Putin's political agenda was to showcase Dmitry Medvedev as a potential presidential successor and catapult a hitherto unremarkable administrator to the levels of national renown and popularity. Paradoxically, Medvedev did not play a personalistic game very well. Unlike Putin, Medvedev failed to turn his reports on the national projects' implementation into publicity events, and his tone was often impersonal and lackluster. In his speech at the Federation Council in 2007, Medvedev gave the impression that investments would be over in a couple of years with the qualitative transformations attained (Medvedev 2008: 265). At the dusk of Medvedev's presidency, domestic commentators sensed his deep disappointment with mega-projects: Medvedev signaled their termination by saying that he was tired to death with victorious and repetitive reports that contradicted disappointing realities (Savina 2010).

Nevertheless, health mega-projects were too good of an instrument in the personalistic toolshed to be abandoned. What happened next was inevitable, perhaps. In their further iterations, national projects remained glaringly political: the authorities relaunched them to buy the citizenry's loyalty while significantly expanding their scope (new targets, for instance, included lowering the prevalence of oncological and cardiovascular diseases). In 2016, the Kremlin strengthened its management architecture for priority projects by creating the Council for Strategic Development and Priority Projects, thus showing the importance of these projects for Putin's political agenda. Unlike many other coordinating bodies (for instance, the task force for import substitution), the regular meetings of the Council always featured Putin, who used every opportunity to underscore the projects' importance for the welfare of the citizens and whip up his subordinates. The numbers point in the same direction: according to different estimates, the government spent somewhere between $10.8 and $43 bn before it decided to offer yet another round of its gingered-up promises.

On the downside, the necessity to press on with these programs, coupled with their low efficiency, ensnared Russian health in the never-ending cycle of renewed promises of social betterment and concealment of failures to attain the declared goals. Notably, the touched-up NPPs were renewed in an executive order "On National Goals and Strategic Objectives of the Russian Federation through to 2024" (No. 204, May 7, 2018). Signed on the eve of Putin's fourth term, it once again gave special prominence to health matters. Echoing his decade-earlier promises, in 2019, Putin continued to advertise the new round of national projects as a major developmental initiative: "The ultimate goal of all these activities is to put the economy on a new track, make it high-tech, increase labor productivity and, on this basis, raise the standard of living of our citizens, and ensure the security of our state for a long historical perspective" (Putin 2019a).

On the one hand, it would be appropriate to single out autocratic centralization that incurred negative implications. The regional governments began accumulating significant debts while struggling to implement the Kremlin's mandate to increase health-related spending and showing their resolute adherence to Putin's questionable metrics (Pomeranz and Smith 2016). Worse, Russia's regions could not introduce the initiatives as informed by the local needs. On the other hand, according to numerous reports, many regional health administrators became particularly good at justifying the need to reequip health clinics while pocketing the kickbacks from the significantly overpriced contracts (Raskin and Makarkina 2013). In 2012 alone, the Prosecutor General's Office reported 46,000 violations that occurred during the implementation of the national health project, while 10,000 people were counseled or arraigned (Rodionova 2013). Following years, violations continued. As a result, the government lost money while local health systems received expensive medical devices they did not need or could not use.

When reading official reports, it is hard to shake off an impression of hard-to-explain discrepancies: on the one hand, the government boasted an increase in life expectancy and a decrease in mortality among Russians from all hitherto prevalent causes, while on the other, it lamented the failure of more than 50% of all specific priority programs (Komrakov 2019). No matter what happened, bureaucrats routinely prepared victorious reports on fully or nearly achieving the assigned metrics, despite failing to show qualitative results of executing Putin's mandate. Top state bureaucrats and regional politicians tend to lie to Putin about the successes of his strategic course so that Putin can reward them for loyalty and then lie to the people. In 2018, the minister of health, Veronika Skvortsova, averred that Russian healthcare improved qualitatively (Alekseev 2018). As noted before, misrepresentation and gaming among bureaucrats are acceptable as long as Putin's subordinates fulfill their part of the tacit contract with a personalistic ruler. Although time and again Putin and his subordinates boasted the decreased general mortality rates in the country, the victorious metrics failed to take into account standardized coefficients such as the population's age structure or social, environmental, and economic determinants of health. According to experts, the construction of hospitals and clinics had no direct connection to diminishing mortality.

It was hard to conceal galloping inefficiencies. In 2019, the State Council members and independent experts alike noted massive deficiencies in allocating resources at the national and local levels. In particular, they highlighted that local hospitals lacked proper equipment and sufficiently trained personnel. Perhaps the best evidence that the megaprojects failed to improve general health outcomes came from none other than Alexey Kudrin, the Accounts Chamber chairman, a former minister of finances, and Putin's close associate since their days in St-Petersburg's city hall in the early 1990s. In 2019, Kudrin offered sharp criticism of the national priorities programs and decided not to disburse the remainder of the money that had already been allocated to NPP Health (Solov'eva 2019). Although he implicitly acknowledged the projects' ineffectiveness and their failure as the motor of development—and many Russians started to pay attention because of Kudrin's status in Putin's informal networks—he hardly said anything that had been hidden from the independent observers (see Taylor 2019). This criticism, almost word for word, echoed the previous exposures of long-known deficiencies, which meant shortcomings in resource allocations became routine (Shubina et al. 2017).

The Kremlin's propaganda machine hailed national health programs as an innovative tool for implementing national development goals of utmost priority and compared them favorably to the period of rapid industrialization in the 1930s. Such a comparison is self-serving and misinformed: the Soviet Union was a strictly predatory state (Osokina 2021) and, despite the grand ambition of its dictator, failed to catch up with the high tempo of economic development typical to the capitalist Russia of the early twentieth century (see Oreshkin 2019). Still, contemporary Russian politicians seem drawn to these comparisons because of a style of personalistic politics that lionizes the leader for everything positive and refuses to pinpoint the leader's obsession with metrics as a cause of health governance inefficiencies.

Inevitably, the flip side of authoritarian spending is austerity. Although Russia benefits from mineral windfall rents, regime principals mobilize resources at the expense of other issues that become neglected and underfunded. As Russian elites lacked a genuine normative vision for improving the national health system, the regime continued to spend half the amount on healthcare compared to industrialized democracies and lagged behind even several European countries that formerly belonged to the socialist block. Austerity, fiscal conservatism, and revenue-maximization are central concerns for the Kremlin. In justifying that routine programs underwent massive restructuring ("optimization" of healthcare by and large implied across-the-board reductions and slashing of funding), the authorities referenced the need to increase doctors' job security and patients' satisfaction with the public health services. More plausibly, "optimization" boiled down to the neoliberal principle: it intended to slash costs by closing rural and hard-to-reach hospitals and medical centers that served relatively few patients.

In 2015, amid big spending on mega-projects in health, the federal budget reduced health care expenditures by 11%. An increase in the share of paid services in the public sector and prescribing cheaper treatment regimens accompanied these slashes (Malysheva 2016). Ordinary patients, especially in rural areas, kept lamenting the limited availability and low quality of medical care, noting the reduction in the number of medical organizations and personnel, both in urban and rural settlements (Makarova 2015). Another major problem concerned problems with the artificial shortages of qualified medical personnel. By 2015, 90 thousand medical workers, an incredible number in a country that faces shortages of well-trained professionals, were fired. All across the country, and especially in smaller towns, scores of medical professionals quit their jobs, worked to rule, or changed places of their residence. Predictably, the reduction of medical workers in Russia's regions doubled the waiting time for medical care compared to the Ministry of Health's official benchmarks.

Reductions in the total number of medical organizations did not go unnoticed. In 2000, there were more than ten thousand hospitals; in 2013, the number fell below 5 thousand; and by 2021, Russia ended up with less than 3 thousand hospitals. Cuts in the available rural outpatient clinics and inpatient emergency and primary healthcare centers in rural areas (known as FAPs) followed (Zvezdina 2017). The decrease in the availability and quality of medicine in the small towns and rural areas almost doubled the mortality rates among rural residents compared to urban dwellers. Several Russian provinces, such as the Republic of Udmurtia, Perm, Chelyabinsk Oblast, and Zabaykalsky Krai, were hit especially hard. In general, healthcare optimization triggered massive closures and decreased access to medical care in Russia.

Given the fundamental constraint of electoral authoritarianism that requires a ruler to guard his popularity, Putin had to react to the optimization's negative outcomes, projecting an image of a competent and benevolent leader. At the Meeting of the Council for Strategic Development and Priority Projects, March 21, 2017, Putin noted that "people rightly and justifiably talk about the shortage of doctors, especially in small towns and <rural> settlements. It is necessary to increase the prestige, status, <and> financial situation of medical workers, to strengthen their protection, including legal. Health care, like education, is not just a service sector: doctors, teachers carry out the most important work for the future of the country and society." Putin advertised massive salary increases to address the problem, but the government resorted to another gaming strategy.

Heeding Putin's demands on paper, the government decided not to increase the total wage fund, which meant that salary increases would entail personnel cuts and additional in-load responsibilities without adequate compensation. In reality, in 2019, 50 provinces failed to increase medical professionals' salaries. According to numerous reports, the shortage of personnel increased overwork and perpetuated the unfair structure of compensation. Thus, the local authorities achieved Putin's questionable metrics by increasing and doubling the workload. Meanwhile, medical professionals started taking their dissatisfaction to the streets (Chernova 2019). In 2018, Putin tried to convince the citizens that he was about to correct another shortcoming of the far-flung optimization. He appealed to the political class to return the necessary medical facilities to villages and other small towns. Several years later, however, despite hundreds of proposals sent to the presidential administration and the Ministry of Health, the problem intensified, and medical facilities' closures continued unabated (see, for instance, Andreeva 2019; Berdnikova 2019).

Undoubtedly, delivering fundamental economic goods (pharmaceuticals and medical devices) and public services (public procurement of medicines) is a complicated and uncertain endeavor when severe budgetary constraints and a low starting point plague the country. However, the real problems stem from the Kremlin's priority of political survival and revenue-maximization rather than the objective lack of requisite resources. The overall high tax burden on the economy increased over Putin's rule, but the Kremlin closely guarded its bulging pockets and, therefore, failed to develop a welfare system, improve its national health system, and alleviate the economic burden of COVID-19. Detrimental to social welfare, the 2021 federal budget proposed deep spending cuts even amid the untamed coronavirus epidemic.

By 2019, it became evident that the politics of austerity generated massive social costs and, according to Leonid Roshal, became a threat to emergency preparedness. Roshal's fire alarms were not unfounded: once the epidemic of COVID-19 got in full swing, the authorities of the Lipetsk, Samara, Rostov, Khabarovsk, Altai, Novosibirsk, and Tyumen regions reported the routine medical care suspended and medical care denied (Dzutstsati 2020). Worse, many hospitals in Russian provinces suffered from the shortages of underpaid medical professionals, many of whom either got fired or resigned, while some dead coronavirus patients were left in hospitals' hallways due to the shortages of morgues (Pugachev 2020). It is shocking that an industrialized country with a decent state capacity still lacks an adequate supply of medical oxygen for two years in the COVID-19 pandemic.

To summarize, instead of alleviating inequalities in access to health and initiating extensive equalizing social transfers, the state chose to allocate scarce resources by heavily investing in some areas of public health that were deemed politically necessary. A string of decade-long investments in health benefited Putin disproportionately: they gave him ample opportunities to showcase his generosity while the immediate benefits for the citizenry and medical professionals remained mixed at best.

BENEVOLENT PRESIDENT: PROVIDING PARTICULARIZED GOODS

There is some theatrical expression of the autocrat's desire to bolster popularity: Vladimir Putin incessantly appears in front of cameras that televise on home TV screens any event wherein Putin scolds his subordinates for insufficient attention to the needs of the ordinary people and takes credit for any breakthrough in health governance. To wit, Putin frequents staged appearances either to showcase the increased domestic capacity to make original drugs and technologies (for the case of Vancomycin, see Yushkov 2019) or publicly praises specific products during his widely covered visits to the local drug stores (for the story on Arbidol, see Sedakov 2015). Indeed, scores of grateful insiders enjoy Putin's leadership; and the sense of gratitude is supposed to infect the rest of the citizens. Such behavior is understandable but somewhat ridiculous as it imitates Viktor Pelevin's artistic imagination. The famous novel, Generation P (1999), published on the eve of Putin's ascension to the top executive position, portrays a mysterious political and social master puppeteer who manipulates the media behind the scene and stars in nearly all news, commercials, and TV shows.

The remainder of this section discusses the Direct Line with President (*Pryamaya Liniya*), a regular, high-profile TV broadcast, highlighting another essential aspect of personalistic governance. During these broadcasts, ordinary citizens pose a wide range of questions about politics, complain about individual problems, pull fire alarms on regional authorities, and ask the president to interfere on their behalf to ensure the delivery of social services at the local level. Overall, there is not much to be said for the view that the issued microscale mandates could help common people, alter the inner workings of the government, and correct the regime's institutional ineffectiveness. Although the microscale mandates attempt to bear the image of the president's benevolence against the sagging healthcare system and regional authorities' callousness, they hardly have any positive effects.

It appears that not all the Direct Line calls are staged. In June 2017, 24-year-old Darya Starikova told President Putin that there was no hospital in the city in her hometown of Apatity, a northeastern town populated by almost 60 thousand people, and she also complained that because of the lack of healthcare specialists, she had been misdiagnosed, losing the critically important time to treat her stage four cancer (Boiko and Fokht 2017). In Starikova's words, "We do not have enough narrow specialists, thanks to which it would be possible to diagnose people on time. Our maternity hospital was closed, our surgical department was closed, and our cardiology department was closed. Everything was transferred to Kirovsk, a neighboring city" (cited in Prosina et al. 2018). Putin appeared sympathetic: he said the same thing happened to his father and promised he would take care of the young woman personally. A week later, he instructed the Russian government and the Murmansk authorities to take the necessary measures to provide affordable medical care to the Apatity population and report back to him. In the meanwhile, Starikova ended up in intensive care, first in the regional capital, Murmansk, then in the Moscow research institute of oncology. After several surgeries, she died.

According to the independent media, Starikova's tragic story highlighted the underlying problems in the Russian healthcare system. Given the significantly increased workload, it is misleading to blame doctors for making the diagnostic mistake. The root of the problem was that although the federal Ministry of Health instructed that all patients with cancer must get free treatment, the regional authorities lacked the requisite funds to do so and often canceled treatments in the local hospitals, referencing budgetary deficits. In June 2018, on yet another annual direct line with the president, Alevtina Kiseleva reminded Putin of Starikova's case. Kiseleva also pulled fire alarms, indicating that the grave problem was the lack of oncology centers in the regions, the lack of essential medicines in hospitals, and the deficits of ambulances (Misnik 2018). In response,

Putin brushed her off, claiming that oncological prophylaxis was a story of successes and, once again, promised to initiate a federal program for the construction of new oncological centers and the re-equipment of the old ones. Echoing the president's words, Veronika Skvortsova averred that the incidence of cancer detection had sharply dropped since Putin took a personal interest in Russian healthcare. However, massive reductions in healthcare were not reversed, and the hospitals in remote areas are still absent. It remained unclear if any state official got punished.

A similar story, exemplifying the inconsequentiality of Putin's microscale mandates, unfolded in the Vladimir oblast when the Accounts Chamber revealed the regional authorities' failure to comply with the presidential instructions to repair and reequip the hospital in the local town of Strunino. Strunino is a small town in Vladimir oblast, Russia, located 131 kilometers northwest of Vladimir, the oblast's administrative center, with a population of 15 thousand people. In June 2018, again on the Direct Line, the local residents complained to the president about the closure of the town hospital's surgical, gynecological, infectious diseases, and pediatric departments. They appealed to Putin to interfere and prevent the closure of the only hospital servicing 30 thousand people. Putin instructed Governor Svetlana Orlova to repair and reequip the hospital by the end of the year. When the deadline approached, the new governor, Vladimir Sipyagin, applied to the federal Ministry of Health, requesting to delay the implementation timetable. Sipyagin promised that he would complete the President's order in a year. When the time came, the governor visited Strunino and stated that Putin's directives to repair and reequip the medical facility had been completed (Artyukh 2020). Despite the governor's victorious reports, the federal audit indicated that Putin's mandate had not been effectuated and noted multiple spending violations. The hospital was neither repaired nor reequipped. Formally, Sipyagin got punished for the radical decrease in his popularity ratings, but he found himself a sinecure in the State Duma several years later (Galimova 2021).

Further, personalistic leaders might benefit more from providing personalized "gifts" to their people than from reforming the ineffective mechanisms of governance. Such behavior is eerily reminiscent of an archaic practice of African personalistic leaders whose "presidential 'gifts' create bonds of dependence between leader and follower and contribute to the leader's ability to maintain his power and control" (Schatzberg 1988: 79). It is also similar to particularized benefits Latin American presidents doled out in the 1960s through the 1980s (Geddes 1994: 135–136).

An illustrative case in point is Putin's promise to finance the treatment of orphan diseases in children using a newly created tax on wealth (Kozlova 2020). The timing was impeccable: Putin made this self-seeking pledge in the context of constitutional amendments, which de facto made him a president for life. To institutionalize Putin's promise and at his behest, the government created a charitable foundation, The Circle of Kindness, which became the privileged recipient of the public funds specifically earmarked to help children with orphan diseases. Most funding would go to purchasing brand new foreign medicines (such as Zolgensma) against spinal muscular atrophy, a genetic disorder characterized by wasting skeletal muscles and losing control over muscle movement. Except for the commonly accepted view that the foundation owes its creation to Putin's sensitivity to the increased public demand for social justice, there is no consensus regarding its performance effectiveness and the overall impact on health governance.

It appears that the Circle of Kindness was designed as a pocket of efficiency, directly handled by the presidential administration, and was legally allowed to circumvent red tape and cumbersome regulations. Although the fund could not cover all patients in need, it alleviated the threatening inability of the provincial authorities to provide orphan drugs. However, there was a malefic side to its activities, too. The fund closely guarded information about its purchases, which also appeared to fall behind schedule (Reiter and Zholobova 2021). The Circle of Kindness exerted behind the scenes influence, preventing some independently funded patients from being allowed to purchase a life-saving injection of Zolgensma. Overall, the foundation does what the regional authorities are supposed to do but cannot because the federal government, delegating the responsibility for paying for 17 orphan diseases, does not leave enough resources at the regional level.

On balance, Putin's microscale mandates are almost always at the center of public attention, although their implementation does not attest to the improvements in the quality of health governance in the country.

Conclusion

Unlike doling out, no matter how attractive, promises to constituents, governing health for the benefit of all is not easy, and, as the chapter shows, the nature of Putin's promises and mandates inversely correlates with realistic chances of having good health governance. Personalistic rulers must appear to work in the interest of people but, failing to do so, might find it in their best interest to fake progress and manipulate information. The outcomes for each health governance episode discussed in this chapter are disappointing. Self-promotion and positive publicity aside, regulators triggered perpetual drug shortages and left patients needing medicines. Contrary to the buoyant rhetoric of federal officials, the poorly managed transition to pharmaceutical sovereignty gave few benefits to the patients but many to the regime's agents who showcased their fidelity to the principal. Health mega-projects improved little while the public absorbed the costs of the decreased equalities in access to health services, and health professionals faced massive cuts in the hospital sector.

Despite a notable degree of official disillusionment that marred the recent years of Putin's economic and social leadership (Butrin 2018), those on the government's dime continued to praise the government's extraordinary competence and ability to govern well (see, for instance, Bednyakov and Mierin 2019). On balance, that kind of PR has nothing to do with discernible improvements in the national health industry and serves only Putin personally. The deceptive strategy of informational autocracies works out as intended. Many ordinary people have yet to realize these appearances are self-serving and that their authoritarian ruler hardly has a credible commitment to their welfare as he sheds any constitutional constraints on his power. Still, people's perceptions change, sometimes drastically, although negative perceptions and grievances do not automatically engender a mass protest and regime change. Consider one telling example. In 2007, Boris Akunin, arguably one of the most iconic Russian detective fiction writers, who was also prominent during the opposition protests of 2011, famously said that "With Putin in power, success is finally possible without compromise." He praised Putin for constructing a governance system wherein anyone could reap the benefits of their labor without compromising moral integrity and rejected the idea that any kind of totalitarianism is in Russia's future. Today, he does not think so anymore; he concedes that he was mistaken.

This chapter has investigated how the regime's institutional setup incentivized the ruler to spawn big promises and its agents to resort to bureaucratic gaming and faking. This research fits conceptually the trend that seeks to explain the sources and consequences of governance inefficiencies within nondemocratic systems. Among nondemocratic regimes, China, understandably, has been in the spotlight. Two recent books explain that China's social and health programs are deeply flawed for two reasons. First, strategic calculations inform the distribution of resources, such as balancing benefits between elites and masses, wherein enlarging the beneficiary groups is more important than considerations of fairness and equity (Huang 2020: 5). Secondly, autocrats' commitment to preserving extant political order incentivizes local administrators to allocate resources to control individuals (Pan 2020: 4–5). These kinds of trade-offs are at the heart of any authoritarian regime. That rulers intervene in markets to provide goods, services, and various subsidies to those who possess organizational capabilities and thus could foment potentially detrimental unrest is already part and parcel of many academic investigations of the developing world (Thomson 2019: 3, 8). Further, Ratigan (2022) uncovered factors that alleviate the vulnerability of Chinese authoritarian regimes even in the context of inadequate provision of healthcare.

Still, many questions persist. Most importantly, is Russia's personalistic regime and its principals capable of rewarding those who demonstrate indubitable successes in health governance and punishing those who consistently show a lack of positive results? Could the regime construct a rational and outcome-based system of impartial incentives in the form of rewards and punishments? Could the regime constrain or deracinate the networks which transcend the public sphere, private sector, and informal connections and ties? Do state officials govern more effectively when the principal abolishes hard controls? The ensuing chapter probes these questions in detail. In essence, the next chapter shows that the Russian regime lacks an institutional setup that could compel state officials to refrain from pursuing self-interest and, instead, serve in the interest of society as a whole.

References

Abbott, K.W., et al. 2020. Competence–Control Theory: The Challenge of Governing through Intermediaries. In *The Governor's Dilemma: Indirect*

Governance Beyond Principals and Agents, ed. K.W. Abbott, et al., 3–36. Oxford: Oxford University Press.

Abbott, K.W., et al. 2021. Beyond Opportunism: Intermediary Loyalty in Regulation and Governance. *Regulation & Governance* 15 (S1): S83–S101.

Alekseev, P. 2018. Nasha meditsina perekhodit na kachestvenno inoi uroven. *Meditsinskaya Gazeta* No. 28, 18 July.

Andreeva, N. 2019. Letal'naya optimizatsiya: Detskie meduchrezhdeniya zakryvayut, chtoby vypolnit' maiskie ukazy. *Novaya Gazeta* No. 7, 23 January.

Antonova, E. 2018. Zapret na import lekarstv reshili ubrat' iz zakonoproekta o kontrsanktsiyakh. *RBC*, 11 May.

Artyukh, D. 2020. Schetnaya palata vyyavila nevypolnenie porucheniya prezidenta Putina vo Vladimirskoi oblasti. *Zebtra-tv.ru*, 2 April.

Auzan, A. 2005. Grazhdanskoe obshchestvo i grazhdanskaya politika. *Polit.ru*, 1 June.

Barabanov, I., and N. Morar. 2007. Putin topless. *The New Times*, 27 August.

Baranova, O. 2013. Besporyadochnost' spiska. *Farmatsevticheskii Vestnik*, 24 December.

Batalova, A., and T. Bateneva. 2019. Nadezhnyi partner udvaivaet sily: Mezhdunarodnye kompanii dali moshchnyi impul's razvitiyu farmotrasli Rossii. *Rossiiskaya Gazeta*, 4 June.

Bednyakov A., and L. Mierin. 2019. Natsional'nye Proekty Rossii: Problemy i Resheniya. *Izvestiya Sankt-Peterburgskogo Gosudarstvennogo Ekonomicheskogo Universiteta*, No. 4.

Berdnikova, E. 2019. Dubinki i palochki. *Novaya Gazeta* No. 117, 18 October.

Blackburn, M. 2020. Political Legitimacy in Contemporary Russia 'from Below': 'Pro-Putin' Stances, the Normative Split and Imagining Two Russias. *Russian Politics* 5 (1): 52–80.

Boiko, V, and E. Fokht. 2017. Pochemu vrachi protiv bol'nitsy, kotoruyu patsienty prosili u Putina. *Russian service BBC*, 30 June.

Butrin, D. 2018. K natsproektam predyavleny gospretenzii. *Kommersant* No. 214, 21 November.

Carnaghan, E. 2007. Do Russians Dislike Democracy? *PS: Political Science & Politics* 40(1): 61–66.

Chernova, N. 2019. Lyudi v belykh zaplatakh. *Novaya Gazeta* No. 102, 13 September.

Croissant, A., and O. Hellmann. 2017. Introduction: State Capacity and Elections in the Study of Authoritarian Regimes. *International Political Science Review* 39 (1): 3–16.

Deryabina, A. and I. Vittel'. 2016. V Rossii stalo men'she deshevykh importnykh zhiznenno vazhnykh lekarstv. *RBC*, 12 February.

DSM Group. 2019. Analiticheskii Otchet: Farmatsevticheskii rynok Rossii: Itogi 2018 g.

Duckett, J., and G. Wang 2017. Why do Authoritarian Regimes Provide Public Goods? Policy Communities, External Shocks and Ideas in China's Rural Social Policy Making. *Europe-Asia Studies* 69 (1): 92–109.

Dzutstsati, A. 2020. Ponimaete, ya do pyatnitsy prosto ne vyzhivu. *Current Time*, 12 November.

Evropa. 2007. *Prioritetnye Natsional'nye Proekty: Tsifry, Fakty, Dokumenty*. Moskva: Evropa.

Gaaze, K. 2014. Poker dlya odnogo. *The New Times*, 1 September.

Galieva, D. 2020. Natsproekty perenatselyat na 2030-i: Srok realizatsii obnovlennykh programm prodlevaetsya na shest' let. *Kommersant*, 13 July.

Galimova, N. 2021. Gubernator Vladimirskoi oblasti Sipyagin ushel v Gosdumu. *RBC*, 29 September.

Geddes, B. 1994. *Politician's Dilemma: Building State Capacity in Latin America*. Berkeley and Los Angeles: University of California Press.

Gritsenko, P. and A. Osipov. 2019. Rodnye i blistery: kak razmenivalis' byudzhetnye milliardy, vydelennye na lekarstvennoe importozameshchenie. *Vademecum*, 3 June.

Grozovskii, B. 2016. Dryakhleyushchii obshchestvennyi dogovor. *Vedomosti*, 17 January.

Guriev, S., and D. Treisman. 2019. Informational Autocrats. *Journal of Economic Perspectives* 33 (4): 100–127.

Hale, H.E. 2011. The Myth of Mass Russian Support for Autocracy: The Public Opinion Foundations of a Hybrid Regime. *Europe-Asia Studies* 63 (8): 1357–1375.

Hale, H.E. 2015. *Patronal Politics: Eurasian Regime Dynamics in Comparative Perspective*. New York: Cambridge University Press.

Hale, H.E., and T.J. Colton. 2017. Who Defects? Unpacking a Defection Cascade from Russia's Dominant Party 2008–12. *American Political Science Review* 111 (2): 322–337.

Han, K. 2020. Autocratic Welfare Programs, Economic Perceptions, and Support for the Dictator: Evidence from African Autocracies. *International Political Science Review* 42 (3): 416–429.

Hanson, J.K. 2017. State Capacity and the Resilience of Electoral Authoritarianism: Conceptualizing and Measuring the Institutional Underpinnings of Autocratic Power. *International Political Science Review* 39 (1): 17–32.

Huang, X. 2020. *Social Protection under Authoritarianism: Health Politics and Policy in China*. New York: Oxford University Press.

Hutcheson, D.S., and B. Petersson. 2016. Shortcut to Legitimacy: Popularity in Putin's Russia. *Europe-Asia Studies* 68 (7): 1107–1126.

Interfax. 2009. Putin prolechil farmatsevtov, 9 October.

Ivanov, M. 2015. Pravitel'stvo eshche podumaet o zaprete goszakupok inostrannykh medmaterialov. *Kommersant*, 20 August.

Izvestiya. 2020. Putin poobeshchal razobrat'sya s obespecheniem lekarstvami ot COVID-19, 17 December.
Kalinovskaya, E. 2019. Ekspert: V 2019 g. pri goszakupkah lekarstv nachnut primenyat'sya referentnye tseny. *Farmatsevticheskii Vestnik*, 9 January.
Kolesnikov, A., and D. Volkov. 2020. Russians' Growing Appetite for Change. *Carnegie.ru*, 30 January.
Kommersant. 2010. Na modernizatsiyu zdravookhraneniya planiruetsya vydelit' 460 milliardov rublei. *Kommersant-Online*, 23 April.
Komrakov, A. 2019. Natsproekty osvoili lish' polovinu deneg. *Nezavisimaya Gazeta*, 7 November.
Kotlyar, E. 2020. Morg perepolnen. V skoruyu zvonit' bespolezno. *Current Time*, 29 October.
Kozlova, D. 2020. Ukol shchedrosti. *Novaya Gazeta*, 27 October.
Kukulin, I., and V. Kurennoi. 2017. Shkola Shchedrovickogo i ee nasledie. Chast' 1. *Polit.ru*, 31 March.
Kuz'mina, B., and M. Perevoshchikova. 2021. Klubni po interesam: vlasti predlozhili mery po stabilizatsii tsen na borshchevoi nabor. *Izvestiya*, 12 November.
Labonté, R., and A. Ruckert. 2019. *Health Equity in a Globalizing Era: Past Challenges, Future Prospects*. Oxford, UK: Oxford University Press.
Levkovich, A. 2018. Zakon o kontrsanktsiyakh vstupil v silu. *Vademecum*, 4 June.
Makarkina, O., et al. 2014. Kartina: korzina, kartonka. *Vademecum*, 10 November.
Makarova, E. 2015. Deputaty razrabotali zakon o zaprete likvidatsii sel'skih bol'nits. *Vademecum*, 16 December.
Malysheva, E. 2016. Meditsina: novaya volna optimizatsii: Finansirovanie rossiiskoi meditsiny vnov' poidet pod nozh. *Gazeta.ru*, 09 January.
Markina, E. 2011. Potrebitelyam ne podstelili aspirinku. *Farmatsevticheskii Vestnik*, 25 January.
Martin, A., et al. 2022. Does Process Matter? Experimental Evidence on the Effect of Procedural Fairness on Citizens' Evaluations of Policy Outcomes. *International Political Science Review* 43 (1): 103–117.
Medvedev, D. 2008. *Natsional'nye Prioritety: Stat'i i Vystupleniya*. Moskva: Evropa.
Medvedev, D. 2009. Rossiya, vpered! *Gazeta.ru*, 10 September.
Merzlikin, P. 2019. Ya ne znayu, chem lechit' rebenka. *Meduza.io*, 28 November.
Misnik, L. 2018. Putin rasskazal o sredstvakh, vydelyaemykh na bor'bu s onkologiei. *Gazeta.ru*, 7 June.
Moynihan, D. P. 2010. The Promises and Paradoxes of Performance-Based Bureaucracy. In *The Oxford Handbook of American Bureaucracy*, ed. R. F. Durant. New York: Oxford University Press.

Mukhina, A. 2019. Eto ne panika, eto katastrofa. V Saratovskoi oblasti bol'nye ne mogut poluchit' besplatnyi insulin. *Meduza.io*, 03 June.

Nikishina, M. 2021. Farmproizvoditeli vyrazili opaseniya iz-za vvedeniya pravila vtoroi lishnii. *Vademecum*, 14 April.

Nikolskaya, A., and M. Dmitriev. 2020. The End of the Crimean Consensus: How Sustainable Are the New Trends in Russian Public Opinion? *Russian Politics* 5 (3): 354–374.

Novaya Gazeta. 2021. Lyubov k otecheskim grosham, 23 February.

Olevskii, T. 2019. Sposob, kotoryi primenyaetsya pri voinakh i epidemiyakh. *Curent Time*, 5 December.

Oreshkin, D. 2019. *Dzhugafiliya i Sovetskii Statisticheskii Epos*. Moskva: Mysl'.

Osipov, A., and N. Kostarnova. 2021. Immunoglobulinovyi krizis perekhodit v kollaps. *Kommersant* No. 197, 28 October.

Osokina, E. 2021. *Stalin's Quest for Gold. The Torgsin Hard-Currency Shops and Soviet Industrialization*. Ithaca: Cornell University Press.

Owen, C., and E. Bindman. 2019. Civic Participation in a Hybrid Regime: Limited Pluralism in Policymaking and Delivery in Contemporary Russia. *Government and Opposition* 54 (1): 98–120.

Pan, J. 2020. *Welfare for Autocrats: How Social Assistance in China Cares for its Rulers*. New York: Oxford University Press.

Paneyakh, E. 2014. Faking Performance Together: Systems of Performance Evaluation in Russian Enforcement Agencies and Production of Bias and Privilege. *Post-Soviet Affairs* 30 (2–3): 115–136.

Pelevin, V. 1999. *Generation P*. Moskva: Vagrius.

Pomeranz, W. E., and K. Smith. 2016. Commentary: Putin's Domestic Strategy: Counting the Trees, Missing the Forest. *Reuters*, 20 May.

Prosina, E., et al. 2018. V Apatitakh pokhoronili Dar'yu Starikovu. *Kommersant*, 24 May.

Pugachev, A. 2020. V bol'nitse v Kamenske-Ural'skom iz-za koronavirusa ostalas' tret' medpersonala. *Current Time*, 30 October.

Putin, V. 2002. Tret'e Poslanie Federal'nomu Sobraniyu Rossiiskoi Federatsii, 18 April [Published in Pavlovskii G.O. 2007. *Plan Prezidenta Putina. Rukovodstvo dlya Budushchikh Prezidentov Rossii. Sbornik*. Moskva: Evropa, pp. 97–125].

Putin, V. 2007. Stenogramma pryamogo tele- i radioefira ("Pryamaya liniya s Prezidentom Rossii"), 18 October. http://kremlin.ru/events/president/transcripts/24604.

Putin, V. 2008. Bol'shaya press-konferentsiya Vladimira Putina. Otvety prezidenta RF Vladimira Putina na voprosy zhurnalistov. *Lenta.ru*, 14 February.

Putin, V. 2009. V.V. Putin provel v Zelenograde soveshchanie "O strategii razvitiya farmatsevticheskoi promyshlennosti", 9 October. http://archive.government.ru/docs/7859/.

Putin, V. 2010. Razgovor s Vladimirom Putinym. Prodolzhenie. Polnyi tekst programmy, 16 December. https://www.vesti.ru/article/2072038.

Putin, V. 2012. Press-konferentsiya Vladimira Putina, 20 December. http://kremlin.ru/events/president/news/17173.

Putin, V. 2017. Bol'shaya press-konferentsiya Vladimira Putina, 14 December. http://kremlin.ru/events/president/news/56378.

Putin, V. 2018a. Poslanie Prezidenta Federal'nomu Sobraniyu, 1 March. http://kremlin.ru/events/president/transcripts/56957.

Putin, V. 2018b. Soveshchanie po voprosam povysheniya effektivnosti sistemy lekarstvennogo obespecheniya, 16 November. http://special.kremlin.ru/events/president/transcripts/59143.

Putin, V. 2019a. Pryamaya liniya s Vladimirom Putinym, 20 June. http://www.kremlin.ru/events/president/news/page/91.

Putin, V. 2019b. Zasedanie Soveta po razvitiyu grazhdanskogo obshchestva i pravam cheloveka, 10 December. http://kremlin.ru/events/president/news/62285.

Raskin, A., and O. Makarkina. 2013. Otsvechivai i ne sidi. *Vademecum*, 17 June.

Ratigan, K. 2022. Riding the Tiger of Performance Legitimacy? Chinese Villagers' Satisfaction with State Healthcare Provision. *International Political Science Review* 3 (2): 259–278.

Reiter, S., and M. Zholobova. 2021. Pishite podobree, oni delayut takoe khoroshee delo. *Meduza.io*, 19 December.

Rodionova, A. 2013. Prokuratura vyyavila 46,000 narushenii pri realizatsii natsproekta Zdorovie v 2012 godu. *Vademecum*, 26 February.

Rodionova, A. 2014. Vavilonskaya basnya. *Vademecum*, 31 March.

Rosenau, J.N. 2003. *Distant Proximities: Dynamics Beyond Globalization*. Princeton and Oxford: Princeton University Press.

Ryakin, S. 2019. Chtoby men'she provalivalos'. *Farmatsevticheskii Vestnik*, 26 November.

Savina, E. 2010. Prezident otsovetoval natsproekty. *Gazeta.ru*, 28 September.

Schatzberg, M.G. 1988. *The Dialectics of Oppression in Zaïre*. Bloomington: Indiana University Press.

Sedakov, P. 2015. Zhizn' posle Arbidola: Kak Viktor Kharitonin zavoeval rynok farmy. *Forbes*, 12 May.

Shevtsova, L. 2015. Itogi goda. 2014 god—konets illjuziona? *Ezhednevnyi Zhurnal*, 1 January.

Shubina, D., M. Sidorova, and E. Rechkin. 2017. Chego boyatsya ispolniteli goskontraktov na postavku meditsinskikh izdelii. *Vademecum*, 8 August.

Shubina, D., and E. Rechkin. 2017. Pochemu ne rabotaet importozameshchenie na rynke medizdelii. *Vademecum*, 09 August.

Solov'eva, O. 2019. Effekta ot natsproektov tri goda zhdut. *Nezavisimaya Gazeta*, 13 November.

Sperling, V. 2014. *Sex, Politics, and Putin: Political Legitimacy in Russia*. New York: Oxford University Press.
TASS. 2019. Istoriya natsproektov v Rossii, 11 February.
Taylor, B. D. 2019. Putin's Fourth Term: The Phantom Breakthrough. PONARS Eurasia Policy Memo No. 602.
Thomson, H. 2019. *Food and Power: Regime Type, Agricultural Policy, and Political Stability*. Cambridge and New York: Cambridge University Press.
Treisman, D. 2011. Presidential Popularity in a Hybrid Regime: Russia Under Yeltsin and Putin. *American Journal of Political Science* 55 (3): 590–609.
Truex, R. 2017. Consultative Authoritarianism and Its Limits. *Comparative Political Studies* 50 (3): 329–361.
Vedomosti. 2019. Lokalizuite eto: Kak vernut' inostrannykh investorov v proizvodstvo lekarstv v Rossii. *Vedomosti*, 30 October.
Visloguzov, V., D. Nikolaeva, and D. Butrin. 2010. Bol'she gippokratii, bol'she sotsializma. *Kommersant*, 21 April.
Yasakova, E. 2021. Syr'e moe: novyi mekhanizm goszakupok mozhet privesti k defitsitu lekarstv. *Izvestiya*, 14 April.
Yushkov, I. 2019. Vankomytsin dlya prezidenta. *Daily Storm*, 19 February.
Zvezdina, P. 2014. Bez posrednikov. *Farmatsevticheskii Vestnik* No. 32, 14 October.
Zvezdina, P. 2017. Eksperty predskazali sokrashchenie chisla bol'nits do urovnya 1913 goda. *RBC*, 7 April.

CHAPTER 3

Managing Actors: Faulty Controls and Flawed Performance

I am deeply convinced that constant rearrangements will not make things better. Neither for work nor people… And most importantly: I clearly understand that those who replace the dismissed will be the same as their predecessors: someone will know the essence of the problem worse, someone better, someone will not understand anything at all. In the end, the result will be the same as it was, if not worse.
—Vladimir Putin in his essay "Pochemu trudno uvolit' cheloveka" [Why it is difficult to fire a person], *Russkii Pioner*, 16 June 2009.

I will sincerely say that we are greatly impressed by what we have heard, by your substantive report, Vladimir Vladimirovich, imbued with concern for our citizens and our country's development. We received clear guidelines for our upcoming work today [and], I would say, optimism and a powerful energy charge. All the tasks set by you will undoubtedly find concrete reflection in our plans.
—Valentina Matvienko, the Chair of the Federation Council, during senators' meeting with Putin on 23 September 2020.

INTRODUCTION

This chapter continues fleshing out my main argument: the features that inhere in a personalistic rule circumscribe the effectiveness of governance. The central theme of this chapter concerns the process and consequences of strategies the Kremlin deploys to manage the multitude of health actors: constructing incentives and constraints for top state officials, exercising manual control, and disengagement from active leadership.

One famous story that highlights how the Kremlin deals with subordinates concerns the dismissal of Vladimir Yakunin, the ostentatiously wealthy, long-serving head of the state-owned enterprise, Russian Railways, who was also a prominent member of Putin's inner circle since their days in St-Petersburg. Arguably, Yakunin lost his lucrative job not because he mismanaged the railroad industry for personal gain and not because he flaunted his wealth, including the infamous "fur-coat-repository" (*shubokhranilishche*) in which he turned one of his rural residencies (Filipenok 2017). However, Yakunin's failure to maintain a well-functioning and affordable railway transportation system, which many ordinary Russians relied on to get from home to work, triggered large-scale social unrest. Instead of permanently dismissing Yakunins' services, Putin assigned him new tasks: he was now in charge of developing pseudo-academic narratives and international symposia, which lionized the regime and promoted the Kremlin's agenda abroad. Enjoying less financially rewarding but still prestigious and high-profile sinecure, Yakunin remained one of the most vocal acolytes of the regime.

Like any authoritarian regime under personalist rule, Russia faces a central problem of developing and applying an appropriate set of incentives to shape the behavior of its officials, private actors, and noncommercial organizations to protect the citizens' needs (Geddes 1994: 193–194). Because personalistic regimes are institutionalized weakly, the leader cannot rely on formal, impersonal institutions to maintain compliance among the elites. Lack of strong formal organizations pushes the ruler to maintain a system of personalized bargains with his state and private actors treated first and foremost like clients. Patron-client relationships cement the dominant coalition (defined as the organization of network leaders that permeate the state, see North et al. 2009: 35–36) on which the regime hinges.

The ruler then is not only a principal who issues bureaucratic mandates, charging his agents with concrete governance tasks, as a standard principal-agent account has it, but also a patron who grants access to valuable resources and activities. At the same time, the main actors involved in health administration are not mere agents, regulators, intermediaries, or private firms but, more consequentially, they are Putin's political clients. Once the principal treats agents as clients, their relationship becomes codependent, and the ruler's ability to effectively manage—reward and punish for the right reasons—his administrators diminishes. Such codependence allows Putin's clients to pursue parochial, self-serving interests and leads to a de facto inversion of systematic hard controls, wherein the regime becomes bound to some of its subordinates. Interdependence between the regime's principals and their clients as the dominant form of political and social relations thwarts efficiency-oriented and problem-solving governance practices. Meanwhile, the objective of working for the public good is alarmingly and perilously compromised.

These considerations are in the first section of this chapter, which discusses severe limitations on the principal's ability to systematically reward his agents for competence and punish them for ineptness and failures. The second section takes a close look at Putin's top health agents, ascertaining their independence and competence. The third section probes into the realities of conducting pharmaceutical business in the country, wherein the Kremlin's manual management style makes privileges and rents and thus wrecks the prospects of a vibrant and competitive pharmaceutical sector. The fourth section explores the flip side of the ruler's outsized influence: the question is what happens when a personalistic ruler disengages from active leadership and manual control while core state actors operate on autopilot.

Faulty Controls: Patronage, Mandates, and Networks

In abstract terms and following a simple formulation of agency theory, there is a "situation where one or more actors (principals) must depend on one or more other actors to perform certain tasks for them" (Wood 2010: 183). Many actors participate in the national governance architecture, including ministers, agencies, governors, the private sector, civil society, members of the inner circle, and street-level medical professionals. The widely agreed-upon finding on the principal-agent dilemma is that dialed-up control diminishes agents' independence and decreases their ability to make competent decisions. As the received wisdom goes, the main problem is that in both democratic and authoritarian regimes, the principal "can maximize either competence or control, but not both." However, this investigation argues that personalistic systems face severe obstacles in achieving either of the objectives.

At first glance, it appears that controls over political leaders, agents, and intermediaries in hierarchical, hyperpresidential Russia are easy to achieve.

The agents surely depend on their ruler for job security, career advancement, and sometimes, via informal networks, privileged access to valuable activities and economic rents, which generate uncompetitive profits and unearned income via public tenders. Undoubtedly, people that comprise Putin's entourage—especially the United Russia partisans, who gradually lose their public appeal—depend on their patron's popularity because it makes clinging to power more feasible. Nevertheless, in reality, Putin must respect the constraints other actors impose on him. Very importantly, when formal institutions are weak, the ability to accumulate and command loyalty via personalized exchanges and particularized bargains is critical since it allows for maintaining a stable or long-lived dictatorship (Wintrobe 1998: 37). These perilous pressures never ceased persisting throughout Putin's tenure in power, and the ruler understands them with clarity. Alluding to the emerging threats to his enduring political domination years ahead of his fifth presidential term, on June 21, 2020, he said: "in two years, instead of normal, rhythmic work at very many levels of government, eyes will begin to scour in search of possible successors. It is necessary to work and not to look for successors" (By making these kinds of statements, Putin also signals the citizens that the government will stop governing without his leadership). Removing executive term limits—in 2020, the Kremlin pushed through a national referendum, which allowed Putin to remain a president for life—tamed domestic elites and signaled his continuing patronal dominance. For now, Tatyana Stanovaya (2020) is skeptical that elites will rebel and alter the patronal pyramid, but the elite's compliance seems to be informed more by following self-preservation instincts rather than genuine clientelistic satisfaction.

To survive politically, a personalistic ruler confronts the necessity of maintaining a single-power pyramid and protecting himself from rising rivals. A split in the elites (and their potential plurality) is a real danger for the regime. Because acolytes and sycophants could defect to an opposing coalition and converge around an alternative patron who is expected to dole out better rewards (Hale 2015), the autocrat must oblige his subordinates' interests and forestall their defection. Putin's subordinates will likely look for a promising patron during critical moments, such as contested—albeit unfree and unfair—elections, which could produce results unpredictable and unfavorable to the regime. What was more, during Putin's short hiatus as a prime minister in 2008–2012, a significant portion of Russian elites began consolidating around Dmitry Medvedev, went public criticizing Putin's illiberal politics, and suggested ways to correct his approach to governance, including health.

It becomes increasingly apparent that Putin does not take even the slightest prospects of an emerging alternative patron timidly: he learned the lessons of the Color Revolutions wherein the split elite opted for an alternative leader-patron in Eurasia all too well. It is not surprising then that Putin has been trying to avoid the lame-duck syndrome and forestall any chances of potential dissent among his subordinates. Any prominent personality who can serve as the focal point of gravitational pull for the opposing forces is removed from politics at the federal and regional levels alike. The mechanisms vary: it could be a personalized bargain (Dmitry Medvedev, replaced at the peak of his popularity in 2012, remained in the hierarchy of power as a prime minister), the arbitrary use of the law (Nikita Belykh, arrested in 2016, and Sergey Furgal, arrested in 2020), or violence (Boris Nemtsov, assassinated in 2015, and Alexey Navalny, poisoned in 2020 and imprisoned in 2021).

In this context, deciphering Putin's reasons for drastic or routine personnel decisions is difficult: punishing administrators for mismanagement and the lack of competence could be why people get fired, but Putin typically avoids explicit signaling or explaining his motives. Still, the impersonal system of rewards and punishments (which could operate well in regimes institutionalized around formal organizations and the rule of law) is antithetical to the personalistic system that circumvents institutions but relies on personalized exchanges. In the context of personalistic rule, strict punishment for underperformance is suboptimal because it sends the wrong signals to the ruler's clients: clients could be punished only for their glaring disloyalty or undermining Putin's popularity among the masses. In contrast, the prospects of being punished for pursuing their self-interest are not inevitable. Moreover, Putin's selective punishments remain rare, and the fired individuals commonly resurface in governmental, legislative, or advisory sinecures. No demotion is desirable for those dismissed from valuable organizational positions, but having less lucrative jobs or diminished access to prized resources and activities is better than being completely removed from the list of Putin's clients. A closer look at the available evidence regarding top bureaucrats' appointments lends credence to the proposition that the Kremlin ignores considerations of corruption and lack of independent administrative abilities as disqualifying parameters.

However, lest Russian voters stop supporting him, Putin must continue to walk the path of plenteous promises, demand the fulfillment of social goals from his subordinates, and keep signaling his commitment to social welfare. In response to these challenges, the Kremlin issued restricted mandates, developed quantifiable but befogged output-based performance indicators, and limited agents' ability to define or interpret their bureaucratic mandates. Narrow mandates and micromanagement are harmful in principle as they erode bureaucratic independence and competence, and such an approach is undoubtedly detrimental to good health governance in the context of electoral authoritarianism. My analysis licenses the standard principal-agent view that general mandates increase bureaucratic autonomy and, possibly, competence. There is a corollary for personalistic regimes: broad mandates require an institutional setup that relaxes the ruler's control over agents and makes autocratic promises less attributed to the ruler personally, which erodes an essential source of his popularity. Therefore, leaders in electoral authoritarian regimes are unlikely to license broad mandates, and it also debilitates an objective assessment of ex ante bureaucratic competence.

The unhurried reading of governmental proceedings indicates that Putin specifically prohibits his subordinates from diverging from narrow mandates, no matter whether independence and initiative could improve health governance and its outcomes. At the Meeting of the Council for Strategic Development and Priority Projects, on September 21, 2016, Putin stressed that point clearly: "We have many tasks, there are enough problems, and we, of course, can formulate them again and again, endlessly, and it will never end, because in any country -- both in a large and in a small and even more so in our large country -- it will be an endless list. We need to isolate the main thing in the work of each department, to formulate and monitor the indicators, how they are implemented."

Putin's subordinates recognize him as the only actor who can formulate strategic solutions. It follows that state agents must carry out governance tasks precisely as formulated, even though these tasks might not be well-suited for increasing people's welfare and health. The centrality of micromanagement and narrow mandates for Putin's approach to governance did not go unnoticed. As Gleb Pavlovsky (2012: 7–17), once Putin's close advisor, insightfully notes, instead of giving his subordinates a new sense of public service mission, Putin wants high-level administrators to worry about specific projects he assigns them. Instead of working toward a common social goal, key participants in the Russian governance system must first and foremost satisfy their principal's political objectives if they want to remain in the system. Predictably, submissive subordination leads to poor performance (Fukuyama 2013: 359).

On the flip side, when the principal's wishes are not clear, when the boss withholds a direct command, or when bureaucratic mandates are too broad-ranging, agents become paralyzed by indecision (for a vivid example of how even a routine situation could create a conundrum for agents, see Taylor 2018: 134–135). It is clear that with attenuated legislative accountability and limited electoral competition, career administrators and elected local officials equally display little incentive to work hard to improve the quality of public goods provision (Zavadskaya and Shilov 2021; Beazer and Reuter 2021). Being on autopilot does not promote independence and professionalism, as a standard account of principal-agent theory holds, but it impairs intent interagency coordination and determined execution.

In the absence of broad-ranging mandates to provide high-quality services in health, imposing rigid, quantifiable indicators of the desired outcomes as the methods of evaluating the efficiency of bureaucratic performance seems only logical. Restrictive mandates and key performance indicators (KPIs) were supposed to preclude dysfunction by incentivizing elites to work in the population's interest and constraints narrow self-interested behavior. Sergey Kiriyenko, hitherto the head of the Russian Atomic Agency and a former prime minister, appointed in 2016 the First Deputy Chief of Staff of the Presidential Administration, is an avid exponent of the Kremlin's managerialism. Russian political observers traced Kiriyenko's philosophy of public administration to Georgy Shchedrovitsky's school of managerialism, rooted in the Soviet past, which prepared future leaders to be creative and transformative and boosted their confidence by rejecting the notion that structural factors constrain outcomes of governance. (One technique was to draw conceptual maps to visualize how to solve emerging problems.) Strangely enough, this school of managerialism attracted the attention of local conspiracy theorists who averred that Shchedrovitsky's disciples consciously planned the stealth state capture, prepared the country for the transition to capitalism, and trained the future political puppeteers (Pryanikov 2016; Gogin 2016). These conspiratorial utterances aside, such an approach indeed resonates with top state administrators in Russia today as it incentivizes accepting Putin's social agenda without giving much thought to the real needs of the Russian people. It views society as an object of manipulation or a mechanism that the regime can fix without triggering externalities, not as a complex environment.

Documentary evidence suggests that Putin's micromanagement intended to restore hitherto falling levels of social trust in various state and public institutions (Nagornykh 2018). Consistent with the logic of particularistic bargains and personalized exchanges between the patron and his clients, it is unclear whether the failure to achieve Putin's mandates or fulfill all key performance indicators leads to the dismissal from employment. This consideration makes me think about imposed metrics not as a mechanism of control over governance actors but as a commitment signal designed to bolster Putin's popularity among the masses (Galimova 2018; Nagornykh 2018). Undoubtedly, "the tyranny of metrics" (Muller 2018) is far from being Russian know-how, but the point is that the developed key performance indicators are inappropriate instruments for increasing bureaucratic accountability and competence. In general, Putin's incentive scheme is at odds with professional ethos and a sense of commitment to impartial public service.

What is more threatening to the quality and competence of the Russian administration, personalistic rulers rely on an informal network of trusted individuals who help rulers govern. That many individuals transcended formal boundaries between the public and private sectors and between different governmental agencies and enterprises is well-understood. Although the intra-elite hierarchy roughly corresponds to the organization an individual represents, few persons—Igor Sechin, Sergey Chemezov, and German Gref—on account of personal proximity and informal connections could convince Putin to steer governance decisions in their favor (Gaaze 2017). The dealings between the informal groupings and networks are about fighting over access, resources, and power (Taylor 2018: 72), and they also dilute the ruler's control over substantive policy implementation.

Controlling informal networks is complicated, too. Manual control practices in awarding contracts to well-connected private actors while undermining the legal tender process are essential to satisfying a spade of clients and thus ensuring the cohesiveness of a single-power pyramid. Putin tends to view his trusted associates and cronies at the helm of state monopolies as indispensable for the purposes of development. The evidence suggests that as Putin becomes increasingly dependent on informal networks for the delivery of goods and services, actors connected to Putin's inner circle ask and continue to receive limitless access to valuable state resources and activities despite their limited ability to deliver. The evidence suggests that Putin and his core Vassals rely on hand-picked domestic firms, but these firms take advantage of the government's strategic directives, despite the multiple warnings the Russian Federal Antimonopoly Service issued. The principal possesses a limited ability to check his clients' effectiveness since providing favors and privileges is his patronal obligation. Almost all state monopolies underperform, and although the principal envisions state monopolies and privileged firms as a vehicle for pharmaceutical development, the government has to subsidize them with taxpayers' money. Although Putin's cronies cannot merely discount the time horizon and pillage ad libitum, ordinary patients do not receive public services as nearly as well as they deserve, but Putin continues his course.

As long as Putin remains popular and in power, political insiders could reasonably expect to remain the regime's beneficiaries. These individuals enjoy considerable autonomy and tend to become "sub-patrons" and spawn hierarchical networks of their own that transcend formal boundaries between the public and private sector and between different governmental agencies and enterprises. Once these informal networks are centralized and fully formed, lower-level clients also become the regime's beneficiaries. This practice shows how Putin's system metastasizes and permeates the Russian state. Over time, especially after trusted individuals receive monopoly privileges, the principal loses his power to control their rent-seeking appetites and improve their performance, which leads to an inversion of authority and further attenuation of the quality of government. Thus, abuse of power and resources, privileges, and rent-seeking inhere on the strength of personalized contracts central to Russia's electoral authoritarianism under personalistic rule. Parts of the story told in Chapter 2 and this chapter are consistent with this view.

To conclude, understanding the complexities of controls over agents and clients in Russia's personalistic authoritarianism could be confounding. On the one hand, Putin cannot completely submit his governance to the growing appetites of political insiders. On the other hand, he cannot undermine his subordinates' welfare lest they start looking for another patron to receive privileges during the next electoral cycle. For political survival, the latter motivation is preeminent, and no personalistic dictator will ever be able to organize the optimal incentive scheme, ensuring the adequate and fair provision of public goods and services. In other words, personalistic rulers face severe constraints in exercising impersonal and impartial control over subordinates and punishing them for incompetence and governance failures. The impersonal system of rewards and punishments is antithetical to the personalistic system, which circumvents institutions but relies on personalized exchanges. The resulting system of governance fails to improve performance by permanently dismissing the bureaucrats that fail to deliver. Instead, it tries to cast a blind eye to the daunting failures of governance and even makes principals cover up their subordinates' mistakes and inefficiencies. This bespoke arrangement is detrimental to the quality of health governance, and in the long term, it makes ordinary patients worse off.

Bureaucrats Endure: Deficits of Quality and Excesses of Loyalty

Forming an acceptable idea about bureaucratic incompetence as the root cause of the poor administrative performance and failure to manage health successfully is challenging. One strain of literature views bad governance as a consequence of the widespread practice of using "informal and personalistic criteria in personnel decisions (hiring, promotion, etc.) rather than more professional or rational-legal standards" (Taylor 2011: 4). Irrefragable is the observation that the longer Putin stays in power, the more frequently he uses informal and personalistic criteria in personnel decisions. For instance, the aging circle of his long-time associates gives way to the new faces, often recruited from the corps of Putin's bodyguards (Nagornyh et al. 2012; Anin 2018; Churakova et al. 2019).

Exposing pitfalls of governance arising from the pathologies of patrimonialism and nepotism in fulfilling vacancies found its rightful place in the governance literature. Rulers resort to patrimonial practices in appointing bureaucrats with insufficient merit for being in charge and creating economic privileges for loyal private actors on the indispensability of patronal obligations to the elite, treated like clients. None of this disposes of the need to further unpack the complexity of the health governance process in the country. Although patrimonial practices contribute to the gravity of the governor's dilemma, a critical source of administrative inefficiency and governance spoliation in Russia is that in personalistic systems, the principal is severely constrained in his ability to exercise impersonal and impartial control over his subordinates and punish them for their incompetence and governance failures.

This section also adds a shade of gray to a deep-seated notion that Russian governance is a clinker because top bureaucrats lack requisite professional qualifications. The confusion about the quality of health administration is unavoidable on account of our inability to construct an objective test of bureaucratic ex ante competencies, delinked from personalistic constraints in which Russian agents must operate. To be sure, Putin's administration designed an elaborate system of key performance indicators, but using Kiriyenko's politicized metric in an academic analysis of the quality of government is not warranted. Nor can we fully rely on the internal—and intently personal—assessment of Putin's top health appointees provided by articulated audiences or nongovernmental bodies. Many incriminations reflect more in-house conflicts and grudges than disinterested statements of competencies and qualifications. The point is that nondemocratic regimes do not always lack Weberian-quality bureaucrats, but the lack of professional independence in implementing narrow, often flawed, and contradictory mandates (as discussed in the preceding chapter) will inevitably make agents look like underperformers.

Regardless of any type of judgment concerning specific individuals and their personal qualities, the faulty system of health actors' management as constructed and maintained by the principal is a case in point. As it appears, all too many facts about senior administrators are indubitably negative, but the principal is not in a hurry to dismiss the ones who failed or underperformed. Let us have a brief look at five ministers of health who served in Putin's administrations since the early 2000s

1. Mikhail Murashko, who received his appointment in January 2020, has a long track record of serving in the healthcare system at the regional level before his appointment to the top position in Moscow. As a regional minister of health, he was implicated in several scandals regarding the alleged misappropriation of health funds intended to purchase foreign high-end medical devices. As a head of federal health surveillance, he distinguished himself by avoiding exposing any pitfalls of Cabinet-level health governance (for details, see next chapter).
2. Veronika Skvortsova, a minister of health in 2012–2020, was an esteemed neurologist and a fifth-generation doctor. Although many health professionals expressed positive opinions about her work, Skvortsova hardly had any administrative clout independent of her boss. She presided over near-disastrous health optimization, wherein

the number of hospitals declined dramatically, and the working conditions of health professionals became near-abysmal.
3. Tatyana Golikova, a minister of health in 2007–2012, promoted an unproven drug, Arbidol, in which she allegedly had a personal financial stake (for which the media not so playfully dubbed her "Madame Arbidol"). Under her supervision, the ministry developed foundational health laws, but these laws were universally considered poorly thought out.
4. Mikhail Zurabov, minister of health in 2004–2007, supervised the ministry's failed programs to ensure universal and uninterrupted access to life-saving medicines. He was also a subject of a criminal investigation that the Prosecutor General's Office opened against the Mandatory Medical Insurance Fund, which Zurabov allegedly lobbied.
5. Out of all five individuals who served as ministers of health under Putin, Yury Shevchenko (in office 1999–2004), who had informal ties to the president since their days in St-Petersburg, was implicated in open fraud, imports of counterfeit products, and personal enrichment (Skorobogat'ko 2004).

Despite their many administrative faults, it appears that unless top state administrators are responsible for triggering mass protests (which challenge the contract between the ruler and the people), they are likely to stay in office. One episode of dismissal from office concerns the fate of Mikhail Zurabov, Minister of Health and Social Development in Mikhail Fradkov's first and second cabinets in 2004–2007. Zurabov failed to implement the necessary but defectively designed reforms to convert in-kind benefits into cash allowances (Wengle and Rasell 2008; Pis'mennaya 2013: 143–151). Specifically, he was in charge of bringing together all social benefits and making proposals for their monetization, the implementation of which caused mass protests. Still, even given his dismal handling of the HIV/AIDS crisis in the country, Putin awarded him another sinecure and kept him in his pool of clients. Tatyana Golikova, too, despite the health industry's critique, stayed in charge of the Ministry of Health for more than a decade, both officially and unofficially. Veronika Skvortsova, although demoted, still found a powerful place in the health governance community.

A study of actual trajectories of top agents lends much support to the proposition that the stasis of cadres is inherent to personalistic authoritarianism. Such stasis of cadres is inevitable, and Putin's most common personnel solution is to reshuffle the same deck of bureaucrats. The extant system of tacit contract and interdependencies among the main actors, the members of the officialdom and those formally outside the purview of the state alike, including those involved in health governance, is calibrated to maintain a status-quo, not effective governance in the interests of the people. It is not by chance that in January 2021, Putin introduced a bill that allowed civil servants appointed by the head of state to work in their posts without age restrictions. By removing age restrictions (which were hitherto capped at 65 years of age), the aging autocrat signaled to his loyal cadres that they would be rewarded for their loyalty for life.

This approach makes sense for Putin because radical demotions or rotations are likely to aggravate his subordinates but are not really functional. Hypothetically, suppose Putin proceeds with culling incompetent and corrupt administrators. In that case, the nature of codependencies and tradeoffs for the dominant coalition, i.e., for people with special privileges they receive as returns on loyalty, defined by the very nature of personalism, will remain the same. Lest the regime's agents choose another patron in case of either mass protests or the emergence of a rival patron during electoral cycles, newly recruited members of the dominant coalition must be provided with concrete, personalized rewards in return for their fealty to the principal. Provided rewards, such as continual access to advantageous positions, valuable resources, and prestigious activities, ensure agents' loyalty to the principal, but they would not improve state quality. Broadly put, the radical rotation of cadres will achieve little to increase the quality of the government. Without radical elite replacement, rotation of cadres simply resets the same perverse incentives that ultimately lead to administrative mismanagement and trigger multiple gaming strategies.

Small wonder, Putin likes to assuage his subordinates' concerns about the stability of their jobs. In one of his well-known essays, Putin openly acknowledged that firing individuals is the measure of last resort and, as such, does not necessarily increase the quality of governance. The first quotation that opens this chapter illustrates the point. In reality, because the necessity to protect key individuals overrides the considerations of their incompetence, the regime principals might dismiss bureaucrats who fail to deliver yet do so rarely and often appoint them to other sinecures.

A case in point is Putin's decision to appoint a new government. At the October 2019 meeting of the State Council in Kaliningrad, Putin expressed his frustration with the government's failure to deliver. Putin indicated the mixed results of the state regulation of the pharmaceutical industry and healthcare and replaced Medvedev's Cabinet with the individuals who, in Putin's presentation, could deliver a national developmental breakthrough. Domestic political observers, too, converged on the idea that Putin dismissed the old Cabinet and appointed a new generation of "technocrats" arguably capable of improving health governance and correcting the shortcomings of Medvedev's government. The majority of old cadres of health bureaucrats remained in the government, although in different positions. Because such administrative reshuffles are more consistent with treating elites as clients than punishing them for underperformance, no substantial changes in the Russian approach to governance are likely. Even absent the exogenous shock of the pandemic of COVID-19, the new cabinet still could have hardly contributed to improving social outcomes.

As argued in the previous chapter, in personalistic regimes, elites, agents, and intermediaries are loyal not to perpetual organizations, coherent ideologies, specific policies, or the public, but they must be unstintingly faithful to the ruler. Putin values loyalty, and he also demands and rewards it. At least in critical situations, anticipatory obedience is an optimizing behavior that can make agents better off. Perhaps the most dramatic illustration is the story of Aleksandr Murakhovky, the chief physician of the Omsk emergency hospital. In 2020 he publicly denied that Putin's sharpest political opponent, Alexey Navalny, was intentionally poisoned and proposed that his health condition was caused by hypoglycemia and other metabolic disorders. Immediately after, Murakhovky became the regional minister of health, which most independent journalists interpreted as a reward for his lies (Solodun and Nikishina 2020). Alarming ambiguities about the case notwithstanding, Putin could not find any better test of his subordinates' fealty than observing their behavior in the wake of the botched attempt of poisoning Navalny.

None other than Leonid Roshal, otherwise a doctor and humanitarian boasting a highly positive reputation among the medical professionals, supported Putin in his attempts to discredit the accurate medical diagnosis supplied by the Berlin clinic Navalny had been admitted to while in a coma (Interfax 2020). As the person who leads a large health intermediary organization, Roshal's anticipatory obedience is an optimizing behavior that allows him to keep his part of the authoritarian bargain. That submissive subordination is widespread in Putin's Russia is irrefragable; however, there is no case to be made that any and all health officials and health intermediaries are emotionally attached to the ruler and remain faithful without dissembling or deceit. After all, any Vassal has a bit of Opportunist in them. Still, an act of open disloyalty could break the career of any official.

What is also alarming for the long-term quality of health governance in Russia is that the regime tends to blame undesired health outcomes on the street-level bureaucrats' alleged wrongdoings. Ordinary medical professionals bear the disproportionate brunt of punishments compared to top provincial authorities, not to mention federal-level regulators and ministers. The executive vertical turned to repressions against those who protested and questioned the Kremlin's administrative wisdom, demonstrating disloyalty and insolence. To quell protests against the distressing "optimization" of the healthcare sector, the regional departments instructed head doctors to eliminate exasperated doctors and nurses. According to the official narrative, medical professionals could not be disappointed in blanket reductions in healthcare unless they share Alexey Navalny's subversive values (Britskaya 2019). Only in 2020, in the middle of the COVID-19 crisis, many regional health officials (in Irkutsk, Omsk, Arkhangelsk, and Kemerovo oblast) and health managers were forced to step down or lost their jobs. The punishment cases for graft, corruption, misdiagnosis, or lack of favorable health outcomes are observable at the provincial and street levels. However, the system of rewards and punishments directed at the top echelon of administrators—and elite, in general—is very far from the rational incentive schemes described in principal-agent theories.

Creating Privileges: Powerful Firms, Poor Services

Central to good health governance is the ability of governments to efficiently allocate state resources so that patients have uninterrupted access to high-quality pharmaceuticals and medical devices in the public sector. In some broad sense, the quality of public services depends on modernized production technologies and a robust and competitive medical sector with a reliable output of drugs and medical devices. But personalistic regimes are not built to achieve that dual task. As authoritarian regimes treat private actors as objects of direct management (consistent with the regime's priority of control over competition and independence), they shore up a public procurement system that depends on hand-picked but often unreliable firms that enjoy unwarranted monopolies.

In today's Russia, only hand-picked and well-connected firms supply—and often on an exclusive basis—medical products: Medpolimerprom provides plastic medical devices (Myl'nikov 2018b); Delrus supplies personal protective coverings (Kobernik and Baranova 2020); Gerofarm supplies import-substituted insulin (Nazarova 2019); Nacimbio is responsible for vaccines; Rostec manufactures coronavirus tests (sold by EMG, see Yakoreva and Ershov 2020) and medical masks. The pervasiveness of manual control over hand-picked firms often imposes unnecessary costs on patients. For instance, the St. Petersburg-based pharmaceutical manufacturer Geropharm secured the position of the sole supplier of home-made insulin (Dombrova 2016), which turned out to be substandard compared to the foreign-made product and caused patients' complaints.

At first glance, the ruler's idiosyncratic proclivities and personal political trajectories are responsible for all of this. Putin's reliance on manual control and personalized networks could be traced back to his days in St-Petersburg city hall when city contracts—in the absence of the formal legal tender process—were awarded to the people personally known to the city's top functionaries. These earlier practices continue on a bigger scale as the ruler consistently chooses to appoint a single operator responsible for producing and delivering a particular product or service in the public sector, ranging from pharmaceutical products and railroad transportation to waste removal. In doing so, Putin single-handedly overrules the Federal Law "On the contract system in the field of procurement of goods, works, services to meet state and municipal needs" (No. 44-FZ adopted on April 5, 2013).

For Putin as the principal, the impulse to control the industry via manual management of private actors and direct involvement in handling social issues offers an expedient but misguided illusion wherein the Kremlin has firm control over outcomes. Putin's faith that he could achieve any policy objectives through hard control and manual management (Pavlovsky 2012: 7–17) results in deliberate choices that decrease the number of competing pharmaceutical companies. Understandably, no individual leader, no matter how well-informed and well-intended, could avoid making errors of judgment in picking the wrong firm. But the story told here is not about individual errors that could be easily corrected or isolated cases of bribes that could be punished.

Most importantly, exercising manual control and creating privileges are inherent to Russian personalism since the regime's weak institutionalization is devoid of other—ideological or partisan—methods of control. From the vantage point of the struggle to maintain authoritarian power, creating privileges and manually managing private firms allows Putin to harvest support across private and quasi-governmental actors.

This practice is part and parcel of the broader trend in the regime's efforts to cultivate the new generation of the deferential business elite, which, according to a renowned observer of Russian affairs, Tatyana Stanovaya (2015), "owns large assets acquired mostly due to access to government tenders or the distribution of projects by large state-owned companies." Manually managing the private sector is not accidental since the alternative approach based on prioritizing free markets and ensuring competition would erode the symbiotic ties between the network of clients and the regime. While top state managers are allowed to hand-pick private actors to carry out the directives they receive, Putin reserves the ultimate right to determine which firms are arguably capable of delivering public goods effectively. Central to the emerging system of pharmaceutical governance are informal networks of small groups of individuals occupying core positions in government and the private sector.

The regime tends to justify this approach citing the need to generate a system of incentives for a fistful of private actors and state-owned enterprises to accumulate profits and invest heavily in domestic industries, thereby increasing the state capacity. In reality, this practice undermines genuine competition between private firms while incentivizing them to increase their profits by seeking privileges and avoiding investments in modernizing the industry. Monopolies seek rents rather than improve the quality of services; the price tag of selecting unscrupulous firms is very high. Further, as Putin allows and encourages the formation of state and quasi-state monopolies with his close associates at their helm, he becomes beholden to his associates as their patron and generally loses an opportunity to backpedal on bad decisions. In practice, such an inversion of authority over public services was a long time in the making: it started in the wake of the global financial crisis of 2008 (Gaaze 2016), and by the end of his fourth presidential term, this inversion became so predominant that it seems natural and immutable.

Documentary evidence suggests that the impulse to appoint a single operator responsible for producing and delivering a particular product or service in the public sector is common to multiple layers of authority, ranging from the regime's principals to the Ministry of Health. During Putin's presidency, the Ministry of Health has been the primary regulator of pharmaceutical products and wielded enormous power over domestic pharmaceutical governance. Minzdrav (short for the Ministry of Health) developed arbitrary barriers for market entry to support several private firms, measures that catapulted a few hand-picked firms to astonishing financial success. The process of medicine procurement is fraught with favors for several companies and firms, state and privately owned alike, some of them closely affiliated to the regime's principals. There is no reason for these companies to achieve market dominance except explicit ministerial backing. The two biggest Russian pharmaceutical companies, whose revenue was almost entirely dependent on winning state contracts and which together captured more than 20% of the total share of state purchases, deserve special attention.

Viktor Kharitonin's Pharmstandard, co-founded by Golikova's husband's long-term subordinates in 2003, is one of Russia's leading drugmakers and one of the largest suppliers of drugs for state purchases. For Pharmstandard, the breakthrough occurred during the epidemic of swine influenza (A/H1N1) in 2009, when Golikova included Arbidol (international nonproprietary name Umifenovir), Pharmstandard's flagship antiviral treatment for influenza infection, on the list of essential medicines, used Ministry's money to purchase it for the public sector, and directed drugstores to sell over the counter, all before clinical trials (Kalinovskaya 2015). (In 2020, Arbidol was fraudulently advertised as an effective treatment against COVID-19 (Batalova 2020), rapidly increasing its sales.) Later on, for undisclosed reasons, Minzdrav allowed the unlicensed release of Gefitinib, an inhibitor of the epidermal growth factor receptor, a product also supplied by one of Kharitonin's firms. Kharitonin's firm enjoyed Golikova's backing despite all too many public fire alarms and won multiple state contracts. In 2018, Pharmstandard and its subsidiaries captured almost half of the federal budget earmarked for the most expensive treatments and orphan diseases.

Another company, Alexey Repik's R-Pharm Group, began as a small start-up with a capital of a few thousand dollars (Sagdiev 2011) and later became a "backbone" health enterprise officially qualified for the large state subsidies. In his interviews, Repik denied the state's partiality to his business (Dranishnikova 2014), but he put its foot in the door by securing small-scale contracts with law enforcement agencies. It is not surprising then that when Minzdrav became the main centralized vendee of medicines, R-Pharm was hand-picked and was often the only firm declaring for public auctions. The company's explosive growth began in 2008 when R-Pharm received several state contracts to supply expensive medications for rare diseases, as its competitors did not declare for auctions. Later on, during the 2013 trading session, R-Pharm emerged as the leading supplier for the federal antiretroviral program. The company also began exclusively supplying five antiretroviral and two interchangeable drugs for viral hepatitis.

By 2015, R-Pharm led in the relative number of state tenders won, effectively controlling about a tenth of all pharmaceutical government contracts. Repik's company also immensely benefited from the new centralized system of antiretroviral purchases, pushing more than a hundred smaller regional companies out of business—although, in theory, Minzdrav got rid of local systems of tenders for the opposite reason, that is, in order to stimulate domestic competition. To be fair, as R-Pharm grows, it also invests in modernizing the domestic productive capacities, conducts trials on generics, and ramps up the production of medicines for larger Western companies. Still, whether the government's hand-picking strategy is optimal or even beneficial for the industry's growth remains questionable. That Repik became the co-chairman of both the Russian Union of Industrialists and Entrepreneurs and Delovaya Rossiya (a national public association uniting entrepreneurs mainly from medium-size businesses unrelated to oil and gas industries) attests to his centrality in the new business elite cultivated by the regime.

Although the president and the government publicly criticized the lack of competitiveness that plagued the system of state purchases (Mereminskaya 2016), they increasingly allowed individuals with special ties to them to become the sole supplier of goods and services and even made disclosure of data on the winners of public contracts optional. Despite many private companies' nonexistent output capacities or lack of value-added for providing health goods, the government's impulse to promote monopolies endures. Two cases worth mentioning here include Medpolimerprom and Stentex: both firms obtained exclusive privileges because of their connections to the regime's principals and reaped exorbitant profits.

In 2017, a hitherto unknown, small, and unconnected firm emerged as a monopolist in supplying disposable medical devices made of polyvinyl chloride plastics (PVC) for public hospitals. Dmitry Medvedev gave the company an effective monopoly over devices for blood transfusion, breathing circuits, catheters, and ventilator filters (Dranishnikova 2017; Zhegulev 2017). Further, the company's top management routinely took an active part in governmental meetings on the industrial policy to which no representatives of other companies were allowed. As it turned out, Medpolimerprom started reselling medical devices from Western manufacturers while failing to build a government-subsidized PVC plant (Shubina 2018). Although the company won nearly all the bids, it could not fulfill its contractual obligations. Several years later, the company's management pled guilty in a criminal case of giving a bribe to an official close to Medvedev's long-time assistant and confidant, Arkady Dvorkovitch (Myl'nikov 2020). Simply put, Medvedev made critical decisions in health governance on the grounds of faulty governance ideas aggravated by pervasive corruption.

A similar story occurred with one of the Russian oligarchs close to Putin, Viktor Vekselberg, who secured the exclusive right to sell stents (a stent is a tubular support device placed temporarily inside a blood vessel) and catheters to the public hospitals. The company jumped on the opportunity to start negotiations with hospitals (the management was under the impression that purchases from Renova's subsidiary, Stentex, were mandatory) but did not bother providing hospitals with products for testing. Essentially, Stentex, much like Medpolimerprom, reaped profits by simply reselling foreign devices. Although other domestic manufacturers fought against the monopolist (Zvezdina and Mogilevskaya 2017), only the international sanctions against Vekselberg made the regulator reconsider the desirability of having a single supplier of stents (Myl'nikov 2019). But for the sanctions, Stentex would remain a monopolist.

Eventually, both companies lost their privileged status: Stentex lost its grounds in the wake of external sanctions (although Vekselberg's Renova continued to receive state subsidies), and Medpolimerprom got hurt by bad publicity and inability to control the narrative (Myl'nikov 2018a, 2018c). Still, no matter how glaring the failures are, the proposition that the government overturned wrong or corrupt decisions because of its desire to improve governance remains unwarranted. Despite the apparent problems with hand-picked monopolists, in 2020, the government started compiling a list of preferred contractors. Some lobbyists suggested that the Ministry of Industry and Trade compile an annual list of manufacturers and suppliers of medical devices, thereby guaranteeing the receipt of purchase orders from state-managed hospitals.

Further centralization and state capture of pharmaceutical governance follow. Some companies' financial success hinges on Putin's favors and his ability to ignore the rule of law. Rostec, a state-owned state military-industrial conglomerate officially known as the State Corporation for Assistance to Development, Production, and Export of Advanced Technology Industrial Product, exemplifies the described trend. This holding is organized on multi-sector principles and headed by Sergey Chemezov, a long-standing member of Putin's inner circle, who got acquainted with Putin in Dresden while working for the KGB before the collapse of the USSR and maintained close relations since. Chemezov's ambition was to expand the reach of Rostec to the civilian procurement of medicines. Like other Russian state-owned monopolies headed by Putin's friends, Rostec gradually came to dominate the defense and civilian economies.

Consequential for Russia's health governance was Rostec's decision to create the National Immunobiological Company (hereafter, Nacimbio) in 2013. The capture of several state-owned pharmaceutical enterprises and the acquisition of monopoly rights to supply many medical products have been central to Chemezov's strategy to reinvent the shell company into a substantial pharmaceutical holding. Chemezov has been granted multiple long-term exclusive governmental contracts without taking part in competitive bidding. In a short span of time, Nacimbio became an exclusive operator supplying medicines to the country's penitentiary system, providing vaccines for the national vaccination calendar, and taking control over medical aviation. Although Nacimbio provides no real benefits for the welfare of the patients, Putin continues to prop the company. In some cases, Putin directly overruled already signed agreements and handed Rostec lucrative contracts to develop a national digital procurement information system and digitize national medical informational services (in 2017 and 2019, respectively). The example amply testifies that personalistic leaders are at the root of many health governance deficiencies.

Although in his recent interview, Chemezov claimed that "the main objective of Nacimbio is technology transfer, creation of joint ventures in Russia, development of its vaccines and drugs" (Lyauv et al. 2018), the reality was different. According to the Transparency International report, Nacimbio is a clearinghouse that fulfills Minzdrav's orders by reselling vaccines and drugs produced elsewhere (Transparency International 2017). In return for Putin's favors, Nacimbio was supposed to invest its profits in modernizing the domestic manufacturing capacities, which it failed to accomplish since the enterprise failed to show real profits. Notably, Chemezov's significance in Putin's inner circle allows him to spawn networks of his own: in 2017, he moved to swap Nacimbio's pharmaceutical assets with the Marathon Group, an investment company privately held by his son-in-law, and create a drug giant with extensive distributional capacities. Thereby Chemezov openly promoted his son-in-law's business interests while signaling Nacimbio's growth as a successful sign.

In summary, contrary to accounts of bad governance that highlight rent-seizing as the dominant coalition's intended and primary collective purpose, this chapter demonstrates that authoritarian rulers create privilege and make rents to ensure private actors' fealty to the regime. The principal also sought to demonstrate his competence in governing effectively and his deep commitment to improving the domestic pharmaceutical sector. In theory, the Kremlin wanted to ensure patients' needs and stimulate the domestic pharmaceutical business, but the outcomes hardly had any indubitably positive impact on modernizing the domestic pharmaceutical capacities or improving patients' access to drugs. In practice, unintended consequences, including product overpricing, drug stockouts, and firms' failure to fulfill their contractual obligations (Latukhina 2017), ensued. Simply put, Putin treated the health sector strategically—more in his political interest rather than in the interest of people's welfare.

The foregoing discussion emphasized one particular feature of the governance process: a limited number of companies came to dominate the supply of medicines and medical devices for the public sector but made health governance less efficient and the pharmaceutical sector less competitive. The final section discusses the governance situation opposite the manual steering practice and investigates how agents behave when the principal removes controls by withdrawing his previously issued mandate.

Officials on Autopilot: HIV/AIDS Crisis as a Nonpriority

Clear is the observation that personalism adds an idiosyncratic twist to governance processes. Most importantly, the outsized role of a leader's persona, the apparent feature of governance in the Russian hyperpresidential system, translates into opportunistic or uncommitted decision-making (Petrov et al. 2014). It is worth stressing that although doubling down on the domestic response to an enormous health crisis is crucial, personalistic leaders do not prioritize substantive policy goals over their political objectives. If they find it politically expedient, they withdraw political support from health initiatives they once heavily stressed. They then avoid reissuing the narrow terms of mandates necessary for agents to govern. Simply, they could lose interest in a particular issue. This section's spotlight is on the flurry of activities and initiatives that boil down to the agents' failure to self-organize and fight the widening epidemic of HIV/AIDS when the rewards of doing so are either not obvious or expected.

The findings in this section develop a corollary to one of the central conjectures of the competence-control theory stating that the removal of controls could be conducive to the actors' and intermediaries' increased assertiveness, competence, and independence (Abbott et al. 2020). Once a principal distances himself from some issues, state officials, too, are likely to loosen their focus even if the policy problem in question is pressing. As previously mentioned, because Putin's promises of social betterment are targeted and particularistic, his mandates are rarely general. In the absence of narrow and time-specific mandates, agents are subject to moral hazard: they will shirk and fail to work together to serve the citizens in a fair manner. Because the principal does not incentivize them properly, they lose independent motivation and abandon "goals, policies, procedures, or tasks." Agents start exhibiting features typical for Opportunists: they become "liable to slacking, slippage, capture, and other forms of agency loss" (Abbott et al. 2021: S89). That there are several Zealots—agents who are faithful to the impartial and thorough implementation of specific policies and strictly follow the tenets of professional ethos—within a broad assembly of regulators who pursue their narrow agendas does not ensure results. Simply put, the flip side of the ruler's outsized influence and manual steering is the collapse of the agents' desire to govern well or govern at all.

There is no denying that since the early 2000s, many Russian politicians have recognized the spread of HIV/AIDS as a significant social problem. Because the scourge of HIV/AIDS poses an objective and imminent danger to human well-being, it is not surprising that Russian authorities took the epidemic seriously. Vladimir Putin announced a crusade against HIV/AIDS at the State Council meeting on April 21, 2006, and reconfirmed his commitment in 2008 at the G-8 summit in St-Petersburg (Putin 2006). He talked about the infection with a sense of urgency and presented the epidemic as a matter of national priority. Further, he called for broad political mobilization to wipe it out. Putin's call ushered in a sustained commitment to providing free antiretrovirals to Russian citizens, massive state-sponsored TV campaigns, and unprecedented construction of AIDS diagnostic and treatment centers. Countless additional examples testify to Moscow's vigorous health interventions to save human lives (Kravtsov 2015: 156–159).

Still, the initial optimism at home ebbed as soon as it became clear that the government did not live up to the pledge, and Putin seemingly forgot about his promise to put an end to the epidemic. Putin's sudden interest in the issue confounded analysts, and so did his sudden absence of leadership. The outcomes of fighting the epidemic of HIV/AIDS after two decades of governance are disappointing. What optimistically inclined observers failed to consider was that the Kremlin's decisions in the health sector reflected its self-serving needs and did not come out of the objective needs of health governance. The regime's principals could single-handedly terminate some promising programs when these do not fit their political interests or press on with the initiatives that consistently fail to deliver. A decision to quietly demobilize in the middle of the surging epidemic of HIV/AIDS is an example of the former, and expanding national priority programs in health accompanied by media fanfares is an instance of the latter. It is difficult to disagree with the argument that Putin's interest in HIV/AIDS waned after he bolstered his international popularity at the G-8 meeting in St-Petersburg in 2006 (Jordan 2010). Personalistic leaders make policy calculations to harvest popularity, but they do not necessarily see through their fair and fruitful implementation. Hence, Putin's lack of concern about forging a comprehensive, evidence-based policy did not put an end to the work of legislative and governmental committees, but that activity was shallow.

As Putin's interest in handling the HIV/AIDS crisis visibly diminished, key Russian bureaucrats and legislators disowned a comprehensive HIV/AIDS policy as they did not expect to receive anything from Putin in return. In this context, the mission of genuine policy entrepreneurs prioritizing the welfare of patients over their self-interest becomes difficult: they find themselves excluded from social practice. It follows that those policy entrepreneurs who decided to push for a comprehensive HIV/AIDS strategy faced indifference and, at times, incurred broad resistance. Routine health programs and the state-guaranteed provision of the antiretrovirals continue to yield tangible results, but all of these are not likely to guarantee an end to the spread of the virus among the generalized population.

In addition, as the next chapter demonstrates in detail, Putin entrusted law enforcement agencies (especially the Federal Drug Control Service of the Russian Federation, FSKN, 2003–2016) with framing the epidemic not as a massive public health crisis but as a crisis of criminal consumption of illicit intravenous narcotics, inspired from abroad. Although heavily disputed by nonstate actors and health professionals alike, FSKN's approach was central to the official position on HIV/AIDS for more than a decade. As a result, none of the Russian officials involved in health governance wanted to lead others against the looming epidemic or bring the fragmented discussions into a coherent framework regarding HIV/AIDS as an urgent public health problem. The remainder of the section examines this episode of governance in detail.

Members of the government followed Putin's all too obvious cues. Initial steps went in the right direction: the government abolished the short-lived Advisory Council of the Ministry of Health on HIV/AIDS (established in 2003) and the Multisectoral Coordinating Council on HIV/AIDS (est. 2004), both dominated by the health ministry officials (Morrison and Wallander 2005: 10–11, 24–25). Instead, the officials formed the governmental commission that would remain operational for the next six years. However, the new body was not without flaws. Although the commission's proceedings might give an impression of a robust interagency process, its commands hardly altered the structure of incentives for individual agencies and did not specify the roadmap for improving public health services. In June 2011, the commission simply approved the National Priority Project Health activity plan. Worse, the commission failed to lead and coordinate; it also withheld information on its workings until its formal termination in 2012. Its fatal flaw was in its design: according to the governmental bylaw, signed by the then Prime Minister Mikhail Fradkov, the committee was chaired by the minister of health (Polozhenie N 608). This resolution went against the common bureaucratic management practice, according to which an executive overseer commonly held a vice-prime-minister rank and was not directly in charge of an individual ministry or agency. This defective design perhaps was not accidental, given Putin's dwindling interest in the subject after 2006.

Another incarnation of a coordinating and overseeing institution, the new Governmental commission for the protection of public health (*Pravitel'stvennaya kommissiya po voprosam okhrany zdorov'ya grazhdan*), formed in October 2012, had a better institutional design since it was

Prime Minister Medvedev who became its chair. Regrettably, this commission chose not to look at HIV until several years later. To be fair, Medvedev had significant experience in health governance; after all, in the second Putin administration, he oversaw a funneling of significant money for antiretroviral treatment in the framework of national priority projects and building brand new AIDS centers. Still, after a short period of "tandemocracy" and once Medvedev concluded his single presidential term, his independence attenuated. Not surprisingly, in the new circumstance, Medvedev's bureaucratic position mirrored Putin's: his multiple interviews lack any substantive discussion of the epidemic.

A sense of urgency was lacking during the commission's routine meeting in October 2015. Although Medvedev acknowledged that the epidemic of HIV/AIDS widened, none of the participants (composed of top bureaucrats and governors but lacking leading domestic health experts) addressed the epidemic as an extraordinary challenge to human security, and the subsequent discussion turned into a formulaic exchange of opinions. The minutes of the commission's meetings give an impression that the government was dealing with unremarkable issues that could not fundamentally threaten citizens' well-being. Nevertheless, concluding the meeting, Medvedev signed the first comprehensive state strategy against HIV/AIDS, which, regrettably, was superficial and declarative.

After two iterations, the new version of the national strategy was officially ready in 2016. Still, independent experts noted that the adopted strategy lacked any logistical or financial backing to make progress a reality (Mishina 2016a; Chernykh 2016) and simply rehashed old health regulations. To make things worse, the same year, the government reduced the regional funding for the antiretroviral treatment by 30% (Mishina and Manulova 2016) and failed to take notice of snowballing ARV's stockouts. It also blatantly ignored the need to devise evidence-based policy to stop HIV and blood-borne infections to which IV-drug users were prone (according to V. Mendelevich, nearly 60% of infections back then were due to drug injections, see Mishina 2016a). Fast forward, in 2020, without any discussion with health experts or AIDS service and advocacy organizations, the government developed a new document which simply replicated its precursor (Mishina 2020).

These outcomes reflect the logic of personalistic regimes, wherein individuals are accountable primarily to the ruler while having few incentives to develop painstaking initiatives and laws to tackle the issue independently and competently. Regrettably, Russian legislators fared no better in attempting to form a comprehensive HIV/AIDS strategy. They failed to develop a consolidated position on the appropriate and comprehensive policy in response to HIV/AIDS. Instead, they buried consolidated evidence-based policy while failing to listen to the health community's concerns and resisted external input from nonstate actors.

Initially, several prominent legislators organized the multi-partisan parliamentary working group to prevent and control HIV/AIDS and other socially significant diseases (*Mezhfraktsionnaya deputatskaya rabochaya gruppa po voprosam profilaktiki i borby so SPIDom i drugimi sotsial'no znachimymi zabolevaniyami*, hereafter MDG). This group united Nadezhda Gerasimova (chair), Mikhail Grishankov, Valery Zubov, Valery Chereshnikov, Artur Chilingarov, and Vladimir Romanov. MDG was very active: in a short span of 2009–2010, it held nine meetings where civil society organizations and health experts were also present. Regrettably, the group's members diverged on the depth of medical and epidemiological knowledge; and their agendas were far from congenial. The former three deputies, the proponents of evidence-based health policy, had an excellent command of the epidemic and its future implications. Neither Gerasimova nor Grishankov dismissed HIV as a problem against which society had to be protected; instead, all their interviews and public appearances highlighted the terrifying fact that the epidemiological situation was far from calm and the spread of the infection was not slowing down. Chilingarov's concern about health matters was nominal, while Romanov's understanding of HIV was barely rudimentary, and Chereshnikov's agenda focused on lobbying for the development of domestic vaccines. More generally, among the State Duma policymakers, only a few of those from the regions hit disproportionately hard by the epidemic had incentives; the rest were either not interested in the issue or expressed their aversion to the proposed solution.

On April 9, 2009, the participants of a joint meeting, held by MDG and Rospotrebnadzor (the Federal Service for Surveillance on Consumer Rights Protection and Human Wellbeing), advocated using all available methods of HIV prevention, including all components of harm reduction, sexual education, and mass-testing. MDG also formed an expert group that developed an analytical report, explaining the principles of harm-reduction programs from the standpoint of evidence-based medicine. Renowned health experts and practicing medical doctors marshaled solid statistical evidence, which one member of the group, Grishankov, sought to include in the national health legislation (Grishankov 2010). During the subsequent roundtable meeting in October 2009, held by the State Duma Health Committee, it became evident that none of the participants now in charge of changing HIV legislation were even vaguely familiar with the compiled materials. After carefully reading the minutes of the Committee's meetings, it is hard to shake off the impression that Olga Borzova, the Committee's head, tried to sabotage the whole process of building an evidence-based consensus. At the beginning of the meeting, she refrained from sharing the recommendations and insisted on the need to examine all perspectives, no matter how dated and unscientific (Gosudarstvennaya Duma 2011).

That was one reason why the flow of common misperceptions and inaccurate data persisted. Not surprisingly, nobody was there to call out bureaucrats from different health agencies who were again able to reassure themselves that the epidemic was under control while articulating their parochial preferences. As a result, the only consensual framing of HIV prevention converged on the promotion of vaguely defined healthy lifestyles, awareness, responsible sexual behavior, and massive blood testing campaigns, which the resolution of the roundtable saw as "the main task of this stage of the fight against the epidemic." It seems like nobody was interested (or able) to grasp that these methods of prophylaxis were irrelevant for stopping the spread of HIV from relatively isolated vulnerable groups to the generalized population. In the next Duma MDG became largely irrelevant, Grishankov opted for the private sector. The momentum was gone: no subsequent legislative activities made a difference.

Such an outcome is consistent with the literature that highlights the role of government as "technocratic" (i.e., insulated from politics, instructed to achieve specific predetermined outcomes in policy, and generally entrusted with a surfeit of confidence in their managerial capabilities, Gel'man 2018) and the limited role of legislatures in policy bargaining and on genuine policy development (Geddes et al. 2018: 136–137). According to a dictum ascribed to Boris Gryzlov, former speaker of the State Duma, parliament was no place for discussions.

Consistent with earlier observations, it is not surprising that those policy entrepreneurs and watchdogs who decide to remain independent are likely to face indifference, bureaucratic inertia, or even broad resistance. Vadim Pokrovsky and Mikhail Grishankov, for instance, for years, kept advocating the adoption of the country-wide evidence-based strategy against HIV/AIDS. After the issue lost political importance to Putin, they confronted federal legislators' obscurantism. More so, despite his stellar record in health promotion, Pokrovsky faced official scrutiny and sharp criticism, while Grishankov's sustained record of fighting HIV/AIDS and high public visibility did not save him from being shut out of the health governance process. Similarly, the Public Chamber's recommendations—a body that in theory provides a societal oversight and independent expertise—had no impact on pushing them to embrace evidence-based methods as a crux of HIV policy (Obshchetsvennaya Palata 2011).

As a result, the state failed to address the epidemic as a pressing crisis undermining the public good. That the official statements and interviews consistently highlighted only successes in fighting HIV/AIDS was very telling. Paradoxically, although the numbers of HIV-positive people in Russia keep climbing, the authorities failed to construct HIV as an existential threat to human well-being. Despite many concerns, the governmental statistics of people living with HIV consistently communicate numbers significantly lower than independent experts. On World AIDS Day in December 2016, the minister of health, Veronika Skvortsova, said that "[T]here is no single criteria to consider an epidemic of HIV... No epidemic has been yet announced in our country" (Skvortsova 2016). A month prior, a health official from Yekaterinburg, the hardest-hit city with the level of infection reaching almost 2% of its population, retracted her previous announcement that the epidemic in the region had become generalized (Morozov 2016). These statements are not surprising since acknowledging the actual scope of the problem would have implied that the government was failing or misleading its populace all along. The greater the societal understanding that the epidemic of HIV/AIDS remained uncontained, the more public officials tergiversated about the health situation, insincere about the epidemic's generalization in the country's most problematic regions.

In summary, Putin's outsized influence and his propensity to set the narrow terms of bureaucratic mandates disincentivizes agents from defining collective objectives together and diminishes their desire for deliberation and input, even at the expense of pushing half-baked strategic decisions in health governance. Not surprisingly, once the ruler withdraws from publicly backing health initiatives and stops demanding concrete results, state actors no longer expect the utility of concerted and decisive action, no matter how grave and objective the health challenge is. A leader's disengagement can mean only one thing in personalistic systems: health actors would be amiss to expect personalized rewards, while proactiveness and success could surely backfire and jeopardize their position in the power hierarchy. Although some faithful and committed policy entrepreneurs ("zealots") continue to push for comprehensive and evidence-based health strategies against the epidemic, the in-house aversion to going above and beyond rulers' explicit injunctions and demands begets regulatory disasters.

Conclusion

In Russia, like any other state, principals rely not only on their country-wide popularity but also on their agents, who are expected to perform administrative tasks for the principal while, at minimum, not sabotaging policy ideas and, at maximum, remaining politically faithful for their patron. The fact that Russia's principal is a patron and the agents are his clients complicates the governor's dilemma, which is generically understood as a trade-off between competence and control. Notably, in the institutional setup of personalistic power, both principals and their agents depend on each other: the personalized exchange of concrete rewards and punishments is central to their relationship. Ultimately, because Putin's personalistic regime relies on personalized contracts and not on strong formal organizations, the leaders are the source of bad governance. The "good" in the observable governance practices is likely to be jeopardized when state officials face a perverse system of incentives.

While state agents and private actors depend on personalistic leaders, who grant them access to valuable activities and state resources, those who participate in health governance also constrain their principals. Lest state agents and private actors start looking for an alternative patron in anticipation of heavily rigged but formally contested elections, the ruler's optimizing strategy is to punish his subordinates only in extreme cases of failures that trigger social protests while tolerating and expecting self-interested behavior. Although Putin's popularity, critical for his political survival in the context of unabolished elections, depends on his agents' ability to improve social welfare, it is more expedient to retain elites' loyalty than satisfy the masses. After all, as Chapter 2 has shown, faking policy success is relatively easy.

Further, if the theory of selectorate (Bueno de Mesquita et al. 2003; Bueno de Mesquita and Smith 2011) is correct, it follows that Putin most likely will be satisfied with prospects of less efficient governance as long as he could keep his subordinates in check through economic spoils and lucrative positions in the government. Somewhat similar problems emerge in non-personalistic electoral regimes wherein authoritarian incumbents avoid deep reforms aimed to improve the quality of the government lest these reforms debilitate the incumbents' ability to use nondemocratic means of staying in power (Bolkvadze 2016). Deep institutional reforms, such as fostering the government's political responsibility and top state administrators, are antithetical to the interests of those who cling to power either in the position of the regime's principals or their clients. It is not by chance that Russian regulators are continually trying to fine-tune, redress, and refine their policies, but they always fall short of undertaking institutional reform.

The next chapter traces how the governance intermediaries hit the wall in their attempts to monitor state administrators' actions and correct the faulty course of their activity. As the chapter will show, the failure is by design; Putin's regime simply resists any societal mechanism capable of independent and meaningful policy oversight. Given multiple low-key flubs and several high-profile disasters, the regime takes the task of overseeing bureaucracy seriously, but it cannot rid the process of inherent features that characterize personalistic authoritarianism.

References

Abbott, K.W., et al. 2020. Competence–Control Theory: The Challenge of Governing through Intermediaries. In *The Governor's Dilemma: Indirect Governance Beyond Principals and Agents*, ed. K.W. Abbott, et al., 3–36. Oxford: Oxford University Press.

Abbott, K.W., et al. 2021. Beyond Opportunism: Intermediary Loyalty in Regulation and Governance. *Regulation & Governance* 15 (S1): S83–S101.

Anin, R. 2018. Dvortsy pod okhranoi. *Novaya Gazeta*, 18 November.

Batalova, E. 2020. Arbidol spaset mir? *Novaya Gazeta*, 20 February.

Beazer, Q.H., and O.J. Reuter. 2021. Do Authoritarian Elections Help the Poor? Evidence from Russian Cities. *The Journal of Politics* 84 (1): 437–454.

Bolkvadze, K. 2016. Hitting the Saturation Point: Unpacking the Politics of Bureaucratic Reforms in Hybrid Regimes. *Democratization* 24 (4): 751–769.

Britskaya, T. 2019. Belye lentochki v belykh khalatakh. *Novaya Gazeta* No. 69, 28 June.

Bueno de Mesquita, B., and A. Smith. 2011. *The Dictator's Handbook: Why Bad Behavior is Almost Always Good Politics*. New York: Public Affair.

Bueno de Mesquita, B., A. Smith, R.M. Siverson, and J.D. Morrow. 2003. *The Logic of Political Survival*. Cambridge: Cambridge University Press.

Chernykh, A. 2016. Pravitel'stvo ne izyskalo novykh sredstv dlya VICh. *Kommersant* No. 199, 26 October.
Churakova, O., M. Zholobova, and R. Badanin. 2019. Zhduny. Rasskaz o tom, kak okhranniki Vladimira Putina ne stali slugami naroda. *Proekt.Media*, 20 November.
Dombrova, E. 2016. Proizvoditel' insulina Gerofarm narastil oborot na 22%. *Delovoi Peterburg*, 14 March.
Dranishnikova, M. 2014. Interv'yu - Aleksei Repik, vladelets i predsedatel' soveta direktorov R-Pharma. *Vedomosti*, 23 September.
Dranishnikova, M. 2017. Lish' odna kompaniya smozhet postavlyat' gosudarstvu katetery i ustroistva dlya perelivaniya krovi. *Vedomosti*, 29 October.
Filipenok, A. 2017. Yakunin rasskazal o svoem malen'kom shubokhranilishche. *RBC*, 15 June.
Fukuyama, F. 2013. What Is Governance? *Governance* 26 (3): 347–368.
Gaaze, K. 2016. Chuzhie zdes' ne khodyat. Igor' Shuvalov i privatizatsiya, kotoroi ne bylo. *Snob.ru*, 11 August.
Gaaze, K. 2017. Sleduyushchii prezident budet iz dvora Putina. Sobchak ili Dyumin – nevazhno. *Biznes Online*, 23 October.
Galimova, N. 2018. Otsenki dlya Kremlya: zachem upravleniya Kirienko vvodyat KPI. *RBC*, 27 November.
Geddes, B. 1994. *Politician's Dilemma: Building State Capacity in Latin America*. Berkeley and Los Angeles: University of California Press.
Geddes, B., J. Wright, and E. Frantz. 2018. *How Dictatorships Work: Power, Personalization, and Collapse*. New York: Cambridge University Press.
Gel'man, V. 2018. Politics Versus Policy: Technocratic Traps of Russia's Policy Reforms. *Russian Politics* 3 (2): 282–304.
Gogin, S. 2016. Chelovek, kotoryi pereigral Sistemu. *RFL/RL*, 9 October.
Gosudarstvennaya Duma. 2011. Materialy Parlamentskikh Slushanii i 'Kruglykh Stolov', Provedennykh Komitetom Gosudarstvennoi Dumy po Okhrane Zdorov'ya v Osennyuyu Sessiyu 2009 Goda, Vesennyuyu i Osennyuyu Sessii 2010 Goda. *Komitet Gosudarstvennoi Dumy po Okhrane Zdorov'ya*, 8 October.
Grishankov, M. 2010. Printsipy Dokazatel'noi Meditsiny i Ispol'zovanie Programm Snizheniya Vreda Dlya Profilaktiki VICh-infektsii Sredi Uyazvimykh Grupp. Doklad Ekspertnoi Rabochei Gruppy, 9 April 2009.
Hale, H.E. 2015. *Patronal Politics: Eurasian Regime Dynamics in Comparative Perspective*. New York: Cambridge University Press.
Jordan, P. 2010. Russia's Managed Democracy and the Civil G8 in 2006. *Journal of Communist Studies and Transition Politics* 26 (1): 101–125.
Kalinovskaya, E. 2015. Delo Arbidola. *Farmatsevticheskii Vestnik*, No. 42.
Kobernik, O., and O. Baranova. 2020. V Rossii poyavitsya edinii postavshchik masok dlya LPU i aptek. *Farmatsevticheskii Vestnik*, 23 March.

Kravtsov, V. 2015. *HIV/AIDS and Norm Diffusion in Putin's Russia and Mbeki's South Africa*. Athens: University of Georgia Press.

Latukhina, K. 2017. Golikova rasskazala Putinu o 899 narusheniyakh v sfere goszakupok. *Vedomosti*, 3 March.

Lyauv, B., et al. 2018. Gendirektor Rosteca: Novye sanktsii vryad li smogut nas podkosit. *Vedomosti*, 17 December.

Mereminskaya, E. 2016. Prezident i pravitel'stvo – glavnyi istochnik neprozrachnogo goszakaza. *Vedomosti*, 3 April.

Mishina, V. 2016a. VICh-infektsii otkazali v umerennosti. Eksperty trebuyut perepisat' strategiyu bor'by s epidemiei. *Kommersant*, 13 February.

Mishina, V. 2016b. Minzdrav nadeetsya na soznatel'nost' narkomanov. *Kommersant*, 18 February.

Mishina, V. 2020. Bez prezervativov i lubrikantov. Minzdrav podgotovil proekt strategii po bor'be s VICh do 2030 goda. *Kommersant*, No. 103, 11 June.

Mishina, V., and A. Manuilova. 2016. SPID ispytyvayut na byudzhetnuyu soprotivlyaemost. Urezano finansirovanie na zakupku antiretrovirusnykh preparatov. *Kommersant* No. 123, 12 July.

Morozov, A. 2016. Epidemiyu VICh obyavili sluchaino. *Gazeta.ru*, 2 November.

Morrison, S., and C. Wallander. 2005. Russia and HIV/AIDS: Opportunities for Leadership and Cooperation. *Report of the CSIS Task Force on HIV/AIDS, Joint Brookings-CSIS Delegation to Russia, 20–26 February*. Washington, DC: CSIS.

Muller, J.Z. 2018. *The Tyranny of Metrics*. Princeton and Oxford: Princeton University Press.

Myl'nikov, M. 2018a. Ot lishnikh boevoi i politicheskoi podgotovki. *Vademecum*, 11 January.

Myl'nikov, M. 2018b. Edinstvennyi postavshchik medizdelii iz PVH vyigral 90% konkursov, v kotorykh uchastvoval. *Vademecum*, 18 July.

Myl'nikov, M. 2018c. Pravitel'stvo lishilo monopol'nogo statusa postavshchikov medizdelii iz PVC. *Vademecum*, 24 December.

Myl'nikov. M. 2019. Liga stavlennikov: Komu iz igrokov rynka medizdelii chashche vezet na rynke goszakaza. *Vademecum*, 2 January.

Myl'nikov, M. 2020. Gendirektor Medpolimerproma Aleksei Borisov priznal vinu v dache vzyatki po delu pomoshchnitsy Dvorkovicha. *Vademecum*, 16 December.

Nagornykh, I. 2018. Vernut' doverie narodnykh mass: Kreml' zadumalsya nad programmoi na 2019 god. *RTVi*, 13 November.

Nagornykh, I., I. Safronov, and N. Korchenkova. 2012. Spetssluzhba personala. *Kommersant*, 3 October.

Nazarova, K. 2019. Vo mnogikh regionakh nachalis' pereboi s insulinom. Bol'nym navyazyvayut novyi otechestvennyi preparat. *Otkrytye media*, 11 January.

North, D.C., J.J. Wallis, and B.R. Weingast. 2009. *Violence and Social Orders: A Conceptual Framework for Interpreting Recorded Human History*. New York: Cambridge University Press.

Interfax. 2020. Roshal' predlozhil sobrat' gruppu medekspertov po Naval'nomu, 5 September.

Obshchetsvennaya Palata. 2011. Profilaktika VICh-Infektsii v Rossii: Problemy i Perspektivy, 24 March.

Pavlovsky, G. 2012. *Genial'naya Vlast'! Slovar' Abstrakcii Kremlya*. Moskva: Evropa.

Petrov, N., M. Lipman, and H. Hale. 2014. Three Dilemmas of Hybrid Regime Governance: Russia from Putin to Putin. *Post-Soviet Affairs* 30 (1): 1–26.

Pis'mennaya, E. 2013. *Sistema Kudrina. Istoriya Klyuchevogo Ekonomista Putinskoi Rossii*. Moscow: Mann, Ivanov i Farber.

Pryanikov, P. 2016. Metodologi - eto totalitarnyi tekhnokratizm. *Tolkovatel'*, 6 October.

Putin, V. 2006. Vstupitel'noe slovo na zasedanii prezidiuma Gosudarstvennogo soveta "O Neotlozhnykh Merakh po Bor'be s Rasprostraneniem VICh-infektsii v Rossiiskoi Federatsii", 21 April. http://kremlin.ru/events/president/transcripts/23547.

Sagdiev, R. 2011. Chempion po goszakupkam. *Vedomosti*, 30 May.

Shubina, D. 2018. Medpolimerpromu ne khvataet deneg na stroitel'stvo zavoda izdelii iz PVC. *Vademecum*, 13 July.

Skorobogat'ko, T. 2004. Klinicheskii sluchai. *Moskovskie Novosti*, 25 March.

Skvortsova, V. 2016. Epidemiyu VICh v Rossii nikto ne obyavlyal. *TASS*, 1 December.

Solodun E., and M. Nikishina. 2020. Nemetskie mediki otkazalis' sotrudnichat' s Natsmedpalatoi po delu Naval'nogo. *Vademecum*, 8 September.

Stanovaya, T. 2015. Biznes i vlast': K novoi modeli otnoshenii. *Politcom.ru*, 28 December.

Stanovaya, T. 2020. The Taming of the Elite: Putin's Referendum. *Carnegie Moscow Center*, 1 July.

Taylor, B.D. 2011. *State Building in Putin's Russia: Policing and Coercion After Communism*. New York: Cambridge University Press.

Taylor, B.D. 2018. *The Code of Putinism*. New York: Oxford University Press.

Transparency International. 2017. Kak gosmonopoliya Nacimbio zarabotala na vaktsinakh i kto ot etogo vyigral: Rassledovanie peterburgskogo otdeleniya Transparency International - Rossiya, 16 October. https://transparency.org.ru/special/natsimbio/.

Wengle, S., and M. Rasell. 2008. The Monetisation of *L'goty*: Changing Patterns of Welfare Politics and Provision in Russia. *Europe-Asia Studies* 60 (5): 739–756.

Wintrobe, R. 1998. *The Political Economy of Dictatorship*. Cambridge, UK: Cambridge University Press.

Wood, D.B. 2010. Agency Theory and the Bureaucracy. In *The Oxford Handbook of American Bureaucracy*, ed. R.F. Durant. New York: Oxford University Press.

Yakoreva, A., and A. Ershov. 2020. Tol'ko odna chastnaya kompaniya v Rossii mozhet prodavat' testy na koronavirus. *Meduza.io*, 28 March.

Zavadskaya, M., and L. Shilov. 2021. Providing Goods and Votes? Federal Elections and the Quality of Local Governance in Russia. *Europe-Asia Studies* 73 (6): 1037–1059.

Zhegulev, I. 2017. Importozamestitel': Kak sozdannaya v 2016 godu kompaniya stala edinstvennym postavshchikom meditsinskogo plastika dlya rossiiskikh bol'nits. *Meduza.io*, 30 November.

Zvezdina, P., and A. Mogilevskaya. 2017. Veksel'bergu otkazali v monopolii. *RBC*, 16 February.

CHAPTER 4

Constructing the Oversight: Organizational Atrophy and Particularized Exchanges

The lack of an effective state administration system. This is the main thing. If this problem is solved, the rest will be surmounted automatically. That is why we should not delve into anything else.
—German Gref, speaking at The Leaders of Russia Forum, March 14, 2019.

Fear "is a bad management method because it is very unreliable. In terms of having contact with society, the best way to govern is by convincing people and using positive motivation. It requires the joint efforts of the people you communicate with. You must not allow any separation of those who make decisions from those who implement them. All people should collaborate in the implementation; that would be efficient joint work with a positive result."
—Vladimir Putin at the plenary session of the 15th-anniversary meeting of the Valdai International Discussion Club, October 18, 2018.

INTRODUCTION

Despite his penchant for self-congratulation, Vladimir Putin publicly, primarily via televised events, conveys his displeasure with the work of his subordinates and demands improvements. In June 2013, Putin criticized the government's lack of professionalism in implementing core presidential decrees. Putin conveyed his impression "that some agencies live entirely in their little world, look solely to their narrow problems and lack any understanding of the common strategic tasks facing our country"

© The Author(s), under exclusive license to Springer Nature Switzerland AG 2022
V. Kravtsov, *Autocracy and Health Governance in Russia*, https://doi.org/10.1007/978-3-031-05789-2_4

(Putin 2013). In the same speech, he also highlighted many shortcomings in the work of the Ministry of Health (hereafter Minzdrav; until 2012, it was officially known as the Ministry of Health and Social Development, Minsotszdrav). More recently, during the governmental meeting on strategic development and national projects, broadcasted by the TV channel Russia 24 on July 19, 2021, Putin noted that "unfortunately, so far, we have not seen an increase in citizens' satisfaction with the healthcare system. We do not need paper reports, but the real state of society and real results for people." In response, health minister Mikhail Murashko acknowledged problems but averred that everything was under control. None of this is particularly new or unusual: that the state apparatus was ineffective Putin acknowledged during his Fourth Presidential Address to the Federal Assembly in May 2003.

Do these types of exchanges mean that Putin sincerely wants to improve the way Russian bureaucracy works? To a certain extent, possibly. Still, these exchanges do not improve the quality of the strategic decisions or day-to-day management of health affairs. Notably, many televised events tell the public that the president closely monitors what his subordinates do, and the failures in health administration are not his fault. Putin certainly knows how to tap into the immortal folk wisdom that "the czar is good, it's the nobility that is bad." In the train, the president's approval ratings remain consistently higher than that of his government (Deutsche Welle 2019).

Even a cursory glance at the state of health oversight gives an impression that something is deeply rotten in the county's monitoring mechanisms. For instance, the Russian Federal Antimonopoly Service (*Federal'naya antimonopol'naya sluzhba*, FAS) time and again exposed malversations in the medicine procurement process fraught with favors for companies and firms closely affiliated to the regime's principals. To the dismay of many, its "patrols" were largely ignored while the agency's long-serving head, Igor Artemiev, was relieved of his post. Russian legislators, too, tried to pull fire alarms on the foundational federal law on the Circulation of Medicines (61-FZ). Although the State Duma hearings revealed that the law was half-baked (and the pharmaceutical industry concurred), it went into effect after the State Duma discussed more than 300 amendments.

Similarly, federal and local legislators pulled fire alarms on the Health Ministry's disastrous reforms in the hospital sector, widely known as "optimization of health." The reform that started in September 2014 massively reduced health facilities across the country, cut down access to medical care in rural areas, and increased workload without sufficient compensation (Krivolapov 2021). The Kremlin's response ranged from ignoring the alarms to small-scale coercion. All this is not that surprising. After all, the Russian legislature's moves to check the executive were not so much about genuine oversight practices as spectacles of regime legitimation and a channel for sectoral lobbying (Whitmore 2010). What is more, the executive vertical turned to repressions: the regional departments instructed head doctors to eliminate distressed doctors and nurses who took their dissatisfaction to the streets. Their disappointment in blanket reductions in the healthcare sector, as the official narrative went, was destructive and instigated by Putin's worthless critics, including Alexey Navalny and his anti-corruption organization, soon dubbed an extremist and subversive agent of foreign influence (Britskaya 2019).

There is nothing random about the regime's adverse responses to these episodes of police patrols and fire alarms; the engine that drives these responses is the underlying logic of personalistic authoritarianism. Politically, "informational autocrats," including Putin, must maintain the credibility of performance rhetoric directed at non-elites. For personalistic rulers, it is essential to convey an impression that the principal does not turn a blind eye to the runaway bureaucracies. The Kremlin faces the need to develop a system of oversight lest the dissatisfaction with incompetent or self-serving bureaucracies transforms into declining electoral support for the regime. However, being bound by patron-client relationships, the political master must fulfill his side of personalistic bargains—protect his loyal subordinates and clients—while shielding his strategic decisions from public scrutiny. What is even more debilitating for the long-term development of oversight structure is that personalistic regimes, being a form of basic natural states, limit the ability of individuals to form perpetually lived organizations. Because perpetual, depersonalized organizations constrain rulers, they prefer to circumvent formal organizations and construct a system of personalized exchanges and particularized bargains.

Further, for formal organizations to achieve common goals, it is essential to maintain an independent corporate identity not reducible to its leaders. However, in Putin's Russia, surveillance agencies and monitoring organizations, both internal and external, suffer from the undermined sense of corporate identity. Unsurprisingly, Putin's personalistic regime fosters further personalization of organized groups. Russian monitors of health, internal and external alike, underwent the process of political personalization in which the political weight of individual actors vis-à-vis the power of the organization increased over time while the centrality and power of the group declined. Thus, although dictators understand the value of governance oversight, their commitment to building a system of monitors functioning in people's interests is not credible.

The story told in this chapter is straightforward. The first section of this chapter highlights the weakness of internal police patrols: top Putin's subordinates subvert the formation of a unified and multi-purpose surveillance organ in health, while the heads of specialized surveillance bodies tend to provide political value for the boss at the expense of informing the principal about the real problems in health governance. The second section briefly surveys how the ruler and his trusted political operatives experimented with different ways of organizing external intermediaries to improve the impression of the regime's credibility among non-elites. It also notes that because the Kremlin never intended to cede control over monitoring intermediaries, a fundamental flaw in external fire alarms is by design. The third and fourth sections profile two intermediary organizations occupying a central position in the architecture of health governance in the country. These sections trace how, why, and to what extent intermediaries hit the wall in their attempts to monitor state administrators' actions and correct the faulty course of their actions while pursuing their self-interest. These two sections also note intermediaries' hard tradeoffs between slim chances of improving the quality of health administration against the certainty of being uninvolved in health governance at all.

Police Patrols: The Pathologies of Internal Oversight

The term "police patrols" describes a centralized, active, and direct approach wherein principals periodically check the behavior of state officials in a particular sphere using some parts of the bureaucracy to do so (for the original definitions, see McCubbins and Schwartz 1984: 166). That presidential administration, a command center within the executive branch, oversees the implementation of presidential decrees is well-known (Ananyev 2018: 33). This section sheds light on the less discussed architecture of internal health oversight, also housed in the executive.

According to the initial institutional design of the Russian executive branch approved during Putin's first presidential term, federal services and federal agencies were managed directly by the Government of the Russian Federation, and they were not subordinate to the relevant ministries, which remained in charge of developing public policy and legal regulation. One of the primary intentions of the administrative reform, which occurred before Putin's irrevocable conversion to personalistic rule, was to ensure the surveillance organs' independence and impartiality. With the expansion of authoritarianism under Putin's third and fourth residential terms, the trend reversed. The architecture of Russian health surveillance organs consisted primarily of three specialized services. Roszdravnadzor is Russia's leading surveillance organ for medicines, Rospotrebnadzor (Russian for the Federal Service for Surveillance on Consumer Rights Protection and Human Wellbeing) is the service surveilling the quality of consumer goods, and Roszdrav was the organization in charge of overseeing medical equipment. Although such a design was sensible, it was also prone to internal vulnerabilities and pathologies.

In general, the idea of an integrated or consolidated health surveillance agency with clearly demarcated sets of responsibilities and independent from ministries seemed functionally warranted because the production and sale of pharmaceutical products, medical equipment, biological additives, and numerous household chemicals could cause direct harm to the consumer and threaten human life. Although I am skeptical that there could be an optimal design of health surveillance organs that would allow for perfect police patrols, the proposed mega-regulator could have enabled more robust mechanisms of internal accountability and horizontal transparency. It stands to reason that, collectively, the government understands the value of impersonal and independent surveillance, but, individually, its members resist its formation. That tension drives part of the story told here. Understandably, the emergence of the independent monitoring service was antithetical to the desires of Putin's immediate subordinates occupying top Cabinet-level positions to remain outside of internal scrutiny.

In 2006, the media unveiled the privileged governmental document, according to which the government entertained the possibility of creating an independent mega-regulator in health akin to the Food and Drug Administration (FDA). The concept proposed to combine three health surveillance services into one new agency. According to the credible media outlet, RBC, the idea originated at Roszdravnadzor, whose head sought to combine three agencies' power (RBC 2007). Yet, the proposed agency was never institutionalized. A similar idea resurfaced in 2015 when the government actively discussed the possibility of transferring the functions of Roszdravnadzor and Rosselkhoznadzor (a surveillance service within the Ministry of Agriculture) to Rospotrebnadzor (Solopov 2015).

Thus, both attempts to establish an independent surveillance agency proved futile; a specialized entity monitoring and regulating health services, the pharmaceutical sector, and medical devices remained only on paper. Worse, since their inception, surveillance agencies underwent multiple reforms that continuously reshuffled their mandates and eventually were either disbanded (as Roszdrav, in 2008) or became directly subordinate to the Ministry of Health and Social Development (as Roszdravnadzor, in 2020). Hitherto, although Rospotrebnadzor remained independent as long as it assisted Putin in his trade wars with European democracies, the media kept circulating rumors about the agency's pending reorganization and its merger with non-health-related surveillance services.

The career stories of Roszdravnadzor's leaders offer an impudent and racy side of the regime's lack of functional internal oversight. Since its inception, the agency has had five leaders: Ramil Khabriev (2004–2007), Nikolay Yurgel (2007–2010), Elena Tel'nova (2010–2013), Mikhail Murashko (2013–2020), and Alla Samoilova (since 2020). As it turned out, the career trajectories of these bureaucrats reflected their organizational ambitions in governing the agency. In a nutshell, Khabriev, Yurgel, and Tel'nova favored an impartial oversight agency to keep the Ministry of Health in check; and their careers in government turned unsuccessful. In contrast, Murashko confined his agency's surveillance efforts to exposing the street-level lawbreaking; and such bureaucratic behavior ultimately brought him a ministerial portfolio.

In 2010, the clash between Minzdrav, which sought to eliminate internal "police patrols," and Roszdravnadzor, which sought to reassert its bureaucratic independence, caused an enormous scandal. In essence, during Tatyana Golikova's tenure (2007–2012), the Ministry of Health acquired enormous administrative powers. By 2011, using her husband's political support (at the time, Viktor Khrsitenko was vice prime minister), Golikova purged her opponents from the ministry (Kotel'nikov 2010) and introduced the legislation that would de jure truncate the independent controlling agencies and put them under her thumb. Roszdravnadzor's attempts to resist backfired: the agency's mandate diminished, and Roszdravnadzor's well-respected leader, Nikolay Yurgel, lost his position (Rybina 2010; Khabriev 2014: 22–23; Yurgel' 2014: 24–25). Formally charged with breaking the law on the civil service, he was booted out by Putin personally for having the audacity to criticize the government in public.

At the center of the conflict was the discussion regarding the new federal law on the Circulation of Medicines (61-FZ), prepared by Golikova single-handedly. The proposed bill was a completely new legal act overhauling the principles of drug regulation in the country. That the State Duma legislators and health experts decried the new law as a lucid example of lousy health governance implies Yurgel's diligence in resisting its passing. Although during its initial discussion in the Duma, the legislators proposed more than 300 amendments, it entered into force in 2010. Given Yurgel's terminated career, few state officials were bold enough to publicly criticize the law and its originator, Golikova, since such criticism implied disloyalty to Putin's policy course. Still, independent health experts continued to link persistent problems in Russian health governance to this law, in which Golikova had played an enormous role. Long story short, Roszdravnadzor lost most of its instruments, while the Minzdrav would hitherto oversee the registration and admission of drugs to the market, and the Ministry of Industry and Trade would control the production of medicines and medical devices in the country. As the foregoing discussion suggests, such an arrangement is faulty.

Elena Tel'nova (in office 2010–2013) was a highly respected administrator who also envisioned the emergence of an independent and consolidated health surveillance organ. Until her death in 2021, she lamented that it would not come to be (Kryazhev 2021). Her stay in the office was short and rocky. According to widespread but not very substantiated rumors, she used her position to lobby for her previous employer (Boris Shpigel, owner of pharmaceutical company Biotech and then-senator in the upper house of parliament), whose interests in dominating the pharmaceutical market went against the interests of companies favored by Golikova (Aleksandrov 2013). Given the agency's powers, the notion that she could have manipulated favors and privileges for private pharmaceutical firms is not entirely disembodied. At the very least, circumstantial evidence points in this direction: with Tel'nova out of office, Biotec failed to emerge as the pharmaceutical monopolist and secure the most lucrative state contracts. Notably, seven years later, before Shpigel was arrested on the charges of corruption and criminal collusion with state officials, Biotech lost the contracts for the high-cost treatment of blood diseases to Kharitonin's Pharmstandard, which had been closely affiliated with Golikova and her family. Those endeavoring to account for the regime's nontransparent decision-making and informal business dealings interpreted the rumors of corruption as symptoms of in-house fighting that Golikova could have used to discredit the extant organization of the internal oversight or, simply, eliminate the internal lobbyist for the pharmaceutical firms, not connected to her personally.

Under the agency's new head, Mikhail Murashko (in office 2015–2020), Roszdravnadzor has not distinguished itself as a powerful internal watchdog; it mainly conducted routine checks in pharmacies and periodically seized batches of substandard drugs but failed to punish their unscrupulous sellers and manufacturers (Kutuzov 2015; Zvezdina 2018). Meanwhile, street-level bureaucrats (including ordinary doctors and their immediate superiors, hospital administrators, and regional authorities) bear the brunt of disadvantageous exposure, frequently followed by questionable incriminations and punishment. Street-level bureaucrats are a convenient target the regime exposed to conceal the low quality of health governance and multiple gaming strategies at the top of the administrative level. Notably, Murashko made a career out of this: in 2020, he became a new health minister.

As noted previously, to survive, health surveillance organs must succumb to gaming or start providing political value to the principal. The story of Rospotrebnadzor (established in 2004 with functions roughly similar to the CDC) is a case in point. This organization could have impartially coordinated epidemiological governance and monitored other agencies' responses to public health crises, including HIV/AIDS, but it resorted to gaming and focused on providing political value to Putin. Its head, Gennady Onishchenko, was the leading spokesperson on matters of public health and the Chief Sanitary Inspector of Russia (in 1996–2013), a position in some aspects similar to the US Surgeon General. To protect the Kremlin's political reputation when Moscow's failure to address the HIV epidemic became evident, he commonly used simple gaming techniques, such as declining to present the undesirable and even incriminating information on the implementation of health policy that existed. For instance, Rospotrebnadzor was in charge of preparing UNGASS reports and providing a detailed description of Russia's domestic response to the widening epidemic of HIV/AIDS. However, HIV advocacy organizations involved in preparing the country report for UNGASS found out that their critical input that exposed Moscow's resistance to the international best practices was simply missing from the final, official version of the 2010 document.

The building of authoritarianism under Putin was also about incentivizing domestic agencies to provide political value for his regime, contributing to the unwarranted mission creep. Notoriously, to provide political value to the boss, Onishchenko toed the line of Putin's course on punishing those post-soviet countries—often referred to as "the near abroad"—that appeared to defy Moscow's foreign policy demands by banning their food exports (Alisova 2013). Onishchenko is best remembered for his bizarre but politically expedient views and blatant health-related accusatory acrobatics. For instance, he spread the canard that the United States was about to start biological warfare against Russia, using Georgia as a military invasion point (Bogdanov 2013). Numerous blunders made him a favorite target of media mockery, and all too many embarrassing moments accompanied his professional activity. Still, Onishchenko was relieved from service not because the independent media pulled so many fire alarms on him (Tagaeva 2013), but because of Medvedev's decision, the then prime minister, who intently disliked him, although the nature of animus remains uncertain.

The new head of the agency, Anna Popova, was little known to the business circles and pundits alike and had no personal connection and access to Putin. For that reason, the media speculated that she would preside over the agency's termination without much bureaucratic fight. Indeed, in 2011, the government had already considered transferring Rospotrebnadzor's core functions to the regional level (Aleksandrov 2013). Contrary to widespread expectation, Rospotrebnadzor was not disbanded and remained valuable to the principal under Popova, too. As before, the agency used its mandate to justify Putin's trade wars, which, understandably, had little to do with genuine concerns for consumer safety and health. Notably, in 2014, Putin introduced a ban on various Western agricultural products in response to international sanctions and restrictive measures that followed in the wake of Moscow's invasion of Ukraine and the Crimean annexation. Popova showed her utility to Putin in a manner similar to her predecessor, although she refrained from colorful and sensationalist statements.

Rospotrebnadzor's head was the primary author of the federal bill that regulated the process of destroying banned products originating in the countries that joined anti-Kremlin sanctions. In 2016, Rospotrebnadzor announced that Ukrainian and Turkish goods, now deemed illegal on Russian soil, would henceforth be destroyed (Chevtaeva 2015). In 2017, after Montenegro joined NATO and supported anti-Russian trade sanctions, the Russian Foreign Ministry warned Russians against traveling to Montenegro because of "the whipping up of anti-Russian hysteria against the backdrop of a general regression in bilateral relations" (Vedomosti 2017). Practical steps ensued. As that small European country ended up on the Kremlin's "counter-sanctions" list, Rospotrebnadzor banned its wine imports. According to the official story, the decision had nothing to do with geopolitics but the unacceptable concentration of pesticides the wines contained. In the ensuing months, Rospotrebnadzor seized more than 16 thousand wine bottles in the Moscow oblast alone. In 2018, Popova bragged that the agency "checked more than 150 thousand objects. 650 thousand products were withdrawn from circulation and destroyed, of which more than 90 percent are vegetables" (Ignatova 2018).

Although this requires a further investigation, Rospoterbnadzor reasserted itself as a valuable agency as it spearheaded the fight against the COVID-19 epidemic in the country. Dealing with this unprecedented challenge to public health, Popova stayed closely attuned to Putin's wishes while de facto abnegating the agency's surveillance responsibilities. In the early stages of the epidemic in the winter of 2020, she heeded the Kremlin's official line that the infection would not warrant any extraordinary measures like massive vaccinations, self-isolation, and mandatory quarantine; and, later on, she misrepresented the number of infected people, using statistical manipulation to divert the attention from the regime's ineffective epidemiological response.

Consistent with the pressures of "informational autocracy," Vladimir Putin aspired to cultivate a regime-friendly image of his rule in Russia and abroad. In the context of an unprecedented coronavirus pandemic, that the Kremlin sought to highlight its success in developing effective vaccines should not be surprising. Showing that Russia had the requisite capacity to rapidly develop cutting-edge vaccines against COVID-19 ahead of global pharmaceutical giants and ramp up their production for domestic and international markets had a critical reputational value to Putin. Consistent with my argument, Popova was ready to heed Putin's tacit commands, and she pushed the development and adoption of a new peptide-based vaccine, EpiVacCorona. Its developer, the Novosibirsk-based Vector Center of Virology, received a generous governmental subsidy. It looked like a success story in the making: in October 2020, the government granted the vaccine emergency authorization, and several months later, Popova claimed that the vaccine was hundred percent effective. In April 2021, regional health authorities started using the vaccine for mass vaccinations, and by the end of May, two million doses of the EpiVacCorona were ready in the vaccination rooms across the country (Tumakova 2021a). Further, in June, Russian pharmaceutical firm, Gerofarm, signed agreements to ship EpiVacCorona to Venezuela and Brazil. Notably, in June 2021, Vladimir Putin was pleased with the breakthrough: he showcased this vaccine as an instance of health governance success during an annual televised event.

Like many other instances of providing political value to the ruler, this episode illustrates the deep pathology of Russian health governance. To everybody's dismay, the independent media pulled disturbing fire alarms: Popova held a patent on EpiVacCorona, and the results of clinical trials were published only in two hitherto unknown domestic journals, one of which was Rospotrebnadzor's in-house operation. Further, The Insider (an independent investigative outlet now under pressure for its anti-regime journalism) revealed that the science behind the vaccine was faulty, and the volunteers participating in the studies failed to develop antibodies (Ponomareva 2021). In the ensuing months, The Insider was joined by investigative journalists from Novaya Gazeta, Vedomosti, Kommersant, and Meduza, independent media outlets, which demanded concrete answers from the government (see, for instance, Kostarnova 2021; Ershov and Matveeva 2022). In June 2021, Rospotrebnadzor responded to the media exposures, dismissing any incriminating concerns. The emerging consensus was that EpiVacCorona was ineffective as a vaccine and even harmful in that it triggered a false sense of protection and thereby caused more infections. What was worse, medical professionals, allegedly aware of the vaccine's uselessness, often replaced the Sputnik vaccine with EpiVacCorona without warning patients (Tumakova 2021b). Despite the widening societal understanding that the vaccine was ineffective, the government kept distributing it for the mass vaccination campaign for nearly half a year after the media pulled fire alarms on it, and nobody got punished for this disaster. Consistent with Putin's style of administrative management, Popova was not fired.

This episode of governance shows that providing political value to the principal is not innocuous: it erodes professional norms, incentivizes gaming and corruption, and is highly costly to the patients. In summary, internal health oversight is deeply flawed, but it intensifies as Putin's authoritarianism consolidates. Putin chooses subservient loyalty over competence and tolerates governance flubs. In contrast, fostering impartial, independent, and robust health surveillance organs constitutes a present danger to the regime because they incriminate the principal and his subordinates as the primary sources of bad health governance. Inculpative exposure could increase the chances of protest voting, too.

Fire Alarms: The Weakness of External Oversight

The term "fire alarms" describes less centralized oversight with less active and direct intervention wherein the principal enables outside actors—including nongovernmental organizations, the media, and self-regulated professional organizations—to inform the principal of a problem and seek remedies (for the original definitions, see McCubbins and Schwartz 1984: 166). Although Russia is unfree, it still features some degree of pluralism: committed individuals, policy entrepreneurs, civil society organizations, and nonstate professional associations are interested in participating in indirect governance and competencies to do so. This interest allows the Kremlin to involve external intermediaries with ex ante authority in the governance architecture. Academics note that "Russian state institutions < ... > have a vital interest in collaboration with civil society, since they rely on the organizations' expertise, resources and skills in order to effectively counter the spread of HIV/AIDS (Pape 2014, p.7). In principle, a robust civil society can monitor health administration and improve the policy course. For attempts to create a distinct tier of independent "meso-regulators" in other countries, see Kaye (2006).

The landscape of external actors and governance intermediaries is complex. Types of actors that participate in health governance in the country include:

- Public councils (more than 25 at the federal level and more than 210 in the regions) and more than 50 ad hoc working groups participate in the work of the central state organs.
- Numerous ex ante authoritative professional communities and associations (e.g., the Alliance of Doctors, the National Medical Chamber, Doctors Defense League) are coopted in or excluded from health governance's national architecture.

- Several multi-issue quasi-state organizations (Public Chamber of the Russian Federation, the All-Russian Popular Front) were created by the Kremlin to solve the principal-agent dilemma.
- More than a thousand patient organizations focus on a particular issue, usually access to medicines and health services, or disease (the International Treatment Preparedness Coalition, the Patients' Control, Patients' League) and several umbrella organizations (like Russian Patients Association, representing hundreds of regional issue-focused patients organizations at the federal level).
- Numerous public experts are involved in all aspects of health governance in an individual capacity.

All these intermediary actors seek (albeit with different degrees of competence and sincerity) to increase the quality of public control over health governance and influence state policy by directly participating in regulation, monitoring the implementation of significant decisions, and providing data and feedback necessary to prepare and implement regulatory documents. In principle, intermediaries, or meso-level actors, formally independent from the state structure, could be helpful in external oversight efforts.

The trend toward cooptation has a long history. Early in his presidency, Putin charged his leading political operators to bring governance intermediaries together. In 2001, Gleb Pavlovsky organized the Civil Forum that brought together representatives of numerous nonstate organizations. As he later reminisced, "The project assumed the creation, along with the extending sphere of expansion of the Russian government, a parallel world of public organizations" (Pavlovsky 2016). At the forum's convention, Putin declared that the government sought to empower civil society, but ex ante authoritative organizations (like Memorial) were skeptical about the nature of the pending collaboration. Although Putin's autocratic inclinations were not evident back then, the skepticism proved warranted. Reminiscing, Pavlovsky, too, lamented that the ideal of orchestration, intended to provide independent input and democratize and improve domestic governance, got wasted as public organizations and nonstate experts succumbed to the government and voluntarily abrogated their agency. Although Putin lost interest in this particular approach to managing civil society, the idea of mobilizing civil society for the regime's goals persisted.

Several years later, the Kremlin put the Public Chamber, a para-constitutional organ giving an institutional forum to the loyal segment of civil society, in charge of providing societal oversight and independent public expertise of government workings and helping to materialize Putin's plans. Although commonly criticized as a smokescreen, the then Duma Speaker Boris Gryzlov described it as "an additional opportunity for the development of civil society in the country < ... > It will have the right to analyze Duma bills, especially bills that deal with constitutional issues. And it will have the right to check the work of the executive" (cited in Bransten 2005). Not surprisingly, the recommendations of the Public Chamber's commission on health had no impact on changing the health governance course. Often, the hearings of the Chamber are challenging to obtain. More consequentially, the Public Chamber was designed as a simulacrum of a well-organized and influential civil society, proving its value for the regime as a "societal" rubber stamp.

At the beginning of Putin's third presidential term and early on in Medvedev's lackluster tenure as a prime minister, the government entertained the idea of institutionalizing an innovative mechanism of external control in order to increase state capacity. As it turned out, these ideas never got political traction. Medvedev's short-lived push for "the open government," in which civil society and experts would monitor the executive, remained exciting but declaratory (Abyzov 2012). In practice, any social oversight was effectively suppressed (Henderson 2011); and the very notion of open government remained orthogonal to the intensifying control over independent civil society.

Further attempts were all linked to the individuals working within the Presidential administration office (for the detailed discussion of how this institution operates, see Burkhardt 2020; Pushkarskaya 2020), most notably Vyacheslav Volodin and Sergey Kiriyenko. There is one particular position in the Russian hierarchy of power, featuring an awkwardly sounding title, with functions and power that cannot easily find equivalency in democracies. As one Russian journalist succinctly put it, "The first deputy chief of staff wields much more power than the title suggests. This person has traditionally controlled parliament, mainstream political parties, pro-regime public organizations, as well as an army of loyal political analysts and sociologists. The first deputy chief of staff also creates official ideology and determines what kinds of freedoms the state will allow its citizens" (Pertsev 2017). In other words, this person makes sure the regime functions smoothly and develops specific tools to ensure that task. These individuals usually have the reputation of the regime's "gray eminence"; and somewhat substantiated rumors and outright canards alike regarding their personalities and predilections widely circulate in Russian society.

Many observers—especially inclined critically toward the regime—carry out the line of reasoning highlighting Putin's aversion to independent noncommercial organizations too far. This section has gone to considerable lengths to substantiate the observation that the regime was keen on enlisting authoritative individuals and mobilizing them in the format of intermediary organizations. Consistent with the literature, personalistic regimes commonly make an effort to coopt those nonstate actors that derive the authority from their professional activities while attempting to control them (e.g., Owen and Bindman 2019; Bindman et al. 2019; Skokova et al. 2018; Flikke 2018). Putin hoped to use select civil society organizations to pressure the state authorities to implement his decisions while expecting loyalty and political support in return (Richter 2009; Vinokurova 2016). As the following sections will demonstrate, Putin supported the formation of one sizable multi-purpose intermediary and cultivated the support of an emerging but authoritative medical association. Bringing these intermediaries into a larger structure of his personalistic rule, not surprisingly, diminished their independence. This choice is also consistent with the broad theoretical observation that orchestration, wherein relatively unconstrained intermediaries have autonomy in regulation, is relatively more likely in democratic than authoritarian systems (Abbott et al. 2016) as a possible strategy for solving the governor's dilemma.

Turning to the core insights of the competence-control theory, it stands to reason that external monitors are effective under nonhierarchical management and with considerable autonomy in interpreting the terms of the principal's grant. Simply put, an effective oversight requires the mode of indirect governance called trusteeship. The problem for personalistic rulers is that trusteeships may invert authority: "the trustor has superior authority ex ante, but may be subject to the trustee's authority ex post" (Abbott et al. 2020: 14–15). However, the informational autocrats must remain in control and prevent the exposure of inefficiencies and policy failures. As a result, the regime designed a solution allowing select professional associations and social actors to participate in indirect governance. However, it also maintained control over them via presidential administration (which makes external "fire alarms" resemble quasi-state or parastatal institutions) and permitted external watchdogs' capacities to decline in effectiveness due to underuse, neglect, or divestment of resources.

In summary, there is no escaping the observation that Putin's approach to constructing health oversight had alarming ambiguities. Over time, he worked to enlist or help construct multiple monitoring bodies that could provide critical input in health regulation, pull fire alarms, and suggest improvements. That was commendable and critically important for constructing good governance. However, the oversight players appointed by Putin perforce were allowed only limited freedom to critique and punish key governmental agents lest the exposed problems and failures indicate the regime and Putin's personal decisions as the source of bad governance, thus substantiating an uncomfortable truth that could cost Putin his popularity. Lest they lose their power to pursue narrow self-interested goals, proximity to the ruler, and status in the hierarchy, intermediaries must be extremely sensitive to Putin's position on core health issues. The following two sections explore how two notable intermediaries operated within the confines of Russia's personalism and what optimizing strategies they adopted.

OVERSIGHT AND QUASI-STATE ORGANIZATIONS: ALL-RUSSIAN POPULAR FRONT

The story of one high-profile intermediary deserves special attention here. The All-Russian People's Front (*Obshcherossiiskii narodnyi front*, hereafter, ONF) is a multi-purpose quasi-state organization officially created as a mechanism of public control over policy implementation (Lassila 2016). Vyacheslav Volodin, who in 2013 replaced Vladislav Surkov as the First Deputy Chief of Staff of the Presidential Administration, is credited with being the leading architect of the Front, although the idea belonged to president Putin. According to Putin, "One of the basic ideas of the popular front was precisely to create the conditions for the direct participation of citizens, various social and professional groups in the development of the national agenda so that people had the opportunity to set tasks for the authorities and press for their execution" (Putin 2013).

The organization functioned as an aggregation of well-known and respected individuals (such as Stanislav Govorukhin, a famous film director), street-level activists, and volunteers who shared Putin's vision for the country. Since its inception, ONF has incorporated 16 national and more than 500 regional nonstate organizations; one of its most gainful acquisitions was the cooptation of the National Medical Chamber and its leadership. The Front claimed a role of a public controller over the governmental functionaries, but the presidential administration directed its actions and purpose. It also served as a public platform for the dialogue between the government and the people. In practice, ONF's independence remains constrained. It works in close contact with the Presidential Control Directorate, a subdivision of the Presidential Executive Office (also known as the Presidential Administration of Russia, *Administratsiya Prezidenta Rossiiskoi Federatsii*), an institution formally in charge of supporting the activity of the president, but widely believed to be the real hub of decision-making. The authoritative newspaper, Vedomosti, conducted several interviews with political insiders, who averred that the Front's executive apparatus was but an external subdivision of the presidential administration. That the chair of the Front's executive committee, Aleksey Anisimov, continued to take Volodin's dictation was an unmistakable indicator of where the ex post control originated. According to investigative journalists, ONF lacked independence, while its decisions regarding substantive goals and personnel management "passed under the hardest control of the administration" (Kozlov and Papchenkova 2015).

It appears that over time, the Front failed to develop a coherent sense of corporate identity and common purpose. Changes in the presidential administration inevitably entailed the tectonic shifts in the objectives the intermediary pursued. In 2016, Sergey Kiriyenko, hitherto the head of the Russian Atomic Agency, who replaced Volodin, pushed his vision of how the Front should serve its principal. Kiriyenko instructed ONF to prioritize social projects and volunteer movements while toning down the discussion of systemic problems in health governance. According to one report, the ONF activists gradually sensed that their main task was "rather not criticize the governors, but, on the contrary, contribute to the dissemination of positive management practices in the regions" (Vinokurov et al. 2019), the task antithetical to the genuine external oversight. Further, as the rotation of cadres indicates, compared to the first generation of top brass, the new set of leaders had less ex ante authority and less proximity to Putin, meaning that the relative power of the organization attenuated, too. The Front became a pool for reserve players, who had to wait for openings within the officialdom; the media also speculated that ONF would replace the discredited ruling party, United Russia (Melikyan 2014; Pertsev 2015, 2020).

Still, the absence of ex post independence does not lend credence to the notion that ONF's activity was pointless and inconsequential. More specifically, Putin commissioned ONF to check bureaucrats' diligence in carrying out presidential mandates, including May Decrees that were supposed to expand social obligations, and their honesty in reporting the results. That task was pretty straightforward: in 2015, the Front faithfully pulled fire alarms on those presidential orders and directives which bureaucrats considered implemented in full but, according to the Front's assessment, were not. One of the prominent functionaries, Nikolay Govorin, reported that "Since 2012, the president has given 185 orders aimed at systemic reforms in the healthcare sector. At the same time, only 69 out of 108 orders < ... > have been removed from control." So the principal was informed, but it was not clear whether any consequences for the underperforming federal and regional authorities followed.

In addition to overseeing the implementation of the May decrees, ONF tried to monitor the efficiency and fairness in the public procurement system, expose corruption among officials and governors, lay bare shortcomings of healthcare reform, and provide a balance sheet of the state's efforts to supply fundamental goods and services. The Front took its job seriously: it organized twenty national investigations, analyzed about 2000 media publications, checked the work of 700 pharmacies and 600 health clinics, and interviewed more than 13 thousand people. In September 2015, ONF followed up on all these monitoring efforts and summoned a national forum entitled "For quality and affordable medicine!" The forum brought together more than 600 participants: doctors, patients, scientists, pharmaceutical manufacturers, heads of relevant ministries. Importantly, it convened amid the widespread dissatisfaction with Minzdrav's administrative performance, which had already provoked public calls to disband the ministry and stop the healthcare sector reforms.

The forum kicked off with a report entitled "People's View on Health Care" presented by Govorin. The report soberly stated that "despite the optimistic reporting of executive authorities in the regions, there is a high level of citizens' dissatisfaction with the lack of changes or even worsening of the situation throughout the country." The official report and subsequent discussion pulled any fire alarm possible, ranging from the exposition of the near-disastrous optimization reform to the appraisal of the increasing prices on pharmaceuticals and medical devices. Govorin and others criticized the minister of health in her presence; it even looked like the participants would press Putin hard to explain the dire health situation in the country. Still, the report ended with a thornless olive branch, saying that it was "impossible to really improve the efficiency of the existing system without an objective public discussion." Suffice it to say that ONF's pleas fell on deaf ears: no healthcare professionals would hitherto participate in decisions concerning the optimization of medical facilities, while the upcoming official roadmap ("Plans for structural transformations of the network of medical organizations until 2020") was barely available. The optimization would proceed in stealth.

When Putin arrived at the forum, he demarcated the boundaries of acceptable criticism directed toward the top officials with exceptional clarity and signaled that ONF should not be too enterprising. As Putin was going through the uncomfortable Q&A session, he quelled the anxious mood of the forum's participants. Instead of heeding the critical concerns and promising to take the fire alarms seriously, he defended the Ministry of Health, relegating the mounting problems to street-level corruption, low professional ethics, insufficient qualifications of Russia's medical professionals, citizens' inability to understand their medical rights, and so on (Putin 2015). The president justified personnel cuts by claiming that the dismissed health professionals were not qualified to work in the modern healthcare system the regime was building.

Although Putin asked the ONF representatives to investigate the situation with the availability of medications and their prices (RBC 2015), at the forum, Putin conveniently shifted the blame from regulators to greedy pharmacies. He brushed off the notion that flawed presidential mandates caused failures. Instead, he demanded criminal prosecution of pharmacies which inflated the prices in their self-interests. That Putin reaction was old news: Since 2009, the government repeatedly accused pharmacies of price gouging and viewed them as saboteurs. Back then, Medvedev famously said that he would not allow pharmacies to go brazen, while Putin coined a harsh dictum: "where are the imprisonments?" ("*gde posadki*").

Worth mentioning is at least one high-profile case in which ONF's monitoring efforts bore fruit. In 2018, ONF sent Golikova a letter requesting to reverse the earlier resolution that allowed only hand-picked companies included in the governmental register to participate in public tenders. Specifically, they highlighted the burdensome problems with the poor quality of domestic polyvinyl chloride (PVC) medical devices and indicated the significant increase in their prices (Myl'nikov 2018). As a result, in December 2018, the government abolished the previous rules and welcomed other firms back into the market for medical devices (Godovannik 2018; Kotova 2018). However, this case is not typical: ONF commonly shied away from challenging other monopolists, such as Chemezov's Nacimbio, exposing Putin's strategic course on import substitution and laying bare the consequences of the limited competition in the pharmaceutical sector (ONF 2019).

Less successful was the Front when dealing with the challenge of vanishing medicines. In 2019, activists of the ONF project entitled "For Fair Procurement" discovered that numerous failed public tenders disrupted public access to medicines, threatening many patients' lives. The Front's leaders appealed to the presidential administration and Minzdrav to take urgent measures to prevent public tenders' failure in the future. Additionally, in the wake of the massive shortages of essential life-saving medicines in the public sector, ONF's functionaries pulled fire alarms on the official strategy of imposing the artificially low price ceiling for pharmaceutical products and criticized the official methodology of calculating reference prices, calling to abolish the extant approach (Pakhomov 2019; GMPnews 2019).

As discussed in Chapter 2, governmental Order No. 871n abolished the ability of public entities to independently calculate the initial maximum contract price on the grounds of assessing the cost of similar purchases or evaluating competing commercial proposals. The idea behind that order was to introduce a unified procedure for all public procurement systems across the country and prevent disparities in prices across different provinces. But negative externalities outweighed the projected benefits of a standardized methodology. It seems that ONF's fire alarms remained useless: the Ministry of Health deflected criticism, pointing to cartel collusion among the suppliers. Still, Anton Getta, the project coordinator for "For Fair Purchases," was on the fence about whether Minzdrav was likely to heed the criticism. He noted that "At the moment, much work is being done to simplify the procurement legislation and remove from it the norms that negatively affect the implementation of the procurement process. But in the procurement of medicines, unfortunately, the situation has reached a dead end. Failed purchases in such quantities will inevitably affect the level of drug supply. We hope that the Ministry of Health will draw conclusions and really rework this document with the involvement of a wide range of experts. There should be no delay in this matter."

The preceding discussion has gone to considerable length to substantiate the proposition that despite all weaknesses, there is no denying that ONF's leadership put its stamp on how health is governed in Russia. At the very least, it drew the principal's attention to the persistent problems in health and solved multiple local problems. Further, ONF distinguished itself at the local level, where its activists are instrumental in solving various individual street-level problems. ONF's street-level activists collected information about inappropriate or ineffective spending of public funds and reported it to the Front's central headquarters and then to the Accounts Chamber (Vinokurova 2016). The actual monitoring practices turned into a far-flung and decentralized version of police patrols conducted by approximately 100 thousand activists at the street level. In practice, they ensured that some patients received the life-saving drugs and inspected the safety and equipment of several primary healthcare sites in the deep province (ONF 2019a, 2019b). Press releases of its provincial branches are replete with peppy reports on volunteers' activities that range from teaching how to hand-craft Christmas toys to scrutinizing the quality of snow plowing. To get a fair sense of ONF's activist work, I systematically read all the press releases from different regional headquarters. Although their record in pulling fire alarms at the federal level is not encouraging, it seems that activists and volunteers successfully solved many small-scale and individual problems. In 2019, for instance, they reported on the availability of subsidized medicines for cancer patients in Moscow pharmacies; helped one resident in the Moscow region to register for disability; helped patients with diabetes in the Moscow region to receive medicines; ensured that the Penza authorities build an obstetric station; made certain that 70 patients received life-saving medicines in the Kirov region.

To conclude, there is no need to deny that ONF turned into a relatively sophisticated public organization (Malle 2016), but it could barely perform the tasks of an independent and competent intermediary. The fact that its leaders were able to bring all too many governance flubs to people's attention and, in some cases, spotlight the ineptness of select Putin's appointees (mainly on the regional level) does not negate the observation that its ability to improve governance remained limited. In practice, the organization's public authority relied on Russia's president, while its independence was constrained and imbricated into the executive and law enforcement organs' structure. Instead of solving the principal-agent dilemma, the Front proved instrumental to Putin to sustain his national popularity and disassociate himself from the ineffectual policy implementation (Vinokurova 2018).

Oversight and Professional Organizations: National Medical Chamber

The National Medical Chamber (*Natsional'naya Meditsinskaya Palata*, hereafter Natsmedpalata, or NMC) is a prominent peak-level professional medical association that emerged ex ante in order to improve the quality of health regulation and protect health professionals' corporate interests. The NMC's story is an example of an ex ante authoritative organization that succumbed to cooptation and therefore lost its independence from the principal while increasing its ability to protect its narrow interests. Since its inception, Leonid Roshal, Director of the Research Institute of Emergency Pediatric Surgery and Traumatology and the former chair of the Public Chamber's committee on health (2005–2009), has been NMC's unchallenged leader.

The rise of NMC was rocky. In April 2011, Minzdrav convened the Forum of Medical Workers in order to create an appearance of broad societal support for the ongoing healthcare reforms. That the government aspired to design a friendly medical association is not surprising. The ministry instructed its regional branches to send in only the loyal delegates supporting the Ministry and the ongoing reforms while failing to invite nonstate medical associations, such as medical unions (Kuravskii et al. 2011). At Putin's behest but against Golikova's expectations, Roshal railed that the healthcare system was severely underfunded, criticized pervasive corruption, decried unprofessionalism in the ministry, and lamented the lack of medical self-administration. The consideration that the outgoing health minister Golikova prioritized financial concerns over public health was central to his vitriol. In response, health ministry officials quickly compiled an orotund letter in which they complained to Putin that Roshal's unconstructive criticism tarnished their reputation and, as they put it, "undermined our faith in the cause to which we give our whole life." Although Golikova publicly backed these complaints, Putin did not defend her (Kara-Murza 2011).

Most independent observers interpreted Roshal's public criticism of Minzdrav as a genuine attempt to pull fire alarms, a *cri de coeur* of a passionate and intelligent professional. At the time, there were no reasons to doubt the sincerity of Roshal's motives. Less discussed was another intention: by going public, Roshal threw NMC in a competition for the privileged position against several alternative peak-level organizations, none of which by 2011 were robust enough to defend the interest of the medical professionals. There was no secret that Roshal desired to consolidate health professionals into a peak-level institution envisioned along neocorporatist lines with the German Medical Association (*Bundesärztekammer*) as a model (Roshal 2011). What happened right after licenses the latter view. Soon after his public "dissent," Roshal signaled that he would submit his organization for the principal's ex post controls. By November 2011, it became clear that Roshal was willing to closely cooperate with the United Russia party and ONF. Once the prospects of cooptation became apparent, Roshal changed his tune: in October 2012, at the 1st National Congress of Russia's Doctors, he praised the new health minister, Veronika Skvortsova, the future architect of the disastrous healthcare optimization reform.

In hindsight, that Putin chose Roshal and NMC as the regime's health intermediary is not surprising. The other alternatives were remarkably unappealing. The Society of Doctors of Russia embodied the first alternative (Rodionova and Sedov 2013; Sedov 2014). The organization was led by Evgeny Chazov (1929–2021), who had boasted a long career in the Soviet health ministry and commanded far-flung professional credibility. However, as a public figure, he was best known for his delusional memoirs, in which he gave disparaging characteristics of the Soviet leaders, both from political and physiological standpoints (he was also keen on republishing them, see Chazov 2014). At the danger of speculation, loyalty driven Putin could not but view Chazov as untrustworthy and underhanded. Unlike Roshal, who was known to Putin since the tragic terrorist attack on the school in Beslan in 2008, the Society of Doctor's octogenarian leader had no personal connection to Putin. Further, Putin would not be amiss to interpret the support of Chazov's organization as Golikova's attempt to forge her clientele in the professional medical community.

The second alternative was even less desirable. It was not in Putin's interest to coopt Alexey Navalny's aggressive watchdog organization, Rospil, which tied all the flubs in the national health governance not to the individual wrongdoings of its agents but rather to the nature of the regime itself and Putin personally (Sedov 2011). At that time, Rospil exposed the alleged corruption and lack of competition in the public tenders for creating a social network for health workers and patients, tenders intended to provide services for HIV infection prevention, and tenders for creating a system for personal health monitoring.

In these circumstances, Roshal thrived. In the ensuing years, NMC underwent a profound transformation from a small forum of concerned professionals to a near-universal organization as it gradually incorporated more than 50 percent of local medical professional non-profit organizations and at least 25 percent of the total number of doctors working in Russia's regions joined the Chamber in an individual capacity. According to Roshal's critics, the Ministry intentionally designed its rules to skew the playing field to make NMC the only professional nonstate organization in the country's architecture of health governance. That should not be very surprising. In 2014, the NMC leaders signed a framework agreement with the Ministry of Health, and by 2019, NMC officially became the exclusive nonstate partner recognized by the government. The National Medical Chamber also joined forces with ONF: according to reports, by 2019, they collaborated on more than 150 joint initiatives submitted to the presidential administration and the Ministry of Health, while medical professionals co-chaired about half of ONF's regional headquarters (ONF 2019). The cooptation of NMC in the regime was complete.

As events unfolded, Roshal proved that the regime could count on him. Despite the absence of dramatic improvements in health administration in the country, Roshal toned down his criticism and tried to discredit unfavorable assessments of Russia's health governance supplied by independent noncommercial organizations (see, for instance, Kruglikova 2015). That in 2018, Roshal served as Putin's surrogate in the presidential election campaign, further confirming Roshal as a valuable asset to the regime. In 2020, Roshal helped the Kremlin to confuse the public about the poisoning of Alexey Navalny, a prominent opposition leader, and tried to discredit the accurate medical diagnosis supplied by the Berlin clinic Navalny had been admitted to while in a medically induced coma (Interfax 2020).

What should we make of all this organizational expansion and political maneuvering? It should certainly be a mistake to accuse Roshal of absolute subservience; on many occasions, he raised the critical problem of healthcare underfunding. Notably, as recently as in 2019, he trained the Kremlin's attention to the fact that the quality of healthcare primarily depended on the financing of the sector. He emphasized that the federal spending should be at least 5%, not the standard 3.7% of the country's

GDP that looked particularly meager compared to some industrialized European democracies, which spent up to 10% of their GDPs on healthcare. Roshal continuously pulled deafening fire alarms about the insufficiency of funding for the healthcare sector but failed to convince the government to dial-up healthcare spending.

There is no denying that the NMC leaders found success in lobbying the organization's corporate interests. First, NMC lobbied to adopt the German model for resolving disputes between a doctor and a patient using an independent medical examination and even started several successful pilot projects. Second, NMC also lobbied to obtain the legal right to conduct medical expertise evaluating the quality and safety of Russian medical care and develop clinical recommendations (i.e., documents specifying protocols for prevention, diagnosis, and treatment of illnesses with a description of the sequence of actions of the health worker in some instances) for approval by the Ministry of Health. As of 2019, NMC was the only nongovernmental organization qualified to do both (Myl'nikov 2019). Third, the task of self-protection loomed large: Roshal tried to influence Russian law enforcement agencies by closely working with Aleksandr Bastrykin of Russia's Investigative Committee (Sledstvennyi Komitet Rossíiskoi Federatsii, SKR). Roshal sought to correct Bastrykin's overzealous push to impose severe criminal liability for medical mistakes (Trifonova 2018). That was an arduous task because there was no legal definition of a medical error, while SKR made medical errors its top-3 investigative priority (Serkov et al. 2018). Fourth, consistent with patron-client relations, the NMC leaders also secured presidential protection that safeguarded medical professionals from unfavorable mass media scrutiny (Shubina 2017).

In summary, because it possessed ex ante credibility and social reputation, the Kremlin found it in its best interest to enlist NMC into its system of governance. In this context, state-sanctioned organizations and peak-level health institutions, as the section shows, can communicate what health professionals think about the desired priorities in and problems with health governance. Nevertheless, they failed to institutionalize meaningful external monitoring processes that could lead to strategic course correction or reverse poor decisions in governing health. Fostering oversight by intermediaries while exercising rigid control over them is counterproductive for the objective needs of Russian patients.

Oversight and Nongovernmental Organizations: Repression and Tolerance

Generally speaking, there is a considerable variation and nuance in the Russian government's relationships with individual nonstate organizations: strategies include outright repressions that target politically undesirable organizations, moderate responsiveness to the neutral NGOs that shy away from the open criticism, and the conscious cooptation of loyal intermediaries into the national architecture of health governance. By enlisting credible intermediaries, the regime demonstrates to the ordinary people that the principal has an enduring commitment to social betterment, generating much-desired political dividends. Overall, the Kremlin seeks to mute critical voices that expose the regime as the root cause of health inefficiencies and reward those who submit to it. According to the cross-country polls conducted by the Russian Patients Association (hereafter, VSP), the plurality of nonstate actors assess the governmental willingness to collaborate with them as unfavorable. The pandemic of COVID-19 exacerbated the trend (VSP 2021: 12). That is not surprising, but it somewhat obfuscates the logic that drives the Kremlin's approaches to intermediaries, ranging from suppression, cooptation, and tolerance. The remainder of this section seeks to articulate this logic.

That the Kremlin intentionally stunted the growth of fledgling civil society, a collection of non-political entities that could monitor health officials' behavior and protect citizens' needs, is well-understood (Crotty et al. 2014). The expansion of authoritarianism under Putin helped weaken independent societal monitors of health governance: Political loyalty was the faultline separating those invited into the oversight system from those who never will be. An increasing number of health-related NGOs—along with multiple individuals, news outlets, polling agencies, election watchers, and political organizations—became politically undesirable and classified as agents of foreign—and pernicious by implication—influence (Kriger 2008; Reprintseva 2016; Zvezdina 2016). The punitive laws steadily expanded the list of "undesirable" advocacy, service, and monitoring organizations and disempowered their ability to monitor state behavior and call out administrators' wrongdoings.

The tag of an agent of foreign influence, and even more so the designation of an undesirable organization, implies that these organizations are in immediate danger of criminal prosecution. The objective was simple: the regime imposed additional controls, whereby any minor mistake in NGO's artificially painstaking quarterly reports or accepting money from abroad would entail criminal prosecution or permanent termination. Notably, in 2018, the Ministry of Justice drafted a new law that would disrupt the work of NGOs engaged in the prevention of HIV infection and accepted foreign funding, however meager. Because domestic health authorities did not underwrite the evidence-based preventive work in the country, the refusal of Western grants was tantamount to self-liquidation. Until recently, despite a generally unfavorable background, some Russian civil society organizations worked with state agencies at the local and regional levels, especially in Tomsk, St. Petersburg, Kaliningrad, and Moscow. There is anecdotal evidence that police, for instance, learn about naloxone and tolerate harm-reduction outreach. Many nonstate organizations, including Transatlantic Partners against AIDS/Global Business Coalition (TPAA/GBC), operated only for a limited number of years.

In this context, many ex ante authoritative and resourceful health organizations unafraid of exposing the regime's malversations find themselves under insuperable constraints. The Alliance of Doctors is a nonstate organization that distinguished itself in defending the rights of medical professionals and exposing multiple problems of health governance in the country. The organization acted primarily as a labor union, presenting a better alternative to the official one, and it also pressured various health authorities and local hospitals to correct their wrongdoings and shortcomings. The members of the Alliance traveled to the exceptionally mismanaged hospitals, demanded explanations from the head doctors, filmed their defiant behaviors, and posted the resulting videos on YouTube. Surely, this strategy was unlikely to inform the principal about local problems of health governance directly, but the key members of the Alliance also harbored no illusion that Putin was not responsible for all the mismanagement they exposed.

Since its inception in 2018, the Alliance of Doctors grew rapidly: three years later, it had 42 regional branches and boasted several thousand fee-paying members. Its founder, Anastasiya Vasil'eva, a professional ophthalmologist, began her political journey after she and her mother, also a medical professional, lost their employment for reasons they saw as related to the governmental ineptness in managing state clinics. She met and treated Navalny when one of the regime's myrmidons sprayed a brilliant green, one of the triarylmethane dyes, in his eyes, causing a dangerous health injury. Very importantly, Vasil'eva sought and received the logistical and legal support of Navalny's organization, also known for its incisive exposure of health mismanagement and ambition to terminate Putin's rule. Later on, she pulled fire alarms on the shortages of medications for COVID-19 patients, monitored scantiness of personal protective equipment in medical institutions, accused health officials of lying about the number of infected people, and decried the government's inability to mobilize the production of medical oxygen. Needless to say, these kinds of fire alarms go against the vital needs of the "informational autocracy" as they discredit the ruler as incompetent and malevolent. Soon after, federal investigators summoned Vasilyeva to explain her activity, which they described as the "spreading of deliberately false information about the coronavirus."

Although the Alliance of Doctors routinely faced thinly veiled police harassment, Vasil'eva campaigned to save Navalny's life during his imprisonment (Kheifets and Dyuryagina 2020; Kostarnova 2021). Waiting being sentenced on politically motivated charges, Vasil'eva wrote a post on her Facebook account, announcing her partnership with Navalny's organization was to end. Trying to explain herself, Vasil'eva noted that Navalny's organization cared more about the struggle for power than physicians' and patients' interests. Her about-face is understandable: in Putin's Russia, such a connection is a political anathema, which precludes any realistic chance of performing intermediary activities. There is little indication that the Alliance of Doctors would not lose its agency; given the Kremlin's frontal assault on all organizations associated with Navalny, the available resources become scarce, and the Alliance's intimidated members try their talents elsewhere.

Although two tendencies—cooptation and repression—sufficiently capture the general trends of how external monitors of health governance function in the country, many independent patients organizations exist in the gray zone; they are not enlisted but remain tolerated. Examples are in order. The International Treatment Preparedness Coalition (hereafter ITPC, founded in 2003 in South Africa and appeared in Russia in 2005) is a decentralized network of people living with HIV and community activists who promote universal access to HIV treatment and other life-saving medicines for related diseases, especially tuberculosis and hepatitis C. The Russian branch ambitiously describes the network's official mission "to maximize the involvement of people living with HIV and their advocates in the decision-making processes that affect their lives—at the international, regional, national and local levels." Most importantly, because the network is issue-driven, it does not aspire to monitor health governance in Russia as a whole. Still, the network distinguished itself by systematically monitoring the outcomes of drug procurement in the country, making information about massive drug shortages public, and initiating numerous inquiries directed at Russian health officials. It exposes the lack of competitiveness, which plagues public tenders, trains attention to the failures of allocating and registering necessary pharmaceutical products to match patients' needs, probes the drastic differences in price points of the same medicines across the country's regions, and trains activists to monitor and analyze public tenders.

Alexey Mikhailov, head of the ITPC monitoring department, is aware of the political challenges that external health organizations encounter and notes that applying political pressure on the regime is counterproductive. He is moderately optimistic about bureaucrats' openness to critical information and their willingness to correct governance shortcomings. For example, in his interview, Mikhailov noted that state officials were responsive to the information about dated medicines causing irreversible side effects and welcomed news about more advanced pharmaceutical products, which were more effective and easier to tolerate by patients. He also noted that the regional health authorities solicited ITPC's help preparing relevant documents for public auctions.

Some ITPC's monitoring information comes from Patients' Control, a social movement that aspires to monitor the quality of medical care in the Russian regions and ensure patients' rights to treatment (Mishina 2020). Many lines of its work are similar to ITPC, and Patients' Control is a smaller organization that monitors Russia's health organs less thoroughly, simply collecting data from those patients who are willing to fill out a form at the organization's website www.pereboi.ru. Its leaders and activists receive information directly from people who encounter interruptions or refusals to treatment and then initiate small-scale protests or write open letters to the government. For example, most recently, the Patient Control wrote an open letter to the Minister of Health Mikhail Murashko, calling him to comment on the shortages of diagnostic tools for patients with HIV and disclose statistics on studies that would help determine which medications are most effective on HIV-positive people. Not too surprisingly, Murahsko did not respond to the letter.

What plausibly saves them from persecution or termination is that neither organization challenges Putin personally and exposes the regime as the originator of governance failures. Although some top state administrators occasionally meet with the representatives of Patient's Control, these meetings hardly indicate the government's attempts to pull it into health governance. While ITPC feels reasonably comfortable with the impact of its monitoring activities, the overall reality for most independent health and social actors is challenging.

Unfortunately, there is no foundation for even cautious optimism for what comes next. Those health entrepreneurs who are reasonably loyal to the regime but fairly critical of its mistakes will fail to implement their organizational initiatives. The real dilemma for both Vadim Pokrovky, who works within the state, and Anastasiya Vasil'eva, who works outside it, is the same: achieving good health governance is unlikely as long as Russian personalism remains intact, but speaking loyalty and heeding Putin's injunctions could moderately help the Russian patient, albeit on the regime's terms. What is worse, open retrogrades like Vitaly Milonov (best known for taking the initiative in criminalizing "satanic" LGBT in the country and trying to sue Madonna and Lady Gaga for doing so) and Elena Mizulina (best known for her campaign for the so-called the Dima Yakovlev Law that bans the US nationals from adopting Russian orphans) act unconstrained.

Conclusion

Lest the low levels of satisfaction with the allocated health goods and services result in the declining electoral support and increasing vulnerability of the regime's rulers, including Putin, in principle understand how to make governance better: police the bureaucracy, develop a system of reliable internal and external oversight, institutionalize information-gathering mechanisms, and involve intermediaries or meso-regulators in the national architecture of health governance. As the Kremlin promised sizable improvements in social welfare provision and allocated significant state resources to health matters, these tasks were paramount for establishing good health governance. Still, in the confines of Russia's personalistic regime, the quality and expanse of oversight are circumscribed.

In brief, the mechanisms of disabling impartial oversight in Putin's system of governance are as follows. Firstly, in Putin's system of governance, any independent internal or external oversight of the Cabinet-level state officials is antithetical to the principle according to which key elites remain shielded from scrutiny and their gaming is tolerated. Putin's key subordinates actively worked to dampen mechanisms of internal, horizontal accountability and pressed their in-house opponents hard to avoid internal discussion and criticism. Secondly, the propensity of internal health surveillance organs and external watchdogs to provide political value for the boss is an optimizing response within the parameters of the tacit authoritarian contract; and it permeates surveillance agencies' institutional routines. At times, the desire to provide political value puts people's health in danger. Third, the inclusion and cooptation of external (societal) actors in the system of health oversight did not sufficiently improve or challenge the personalistic mechanisms of health administration. Directly managed by the presidential administration, coopted intermediaries became quasi-governmental institutions, and they provided political value for the regime's principals in return for special privileges, protection, and access to the state's resources.

On balance, while mobilized intermediaries sometimes exposed insufficient technical competencies of top managers in health, uncovered problems with health policy implementation and outcomes, and identified isolated cases of rent-seeking behavior of select bureaucrats, they were silent about the political underpinnings of bad health governance and failed to question Putin's politics as the source of drawbacks. These intermediaries remained under the principal's control facing the risk of losing their position in the governance architecture to the principal.

The book started with the premise that one needs to understand how the political regime operates in order to explain the ongoing spoliation of governance practices. The preceding chapter elaborated on how Putin and his subordinates sought to provide and regulate fundamental goods while looking after their narrow interests. Undoubtedly, the regime understands the need to institutionalize external monitoring and information-gathering mechanisms. However, as this chapter has demonstrated, no sizable improvements in health governance are likely because monitoring and oversight practices are faulty and exclude the top echelon of administrators from scrutiny.

Brian Taylor notes that in Putin's Russia, the principal prioritizes police patrols and internal oversight housed in the executive, despite that "a fire alarm approach is more likely to improve not only state capacity, but especially state quality" (see, for instance, Taylor 2011: 23, 30). This analysis rings true: the presidential administration introduced KPIs to monitor the performance of political appointees (such as governors) and bureaucrats alike. It also handled formally independent intermediaries, such as

ONF, which Putin instructed to help monitor the behavior of state officials. However, I think the pathology of oversight strategies is broader and rooted in the very nature of Russia's personalistic regime.

Fundamentally, personalistic regimes inhibit the formation of permanently lived organizations to diminish the credibility of their collective demands on the ruler and exposure of commitment deficits. It is not surprising then that Russian monitors of health, internal and external alike, underwent the process of political personalization in which the political weight of individual actors vis-à-vis the power of the organization itself increased over time, while the centrality and power of the group declined. This process plagued both internal and external organizations. Although the Kremlin supported external quasi-state entities, it also incentivized the loyal intermediaries to pursue their particularized and individualized self-interest while forcefully punishing the independent ones. In turn, intermediaries chose to abstain from suggesting course correction because it would signal disloyalty to Putin personally, and they generally avoid exposing pitfalls of the extant governance practices lest the public exposure of governmental malversation diminishes their boss's popularity.

Still, is Putin's ineffective system capable of change and improvement? After all, many of Putin's subordinates are worried about the poor state of governance in today's Russia. There is no need to disagree with German Gref's (currently the CEO of the largest Russian bank and, formerly, a reform-minded minister) assessment that the Russian state administration system is yet to be drastically improved should the government deliver on the grand promise of social betterment (see the opening epigraph). A short answer, all things being equal, is a hard no. Simply, because oversight activities, both internal and external, are imbricated into the system of personalized exchanges between the ruler and intermediaries, no oversight activities could improve how the Kremlin administers health governance. The failure is by design; Putin's regime disables mechanisms of independent and impartial policy oversight.

The subsequent chapter probes into health securitization, an optimizing strategy that multiple state agencies and social actors adopt to protect their contracts with the principal and ensure their corporate survival.

References

Abbott, K.W., et al. 2016. Two Logics of Indirect Governance: Delegation and Orchestration. *British Journal of Political Science* 46 (4): 719–729.

Abbott, K.W., et al. 2020. Competence–Control Theory: The Challenge of Governing through Intermediaries. In *The Governor's Dilemma: Indirect Governance Beyond Principals and Agents*, ed. K.W. Abbott, et al., 3–36. Oxford: Oxford University Press.

Abyzov, M. 2012. Komu i zachem nuzhno otkrytoe pravitel'stvo? *Radiostantsiya Ekho Moskvy*, 27 June.

Alisova, O. 2013. Gennadii Onishchenko - pobeditel' shprot i Borzhomi. *BBC*, 23 October.

Aleksandrov, O. 2013. Roszdravnadzor: shilo na mylo? *The Moscow Post*, 07 March.

Ananyev, M. 2018. Inside the Kremlin: The Presidency and Executive Branch. In *The New Autocracy: Information, Politics, and Policy in Putin's Russia*, ed. D. Treisman. Washington, D.C.: Brookings Institution.

Bogdanov, B. 2013. Onishchenko prizval Gruziyu zakryt' biolaboratoriyu SShA. *Rossiiskaya Gazeta*, 14 October.

Bindman, E., et al. 2019. NGOs and the Policy-making Process in Russia: The Case of Child Welfare Reform. *Governance* 32 (2): 207–222.

Burkhardt, F. 2020. Institutionalising Authoritarian Presidencies: Polymorphous Power and Russia's Presidential Administration. *Europe-Asia Studies* 73 (3): 472–504.

Bransten, J. 2005. Russia: New Public Chamber Criticized as Smokescreen. *RFE/RL*, 17 March.

Britskaya, T. 2019. Belye lentochki v belykh khalatakh. *Novaya Gazeta* No. 69, 28 June.

Chevtaeva, I. 2015. RF budet unichtozhat' sanktsionnye produkty iz Turtsii i Ukrainy. *Deutsche Welle*, 24 December.

Chazov, E.I. 2014. *Khorovod Smertei. Brezhnev, Andropov, Chernenko*. Moskva: Algoritm.

Crotty, J., S.M. Hall, and S. Ljubownikow. 2014. Post-Soviet Civil Society Development in the Russian Federation: The Impact of the NGO Law. *Europe-Asia Studies* 66 (8): 1253–1269.

Deutsche Welle. 2019. After 20 years, is Vladimir Putin's Untouchable Image Crumbling? 08 August.

Ershov, A., and O. Matveeva. 2022. EpiVakKorona - vrednaya pustyshka, registratsya kotoroi dolzhna byt' otozvana. *Meduza.io*, 26 January.

Flikke, G. 2018. Conflicting Opportunities or Patronal Politics? Restrictive NGO Legislation in Russia 2012–2015. *Europe-Asia Studies* 70 (4): 564–590.

Godovannik, L. 2018. Polivinilkhloridnyi skandal doshel do Peterburga. *Fontanka.ru*, 11 September.

GMPnews. 2019. ONF podgotovit predlozheniya po peresmotru mehanizma opredeleniya tsen na zakupki lekarstv, 09 August.

Henderson, C. 2011. Civil Society in Russia State-Society Relations in the Post-Yeltsin Era. *Problems of Post-Communism* 58 (3): 11–27.
Ignatova, O. 2018. Shtraf-menyu: V Rossii khotyat vvesti shtrafy za prodazhu i khranenie sanktsionnykh tovarov. *Rossiiskaya Gazeta* No. 96 (7559), 07 May.
Interfax. 2020. Roshal' predlozhil sobrat' gruppu medekspertov po Naval'nomu, 05 September.
Kotel'nikov, M. 2010. Tat'yana Golikova proizvela zachistku zdravookhraneniya ot imenitykh opponentov. *Skandaly.ru*, 01 June.
Kara-Murza, V. 2011. Spravedlivy li upreki doktora Leonida Roshalya v adres chinovnikov Minzdrava? *RFL/RL*, 20 April.
Kheifets, V., and K. Dyuryagina. 2020. Al'yans vrachei popytalis' razbit'. *Kommersant*, 03 April.
Kotova, M. 2018. Medizdeliya razbavyat konkurentsiei: ONF otodvigaet Medpolimerprom. *Kommersant*, 19 July.
Kruglikova, M. 2015. Natsmedpalata: Fond Zdorov'e provodit fragmentarnyi i tendentsioznyi analiz. *Vademecum*, 30 June.
Kriger, I. 2008. Dura lex: Gosudarstvo posledovatel'no vytesnyaet nekommercheskie organizatsii s pravovogo polya. *Novaya Gazeta*, 24 July.
Kryazhev, D. 2021. Pamyati Eleny Tel'novoi: istoriya odnoi fotografii. *Vademecum*, 29 July.
Kostarnova, N. 2021. Privivai, no proveryai: Populyarizatory dokazatel'noi meditsiny poprosili pravitel'stvo otkryt' dannye o vaktsinatsii. *Kommersant*, 02 Decemebr.
Kaye, R. 2006. Regulated (Self-)Regulation: A New Paradigm for Controlling the Professions? *Public Policy and Administration* 21 (3): 105–119.
Khabriev, R. 2014. Sozdavaya Roszdravnadzor, my sdelali stavku na pravil'nykh lyudei. *Vestnik Roszdravnadzora* No. 5.
Krivolapov, A. 2021. Deputaty oppozitsii vystupili s kritikoi optimizatsii zdravookhraneniya Orenburzh'ya. *Orendgrad.ru*, 26 January.
Kuravskii, P., M. Petrushko, and L. Chizhova. 2011. Minzdrav obidelsya na doktora Roshalya. *RFE/RL*, 19 April.
Kutuzov, R. 2015. Zdorovyi dukh. *Vademecum*, 07 September.
Kozlov, P., and M. Papchenkova. 2015. Kak Obshcherossiiskii narodnyi front vstroilsya v vertikal' vlasti. *Vedomosti*, 29 November.
Lassila, J. 2016. The Russian People's Front and Hybrid Governance Dilemma. In *Authoritarian Modernization in Russia: Ideas, Institutions, and Policies*, ed. V. Gel'man, 95–112. London: Routledge.
Malle, S. 2016. The All-Russian National Front – for Russia: A New Actor in the Political and Economic Landscape. *Post-Communist Economies* 28 (2): 199–219.
Melikyan, T. 2014. ONF god spustya: mulyazh partii ili strategicheskii proekt Kremlya? *Moskovskii Komsomolets*, 12 June.

McCubbins, M.D., and T. Schwartz. 1984. Congressional Oversight Overlooked: Police Patrols versus Fire Alarms. *American Journal of Political Science* 28 (1): 165–179.

Mishina, V. 2020. Lekarstvam dlya VICh-infitsirovannykh vredit COVID. *Kommersant*, 17 April.

Myl'nikov, M. 2018. ONF prizval pravitel'stvo rasshirit' reestr postavshchikov medizdelii iz PVH. *Vademecum*, 18 July.

Myl'nikov, M. 2019. Minzdrav propisal kriterii nezavisimoi ekspertizy kachestva medpomoshchi. *Vademecum*, 21 January.

ONF. 2019. Farmatsevticheskim proizvoditelyam nado predostavlyat' spetsial'nye vozmozhnosti dlya proizvodstva novykh preparatov, 20 September.

ONF. 2019a. V Penzenskoi oblasti posle sryva srokov stroitel'stva vozveden pervyi fel'dshersko-akusherskii punkt, 1 November.

ONF. 2019b. Blagodarya ONF v Kirovskoi oblasti bolee 70 patsientov s nachala 2019 goda poluchili zhiznenno neobkhodimye lekarstva, 5 December.

Owen, C., and E. Bindman. 2019. Civic Participation in a Hybrid Regime: Limited Pluralism in Policymaking and Delivery in Contemporary Russia. *Government and Opposition* 54 (1): 98–120.

Pakhomov, A. 2019. ONF: goszakupki lekarstv sryvayutsya iz-za novykh pravil formirovaniya nachal'noi tseny kontrakta. *Vademecum*, 04 February.

Pape, U. 2014. *The Politics of HIV/AIDS in Russia*. London: Routledge.

Pavlovsky, G. 2016. Ekspertogoniya. Memuar o Grazhdanskom forume—2001, *Gefter.ru*, 18 November. http://gefter.ru/archive/20078.

Pertsev, A. 2015. Privet iz GDR: Kak Kreml' primenit Narodnyi front. *Carnegie.ru*, 09 December.

Pertsev, A. 2017. Volodin vs. Kiriyenko: The Battle for Influence in Russia's Power Vertical. *Carnegie.ru*, 16 June.

Pertsev, A. 2020. Edinaya Rossiya pomenyaet nazvanie i obedinitsya s Narodnym frontom. *Meduza.io*, 25 February.

Ponomareva, V. 2021. Tsena placebo. Afera s EpiVak mozhet stoit' zhizni tysyacham lyudey. *The Insider*, 09 July.

Pushkarskaya, A. 2020. Nesmenyaemee Putina. *Zhurnal Kholod*, 13 November.

Putin, V. 2013. Konferentsiya Obshcherossiiskogo Narodnogo Fronta. Vladimir Putin prinyal uchastie v konferentsii Obshcherossiiskogo narodnogo fronta "Forum deistvii", 05 December. http://kremlin.ru/events/president/news/19787.

Putin, V. 2015. Vstupitel'noe slovo na plenarnom zasedanii Foruma Obshcherossiiskogo narodnogo fronta "Za kachestvennuyu i dostupnuyu meditsinu!" 07 September. http://kremlin.ru/events/president/news/50249.

RBC. 2015. Putin potreboval vyyasnit' prichiny uskorennogo rosta tsen na lekarstva, 7 September.

RBC. 2007. V Rossii poyavitsya megaregulyator potrebrynka, 9 February.

Reprintseva, Yu. 2016. Pochemu gosudarstvo obyavlyaet bortsov s VICh inoagentami. *Novaya Gazeta*, 09 August.
Richter, J. 2009. Putin and the Public Chamber. *Post-Soviet Affairs* 25 (1): 39–65.
Roshal, L. 2011. Zachem nuzhno samoregulirovanie? *Medportal.ru*, 13 April.
Rodionova, A., and K. Sedov. 2013. Ustav ot edineniya. *Vademecum*, 01 July.
Rybina, L. 2010. Nikolai Yurgel' rasskazyvaet. *Novaya Gazeta*, 10 February.
Sedov, K. 2011. Navalny vglyadelsya v monitoring. *Farmatsevticheskii Vestnik* No. 33, 20 October.
Sedov, K. 2014. Britvy titanov. *Vademecum*, 14 January.
Serkov, D., M. Alehina, and P. Zvezdina. 2018. Minzdrav preduprezhdayut: v SKR poyavyatsya otdely po vrachebnym oshibkam. *RBC*, 29 November.
Shubina, D. 2017. Natsmedpalata poluchila prezidentskii grant na zashchitu medikov ot SMI. *Vademecum*, 02 August.
Solopov, M. 2015. Pravitel'stvo zadumalos' o sozdanii megaregulyatora na potrebrynke. *RBC*, 08 September.
Skokova, Y., et al. 2018. The Non-profit Sector in Today's Russia: Between Confrontation and Co-optation. *Europe-Asia Studies* 70 (4): 531–563.
Tagaeva, L. 2013. Pochemu Putin sdal Onishchenko. *Republic.ru*, 25 October.
Taylor, B.D. 2011. *State Building in Putin's Russia: Policing and Coercion after Communism*. New York: Cambridge University Press.
Trifonova, A. 2018. Vrachebnym oshibkam podbirayut tsenu. *Kommersant*, 25 July.
Tumakova, I. 2021a. Operatsya «E»: My vam rasskazhem, chto poluchaet s EpiVakKoronoi chelovek, chto - krolik, a chto - razrabotchiki vaktsiny. *Novaya Gazeta* No. 60, 04 June.
Tumakova, I. 2021b. EpiVakAfera: V privivochnykh kabinetakh nachali zamenyat' vaktsinu Sputnik preparatom EpiVakKorona, ne preduprezhdaya patsientov. *Novaya Gazeta* No. 67, 23 June.
Vedomosti. 2017. V vine iz Chernogorii nashli pestitsidy, 31 May.
Vinokurova, E. 2016. Putin poprosil ne otkryvat' okhotu na elitu. *Znak.ru*, 25 January.
Vinokurova, E. 2018. ONF snova v poiske sebya. *Znak.ru*, 14 June.
Vinokurov, A. et al. 2019. Vitse-gubernatora prizvali na front: Mikhail Kuznetsov mozhet reanimirovat' ONF. *Kommersant*, 12 September.
VSP. 2021. Aktual'nye Problemy Rossiiskogo Zdravookhraneniya v 2020 godu v otsenkakh patsientov i patsientskikh NKO. *Vserossiiskii soyuz patsientov*, 26 April.https://vspru.ru/senter/issledovaniia-analitika-mneniia/issledovaniia.
Whitmore, S. 2010. Parliamentary Oversight in Putin's Neo-patrimonial State. Watchdogs or Show-dogs? *Europe-Asia Studies* 62 (6): 999–1025.
Yurgel, N. 2014. Roszdravnadzor—odin iz kraeugol'nykh kamnei v sisteme natsional'noi biobezopasnosti Rossii. *Vestnik Roszdravnadzora* No. 5.
Zvezdina, P. 2016. Boginya zachistki. *Farmatsevticheskii Vestnik* No. 19, 06 June.

Zvezdina, P. 2018. Roszdravnadzor poimal 56 aptek na prodazhe zapreshchennykh lekarstv. *RBC*, 22 February.

CHAPTER 5

Securitizing the Epidemic: Ideological Adaptations and Illiberal Meanings

[They want to] liquidate Russia, there is a political task to liquidate Russia through drugs and narcotic addiction and HIV infection.
 —Chief Sanitary Doctor of the Russian Federation, Gennady Onishchenko, presenting his report on HIV/AIDS in Russia to the State Duma, April 9, 2009

In terms of its strategic impact, drug production can be compared with weapons of mass destruction, which can, in the shortest possible time, lead the institutions of the state against which drug aggression is unleashed to complete collapse and degradation.
 —FSKN Director, Viktor Ivanov, April 2015

INTRODUCTION

The scourge of HIV/AIDS (Human Immunodeficiency Virus/Acquired Immunodeficiency Syndrome) poses an objective and imminent danger to the population's well-being. Still, after several decades of fighting HIV/AIDS, the matter is less of an extraordinary human security crisis that requires unprecedented health intervention than a routine matter of public health. Last twenty years, Russian health authorities were not idle and did not ignore the issue. Still, they gradually started offering public utterances, which infused the Russian struggle against the epidemic with unique patterns of political significance. The language describing the domestic epidemic gave a strong impression that state actors settled on the notion that the origins, nature, and implications of the epidemic belong to the realm of decaying public morals, intensifying geopolitical confrontation, and the ontological insecurity of the Russian state, not public health.

The quotes that open this chapter belong to two very prominent individuals who enjoy proximity to Putin, and they capture the essence of how many top-tier state administrators and public figures think about HIV/AIDS. These are more than random quotes any indefatigable reader of the official interviews and statements can put together; an unwearied observer of more recent public statements can find similar utterances concerning the epidemic of coronavirus as well. This peculiar discourse of securitization a-la Rus now appears in the belligerent interpretation of another instance of a profound public health crisis. Speaks Valentina Matvienko: "We dealt with COVID better than others, made a vaccine, and we have the most modern weapons. This haunts our partners -- they are once again launching unsubstantiated stories made according to well-known patterns. [They do so] in order to contain Russia and subjugate it. We can't relax" (Matvienko 2020). By "partners," the long-serving Chairwoman of the Federation Council means Russia's external enemies, and by "stories and patterns," she means an external exposé of the wrongdoings or shortcomings in Russian health governance. None of these statements help mitigate public health crises, and yet they seem to dominate the official narratives of disease. There is much indication that the illiberal meaning is at the core of the official health discourse, but what are we to make of these statements, and of what is this all an instance?

This chapter proposes that the observed ideological adaptations stem from the fact that because the ruler has no institutional constraints to his administrative power and is not submitted to the checks of any permanent organizations, all state agencies and societal players involved in the system of governance are remarkably vulnerable to termination, reorganization, neglect, or divestment. Ultimately, the Russian approach to talking about health issues in public (and, broadly, connecting public health issues to politics) reflects actors' desire to protect their contracts with the autocratic principal by creating political value-added for him. Elites not only tap into Putin's illiberal and anti-Western ideas but also give credence to the regime's intensifying illiberal posture. They interpret Putin's self-serving commitment to traditional values and conflict-oriented geopolitical musings as a mandate to find and eradicate ontological threats to the country instead of receiving a mandate to eliminate the public health crisis. Creating facts on the ground for the ruler goes hand in hand with agents' underperformance, and securitization thus becomes advantageous for agents as a self-seeking gaming strategy.

None of this qualifies as good health governance practices. Little wonder, today, the country has fewer tools to constructively respond to a generalized stage of the HIV/AIDS epidemic. The roots of all this inhere in the core features of personalistic authoritarianism. The transactional nature of tacit contracts between principals and agents incentivizes most influential participants in the Russian system of health governance to satisfy their principals if they want to protect their place in the domestic political hierarchy. The focus of this chapter is not only on top elites but also on the meso-level bureaucrats, who actively participate in illiberal ideological adaptations on the account of their particular vulnerability to the threats of disuse, neglect, or dismissal from the internal organizational hierarchy. Adaptations were decentralized and gradually cultivated intersubjective consensus across different levels of aggregation. Widespread ideological adaptations triggered optimizing governance responses which plagued domestic efforts to apply international recommendations and best practices. All this makes eradication of HIV/AIDS an uncertain endeavor with.

The first section explains how a distinct configuration of conditions within Russia's personalism prompted agencies to securitize health issues while adopting and disseminating non-evidence-based solutions to the epidemic. Three empirical sections that follow trace three distinct, but at some point interwoven, stories wherein the main actors in the multi-level health architecture deploy the securitization discourse to ensure their informal contracts with the principal. The second section looks at drug enforcers' efforts to protect the agency from termination and their simultaneous efforts to construct an exonerating discourse of securitization amid an unfolding story of the agency's underperformance. The third section turns to discuss the Ministry of Health's attempts to deploy the securitization discourse to protect itself against external and internal critics that sought to reform or disband the ministry. The fourth section explores the Moscow Patriarchy's role in detailing, crystallizing, and spreading the securitizing discourse with the state as the referent object of security.

Each empirical section of this chapter delineates the sequence of events, from massive corporate vulnerability crises aggravated by the inability to show unequivocally positive health outcomes of agents' work to the incremental construction of agency-friendly and exclusively proper knowledge regarding the epidemic. Although some elements of the resultant health securitization discourse had circulated in society before the agencies' inability to deal with the health crisis became evident, I pinpoint specific moments when domestic actors chose to privilege them as integral to the public representations of their work. Establishing such a sequence is pivotal for the process-tracing methodology adopted here (George and Bennett 2005).

Elites Adapt: Illiberal Meanings and Corporate Vulnerability

In Putin's Russia, ideological discussions resurface when the regime needs them to bolster its legitimacy with the masses. Unlike tacit contracts and personalized exchanges, ideology has little purchase in ensuring the individual elites' consent and obedience, while genuine ideological commitments that impinge on personalized exchanges and bargains could destabilize the regime. However, makeshift ideological frameworks are replete in Putin's Russia, and they genuinely express the ruler's ideological predilections. Unwearied scholars of Putin's discourse will find many significant nuances in his ideological outlook. Still, anti-Westernism and illiberalism are the top ideas on which Putin's romantic sensibilities hinge (Kravtsov 2015: 68–73; Taylor 2018: 15–17, 40). Sergey Medvedev pinpoints Putin's speech on September 4, 2004, (Putin gave a state of the nation address in the wake of the Beslan school hostage crisis in the town of Beslan, North Ossetia) and his subsequent meeting with journalists as the foundational moment. At that juncture in time, the president articulated his belief that Western countries, still informed by the logic of security competition, "pull strings here so that we don't raise our heads internationally" (Medvedev 2004). Three years later, Putin confirmed his heavy conspiratorial suspicions about Western intentions to weaken and demolish Russia in the so-called Munich speech (Baev 2017).

At that time, Putin's political operatives elaborated the president's core ideas, contributing to the development of a normative and moral mission for the country. Starting in 2005, Vladislav Surkov (in office, 1999–2011), misleadingly credited with being "the hidden author of Putinism" (Pomerantsev 2014), proposed three ideological pillars (such as statism, developmentalism, and great-power imagery), commonly known as "the sovereign democracy" doctrine. In his speeches and essays, Surkov consistently pointed fingers at the proponents of liberal values and human rights as a destructive and un-Russian force. In his so-called secret report to the General Council of United Russia on June 17, 2005, he asserted that liberals always failed to pull Russia out of the political turmoil and fed off social chaos (Surkov 2005; Kosachev 2006). In the ensuing years, many prominent members of United Russia echoed Surkov's sentiment, lamenting that the West does not fully understand Russia's uniqueness (*samobytnost'*), does not appreciate Russia as a civilization in a class by itself, and is responsible for the country's distrust toward Europe (see, for instance, Luzhkov 2006; Kosachev 2007). Far from being inconsequential, these carefully constructed illiberal utterances shaped Putin's approach to governance and functioned as obstacles to the diffusion of international health norms and best practices (Kravtsov 2015). As evident from Putin's patter at the 2020 meeting of the Valdai discussion club, the main points of the doctrine linger in his political outlook and reveal his idiosyncratic views (Putin 2020). Later on, the plot thickens.

The regime took further steps on the road of illiberal soul-searching at the moment when the Bolotnaya protests against the heavy-handed electoral manipulations and fraud that erupted during the winter of 2011–2012 threatened the regime's legitimacy (see Hale 2015: 282–291). Putin's need to maintain high levels of popular legitimacy in a rapidly modernizing society (exemplified by Pussy Riot's punk prayer and the subsequent scandalous criminal persecution) required him to push back against the insolent free-thinkers with the discourse of traditional moral values (Sharafutdinova 2014; Wilkinson 2014; Robinson 2017; Edenborg 2020; Waller 2021), of which conservative securitization of the epidemic eventually became a part. References 'Sharafutdinova (2014) and Waller (2021)' are cited in the text but not provided in the reference list. Please provide the respective references in the list or delete these citations.Error during converting author query response. Please check the eproofing link or feedback pdf for details

Allegedly an avid reader and purported admirer of conservative thinkers of the past (Snyder 2018), Putin quickly discovered obsolete philosophical references to justify his social conservatism and anti-Westernism and dubbed them "spiritual clamps" (*skrepy*) that unite all Russians in an organic whole. Nikolay Berdyaev (1874–1948), Aleksey Losev (1893–1988), Ivan Ilyin (1883–1954), and Lev Gumilyov (1912–1992) are on an incomplete list of those conservative thinkers Putin has habitually mentioned in his annual presidential addresses. Contrary to Timothy Snyder's interpretation that these thinkers' ideas genuinely inform Putin's ideological outlook and structure his political behavior, there are few reasons to believe that Putin possesses deep ideological predilections and truly reveres or even reads these authors.

Never mind that the debates about the role of ideas in structuring political actions are entertaining and analytically necessary. What is more consequential than being lured by the hopelessly out-of-date musings is that the conservative voices offer much instrumental and ornamental value for Putin, helping him maintain the foundations of informational autocracy. Instrumentally, conservative discourse justifies further attenuation of liberal democracy, deflects criticism for poor national human rights record (Horvath 2016), and provides a lexicon to speak about geopolitical warfare with the liberal West (Melville 2017, 2018). It could also be used to counterblast domestic vulnerabilities (Tsygankov 2016) and establish a new social contract in which social modernization is sacrificed for the sake of state security (Ostbo 2017). Ornamentally, appealing to the thinkers of the long-gone past could exalt presidential musings and make them appear more authentic and profound than they are.

An astute observer of Russian politics, Catherine Belton, discusses several rationales of Putin's ideological turn (Belton 2020: 258, 260, 420–421). At best, the regime adopted conservative ideology in order to present to the masses as a unifying creed and the expression of national identity in the context when Putin's legitimacy was sliding. At worst, Orthodox/conservative/illiberal values seemed to be adopted as instruments of domination that would help exculpate the regime from any wrongdoings and, in addition, provide a rationalization for the influence operations in the near abroad on the eve of the invasion in Ukraine. According to Belton's sources, unnamed tycoons and devout Orthodox believers who had intimate access to Putin personally, conservative ideology "was conveniently designed to make serfs out of Russian again, and keep them in the Middle Ages" and that "[T]he authorities cannot be guilty of anything. They serve by absolute right." An examination of actual practice—when referencing the hurt feelings of the believers allowed the unscrupulous law enforcement functionaries to prosecute the regime's political opponents—licenses the ideations of Belton's interlocutors. In any case, ideology in Putin's Russia appears to be an instrument of power rather than a deeply internalized and sincerely held system of beliefs that could shape state officials' behavior.

Equally troubling, Putin's conservative and illiberal ideas resonated with diverse audiences, ranging from the proponents of statism, militarism, and obscurantism of the Soviet mold to the young persons who tried to compensate for their lack of social sciences background with eagerness to apply ill-defined conservative principles to make sense of current global and local affairs. The Notebooks on Conservatism, another notable venue, published several thinking pieces penned by persons with proximity to Putin and much higher in the hierarchy of power than most of the articulated audiences. The Notebooks gave a platform for many commentators who "exposed" the ubiquity of external threats and highlighted the importance of upholding traditional (moral-spiritual) values to protect Russian national interest (see, for instance, Morozov 2014; Kiselev 2014). In these circumstances, various outfits—such as Izborsky Club or Tsargrad-TV—provided a basis for establishing an illusion that conservative ideas had engulfed the entire nation (Laruelle 2015, 2016, 2020) while, in reality, they spewed mere pseudo-intellectual schlock.

Domestic judgments regarding the value of illiberal discourses predictably vary due to observers' normative orientations, but their quality and intellectual reach are not very satisfying. The beating heart of the discourse is the notion of ontological insecurity, which highlights the rivalry between Russia, the champion of authentic, time-honored values, deeply ensconced in the national psyche, and the decaying West, the sponsor of immoral norms and deviant behavior. The earliest variant of this simple formula appeared in Nikita Mikhalkov's writings (2010), and the latest iteration of an equally simple but more passionate diatribe is in Konstantin Bogomolov's newspaper publication (2021). Because the notion of conservative values is an entirely artificial construction, the Kremlin cannot help but assert ownership of risible formulas and make them mandatory for non-elites. In January 2022, the Ministry of Culture prepared a draft, "Fundamentals of the State Policy for the Preservation and Strengthening of Traditional Russian Spiritual and Moral Values," which offered an official law-like expression of the regime's illiberalism. According to the draft, "Threat to traditional values is the activity of extremist and terrorist organizations, the actions of the United States and its allies, transnational corporations, foreign non-profit organizations… The activity of the conductors of a destructive ideology objectively contradicts the national interests of the Russian Federation." What really matters is not how intellectually incisive the conservative argument is but how well it justifies the authoritarian rejection of liberalism and civil liberties.

Even more so, any player opposing the Kremlin on esthetical, cultural, or political grounds could now be viewed as a public enemy.

The content of traditional or illiberal discourses helps explain the substance of HIV/AIDS securitization, such as commitment to conservative prevention policy and placing the blame for failing to stop the spread of infection on the West. State agencies blamed the spread of HIV/AIDS on the West and portrayed international recommendations as weapon-like instruments of Western aggression against the country. Although many discursive resources to catapult securitizing rhetoric to the levels of high political prominence existed all along at the societal level, they became valuable only when Putin settled on the conservative illiberal posturing. To be sure, multiple arguments that downplayed the gravity of the epidemiological situation, suggested that HIV/AIDS was a Western foreign policy weapon, and highlighted Western evidence-based prevention strategies as a security threat for the country had been circulating in Russia well before the Bolotnaya protests. However, only after Putin's rhetorical moves did the agencies widely employ these arguments (often engaging fringe commentators) and thus turned disconnected and directionless arguments into a coherent whole.

The question is why jumping onto the questionable narrative and adhering to it resolutely became so prevalent. It is easy to interpret illiberal declarations as loyalists' conceptual tools deployed to develop or rally mass support for Putin's claim to power. Nobody should expect propaganda professionals, such as Vladimir Soloviev, or propaganda outlets like Russia Today, to offer any responsible depictions of the pandemic. However, unusual is that vital public health topics became reinterpreted along ideological lines and strongly embraced by a multitude of state agencies and top state administrators, for whom policy prevarications were not a job requirement. After all, only the Russian Orthodox Church (ROC) could be rightfully seen as a natural carrier of conservative and illiberal values among all participants in health governance (Agadjanian 2017).

The standard line of reasoning presents ideological formulations as directed toward non-elites. Elites communicate conservative values and flesh out illiberal posture to create bonds between non-elites and the ruler (Robinson 2020) and develop a new national identity (Stepanova 2015). As discussed in the introductory chapter, rulers often find it in their best interest to construct ideological frameworks in order to complement material inducements and redirect attention from poor performance.

Although the percentage of nondemocracies with an official ideology, mandatory for all citizens, is low (Guriev and Treisman 2019: 110), ideology-like frameworks endure in many places. They generate norms and make meanings intended to create non-material sources of compliance among non-elites and nurture grassroots sensibilities favorable to the regime. In this respect, the Kremlin's illiberal posturing is functionally similar to other personalistic regimes' efforts to construct an appealing ideological narrative (as it happened, for example, in John Magufuli's Tanzania, see Paget 2020; Talleh Nkobou and Ainslie 2021).

What is unique about how ideological pronouncements function within Russia's personalistic system is that elites readily adopt conservative attitudes to protect their contracts with the ruler and justify their domination over society. Although antithetical to the public interest, ideological adaptations are essential tools in the arsenal of state agents and social actors to reassure Putin of subordination and loyalty. It appears that a wide range of agents, intermediaries, and societal actors adopt Putin's ideas and values. It is easy to observe that Putin's discovery of inward-looking traditional Russian values informed and determined the content of HIV/AIDS securitization across agencies and societal players. Federal narcotic agency (Federal'naya Sluzhba Rossiiskoi Federatsii po Kontroluy za Oborotom Narkotikov, The Federal Drug Control Service of the Russian Federation, hereafter FSKN), joined by the Ministry of Health (Minzdrav) and the Orthodox religious authorities, jumped on the opportunity to securitize the pandemic along those presidential lines. Other authors reached similar conclusions, arguing that illiberal entrepreneurialism or conservative public pronouncements indicate signaling behavior that demonstrates the elite's loyalty and usefulness to the ruler (Waller 2021: 3). Devoted Vassals must comply with the ruler's ideological posturing on account of having a sense of obligation to the ruler rather than for moral or normative reasons, but this line of reasoning should not be carried too far. What is more consequential for personalistic politics is that elites creatively interpret their formal mandates according to the ruler's ideological wishes giving rise to adaptive, optimizing responses that seek to prevent neglect, divestment of resources, and agency termination.

Consistent with Terry Moe's seminal article (1989: 282–284), bureaucracies that face the problem of uncertainty must seek protection from abrupt termination or arbitrary reorganization. In other words, agencies must shield themselves from corporate uncertainty. Corporate vulnerabilities arise when agents believe that the threat of termination is credible or severe reputational damages are unavoidable. Russian agencies' vulnerability to termination, restructuring, and organizational weakening inhere in Putin's approach to governance. There are no institutional checks and balances in personalistic systems that could otherwise protect bureaucratic agencies. Organizational restructuring, agency termination, and arbitrary changes in agencies' missions and mandates are not surprising, given the principal's dominant position in Russia's political system. The incompleteness of contracts and threats to agency survival are essential to the principal's control over subordinates.

In the Russian case, the sources of bureaucratic vulnerability persisted over time: top dominant actors failed to alleviate bureaucracies' fears regarding their corporate futures, while Putin and Medvedev alike tended to radically reorganize the bureaucratic structure and alter agencies' mandates to fit their political designs (Ananyev 2018; Gel'man 2017). There are many (some of them are idiosyncratic) reasons why the contacts remain incomplete. In some cases, mandate ambiguity (newly established agencies' functions duplicated those of the well-established rival ministries or overlapped with them) presented both threats to corporate survival and opportunities to ensure it. Indeed, the government failed to delineate the division of responsibilities between the drug enforcement agency and the police, kept several health surveillance organs and the Ministry of Health in a tug of turf wars, and chose, under the title of National Priority Projects, to bypass the Ministry of Health in order to modernize health infrastructure and improve particular health outcomes, such as maternal health, that were deemed especially salient for the overall population health. Only some agencies (Rosgvardiya, the Federal Security Service, FSB) are more secure at the corporate level than others (the Ministry of Health; the Federal Penitentiary Service, FSIN; the Federal Drug Control Service, FSKN) because they are needed to suppress dissent if the contested elections occur. Those less secure must provide value-added beyond simple gaming strategies that prevent domestic observers and ordinary patients from observing the regime's governance failures. Broadly speaking, although bureaucratic redundancy is not necessarily wasteful (Ting 2003), it implies that the principal might terminate a redundant agency without inflicting severe damages on the state's routine operations.

Internal conflicts accompany the incompleteness of contracts. All agencies under investigation are involved in situational conflicts with society, which might broadly undermine the popularity of the personalistic regime in general since these conflicts expose the fundamental weakness of the regime's ability to govern effectively. Situational conflicts are hardly avoidable, given the multiplicity of divergent interests combined with underperformance and the Russian state's low capacity in general (Hashim 2017). It is difficult to predict how Putin will respond to these conflicts, and his reactions could be subjective through and through. Sometimes, Putin could be pretty accommodating. In 2009, he explained his approach to intra-regime conflicts: "In principle, there is nothing wrong with the conflict as such. It just has to lead to an optimal solution [of managing an issue]. And if it is possible to use the conflict to make the situation more manageable so that administrative decisions are more balanced, thoughtful, and calculated, this is good. And if the conflict ultimately leads to squabbles and the destruction of the system, it means that people lack intelligence, experience, and character. Here, the importance of all three components is about the same" (Putin 2009b).

However, sometimes he allows intra-elite conflicts to unravel. Mere two years after the Russian drug enforcement agency—a key actor in HIV/AIDS governance—began its operations, the legislators gathered to discuss FSKN's unimpressive performance and recommended its termination. The head of the federal narcotic agency could never conceal his intrigues which fueled public conflicts with other representatives of law enforcement agencies and their lobbyists in the State Duma. These conflicts were dangerous to Putin because they exposed hitherto concealed systematic corruption and illegal activities of those supposed to uphold the law. Democratic whistleblowing, which in a personalistic regime looks more like exposing dirty laundry, gets one fired, as the first head of FSKN was soon to figure out. It follows that different protective strategies, as duly adopted by the second head of the drug enforcement agency, were in order.

Another core actor, the Ministry of Health and Social Development (hereafter Minzsotsdrav, as the ministry was officially known until 2012), all too often found itself in the middle of perpetual conflicts, if not scandals. Its inability to manage its main assigned tasks drew internal (street-level bureaucrats) and external (health activists and public health experts) disapproval that culminated in the agency's perceived need to constrain its critics (Kravtsov 2015: 115–118). Severe situational conflicts included the prolonged battle between Zurabov and the legislature and between the Ministry of Health central apparatus and health activists who in 2010 initiated mass protests in response to the ministry's inability to supply drugs for all patients who needed them. The Russian Orthodox Church is the third leading health actor discussed here. Notably, at the time of Patriarch Alexy II's death in 2008, the Church was institutionally weak (Papkova 2011) and had yet to prove its political usefulness to Putin. Because its leaders value what Putin has to offer, they heed his desires, as they depend on Putin's favors and privileges.

It follows that state agencies involved in health must provide value to their principal beyond simple gaming strategies and mere imitation of effective health governance. Basic gaming techniques, discussed in Chapter 2, are frequently sufficient for top administrators to survive in their extant positions, but molding their public image, mission, and organizational routines in line with Putin's quasi-ideology is a new level of subservience and an expedient strategy of corporate survival. The transition from situational usefulness (such as justifying the president's political moves in geopolitical confrontation) implies that agency leaders must find a more systematic approach in which the whole agency appears to support the principal. Core domestic actors involved in the health sector, including FSKN, the Ministry of Health, and the Church, adopted securitization discourse to create value for Putin as corporate entities. Ideological adaptations to illiberal posture also allow Putin's subordinates to exculpate their inefficiencies, while eager propagandists use ideological constructs to blame the regime's malperformance on its opponents, whether real or invented.

The necessity to respond to incomplete contracts, inherent vulnerabilities, and intensifying internal conflicts strongly incentivizes public officials and senior bureaucrats to "go public" proactively and defend agencies against their critics by framing the issue in their interests. Most actors sought to benefit from practicing "megaphone governance" as they shaped their public utterances to convince Putin of their overall political value for the Kremlin. Besides predictably mirroring Putin's policy preferences, actors also create facts on the ground that reify his illiberal vision. In the age of media proliferation, all bureaucratic leaders govern in public (Grube 2019: 29), even those in nondemocracies. HIV/AIDS is likely to be a front-page story, and commanding the public's attention, as well as shaping the public's perception of the issue, is preferable to silence, which is disadvantageous as it allows the media to focus on the agencies' underperformance and even be critical of Putin's policy course. Such a move allows actors to preempt the image of their failure.

Although the picture painted above is rationalist, it is compatible with the constructivist rendition of securitization. According to the constructivist line of thinking, health-related actors and state agencies are corporate entities. They possess self-interests (organizational survival within the overarching bureaucratic structure, or "physical" survival) and identity (the ability to distinguish themselves from other agencies and nonstate actors. Agents also exhibit the need to maintain shared knowledge to hold unity and act intentionally (the ability of bureaucracies to act on behalf of themselves and pursue interests given their environmental constraints). Corporate vulnerability elevates the need to demarcate enemies and supplant the external accusatory narratives of underperformance with self-affirming public representations of the agency's work (Klotz and Lynch 2007: 45, 65), in this case, constructing a corporate-friendly discourse regarding the existential dangers of an epidemiological threat. This behavior is consistent with the constructivist hypothesis that maintaining shared knowledge is crucial for upholding the sense of corporate identity (Wendt 1999: 215).

As this section suggests, the distinct conditions working together—Putin's illiberal ideations and pervasive organizational vulnerability—account for the resultant securitization of the epidemic. Then, the need to create value for the boss is the engine that drives the process of securitization. This optimizing response triggers mission drifts, which compromise the attainment of substantive goals. Initial mandate ambiguities allowed agencies to change their missions (mission leap) while entering the public domain proactively and leveling specific justifications for the necessity of doing so. Thus, FSKN and ROC, in their mission leap, decided to include HIV/AIDS in their work, even though eliminating AIDS was not entirely congruent with their chief mission or issued mandate. FSKN rightfully became a securitization entrepreneur among all those, as its attempt to securitize health was in the others' vanguard. Adopting expedient ideologies provides a correlation of political goals between the principal and agents, but it could not increase agents' competence, let alone the sense of professional ethos and public-service mission. The question remains whether creating ideological value for the boss is indeed an advantageous instrument in alleviating corporate vulnerability. To a certain extent, this strategy worked as intended. Viktor Ivanov, the director of the disbanded FSKN, prolonged its lifespan by nearly a decade. Minzdrav's central apparatus consolidated its bureaucratic position vis-a-vis health surveillance organs and internal critics. The Moscow Patriarchy remains in Putin's good graces and takes on greater social significance.

In summary, this section described the main ingredients leading to the self-serving strategies of securitizing the epidemic in Putin's personalistic regime. Broadly and consistent with the overall line of arguing in this book, agencies' propensity to develop securitization discourses reflects an intentional optimizing response to their institutional setting. Three sections that follow, respectively, explore securitization dynamics developed by three core actors, FSKN, the Ministry of Health, and the Orthodox Church. These actors engulfed the public in all too many statements lionizing their resistance against those who wished to eliminate Russia by subversion: spreading the infection, promoting alternative lifestyles, and legitimizing narcotic addiction. My discussion highlights not so much how exactly the agents support Putin's geopolitical imagery as their public behavior (issuing media releases, doing interviews, sponsoring ultra-conservative opinions and conspiratorial voices on the epidemic), thereby simultaneously creating value for their principal and concealing their underperformance.

FSKN: HIV/AIDS as a Case of Narcoagression

This section looks at drug enforcers' efforts to solve the problem of their underperformance and their subsequent efforts to construct an exonerating discourse of securitization amid a credible threat of the agency's termination.

Quickly after its creation, FSKN moved to establish itself as one of the leading players in HIV/AIDS governance and chose to securitize the epidemic. Plagued by uncertainty about its future, FSKN entered the policy arena to alleviate its bureaucratic redundancy and offer Putin political value. It prioritized the fight against narcotics but riled up against harm reduction, rehabilitative measures, and independent nonstate actors. The agency securitized HIV/AIDS and the widespread narcotic addiction as a means to an end: it helped the agency exculpate itself from the accusations of underperformance and survive as a corporate agency amid the calls for its termination.

From 2003 through 2016, throughout the entire period of its existence, the Federal Drug Control Service was in turmoil. Organizationally, it evolved from the Ministry of Internal Affairs, which has traditionally been one of Russia's core law enforcement agencies, but its personnel and material resources came mainly from the previously disbanded tax police. Unlike its rough equivalents in other countries, Gosnarkokontrol was not originally designed to perform the duties of an elite drug enforcement force whose mission otherwise would have been to eliminate the nationwide nets of narcotic distributors and fight transnational cartels. Instead of concentrating its efforts on destroying the supply side, since the onset of its creation, the agency predominantly focused on essential policing functions, fighting drugs on the streets, and thus directly competed with the counter-narcotic branch of the regular police force and duplicated its work, often with less than plausible results. Merely two years into the agency's existence, in November 2004, the Russian legislators gathered to discuss its unimpressive performance and recommended its termination.

Viktor Cherkesov, the agency's first director, weathered numerous scandals that accompanied the agency's routine work. In 2004, the agency undertook massive raids on animal hospitals and harassed veterinarians who lawfully used ketamine, the synthetic opioid. However, the courts found only one individual guilty of illegal possession of the substance due to those raids. Although Cherkesov was seemingly able to defuse the ensuing public outrage by offering a public apology for his inexperience and over-zealousness (Stenin 2004), in October 2007, the arrests of several senior officers implicated in corruption brought the agency under public and administrative scrutiny and precipitated Cherkesov's fall.

Against the backdrop of Cherkesov's failure, the agency's new director, Viktor Ivanov, raised political stakes. Part of his strategy was to convince his audiences that Gosnarkokontrol's role in stopping the spread of the human immunodeficiency virus from rapidly spreading in the country was pivotal (Ivanov 2016). The cardinal measure advocated by Ivanov was seductively simple: to punish IV-drug users and extinguish the demand for narcotics in the country. It is true that even in 2016, 55% of all new infections happened as a result of sharing hypodermic needles among IV-drug users. Ivanov and the agency's spokespeople habitually ignored the notion that harm-reduction programs could mitigate the spread of the infection to others and that non-injected methadone treatment (opioid substitution therapy) could decrease sharing of contaminated needles. Pragmatic and evidence-based responses to the disease as a public health crisis disappeared from the agency's action repertoire.

Furthermore, while Russian drug enforcers highlighted potential medical side-effects of harm-reduction programs and maintained that the distribution of syringes promoted drug use, they remained unclear on which alternative rehabilitative and preventative measures would be desirable. The practical balance sheet of FSKN's performance was far from perfect: the consumption of the controlled substances increased, and the intravenous injection of drugs remained the leading vector of the infection spread. Thus, Russia remained the hotbed of the generalized epidemic, which was on the verge of being unstoppable.

In principle, FSKN could have learned how to improve its performance. Despite a generally unfavorable background, some Russian civil society organizations have collaborated with state agencies at the local and regional levels, especially in Tomsk, St. Petersburg, Kaliningrad, and Moscow. There is anecdotal evidence that street-level officers learned about naloxone, a vital medication intended to reverse an opioid overdose, and tolerated harm-reduction outreach efforts. However, for the system-level officers working with health activists was not desirable politically. To a loyal bureaucrat, harm-reduction outreach programs looked like some self-appointed individuals distributing needles, syringes, and condoms at shady city spots. Regrettably, Andrey Ryl'kov's Foundation (Fond Andreya Ryl'kova, hereafter FAR), which focuses on harm reduction and is openly critical of Putin's regime, had failed to prioritize teaching the drug police about the public health dimension of narcotic consumption. As a result, Gosnarkokontrol felt antagonized and considered its work against the spread of HIV sabotaged.

Further scandals revealed that some FSKN officers consumed confiscated narcotics in their field offices. Later on, in the Spring of 2010, in the remote region of Perm, the agents lost (or perhaps sold on the black market) about two tons of metilbenzilketon, a precursor used in the illegal production of amphetamines. In the ensuing months, the then-President Dmitry Medvedev fired seven generals, heads of the agency's regional divisions. Astonishing cases of fabrication of evidence and extortion perpetrated by the FSKN officers in Ul'yanovsk trucked public attention in 2011 (Titov 2011).

Against this background, the key FSKN agents jumped on the opportunity to construct a discourse in which the scourge of the HIV/AIDS epidemic appeared as part and parcel of a comprehensive attack on Russia. To subjugate Russia, Russia's geopolitical rivals and the agents of foreign influence condoned the use of narcotics and promoted harm-reduction therapy. By doing so, Russia's enemies undermined the fruitful domestic efforts to stop the spread of HIV and unleashed an assault on domestic political stability.

Further, against the standard account of the Ukrainian Revolution of Dignity, which put an end to the corrupt and ruthless rule of Viktor Yanukovich in 2014, Ivanov claimed that the harm-reduction proponents were instrumental in overthrowing the legitimate government in Kyiv. He also noted that the Ukrainian nationalists recruited drug users to join death squads that operated in predominantly Russian-speaking separatist regions (FSKN 2015). The reporters of Rossiiskaya Gazeta, an uncritical pulpit of the federal government, favorably covered the drug agency's arguments. It reported that the spread of harm-reduction programs in Ukraine led to a sharp decline in the population's health, spurred criminal activities, and increased the number of addicts twofold (Vinnik 2015). The implication was that the countries heeding Western recommendations endanger their security. Even more ominously, Ukraine was portrayed as the primary source and transit hub of narcotic smugglers into Russia (Bogdanov 2017a). It would be somewhat fiction to disagree that the traffic of opiates and synthetic drugs from the neighboring countries was negligible. After all, FSKN did stop several smuggling schemes that originated in Ukraine. Nevertheless, all of these claims aimed to lionize the agency's programmatic success and deflect attention from its inability to slow down the unfolding public health crisis.

These conspiratorial utterances resonated with the outlandish accusations that the US government had been encircling Russia's borders with the outposts that secretly produced biological weapons (Vladykin 2016; Romanova 2016). Kirill Smurov, the deputy head of the anti-narcotics division of the MVD, offered similar remarks at the Shanghai Cooperation Organization in April 2017 (Bogdanov 2017b). It is not yet clear whether the notion of "external narco-aggression" will become a future master frame for discussing the ongoing spread of HIV in the country. Weirdly enough, in February 2022, in the beginning of the war with Ukraine, Putin referred to Ukrainian resistance forces as narcotic users.

In the broad sense, the regime's agents are at the mercy of the principal, and there is little they can do to change the principal's mind. Still, state agencies can surely put up a public fight when significant situational conflicts send principals' the message of their ineptness. In 2013, the possibility of disbanding FSKN was the center of public attention and seemed all but certain. With the agency's demise several years later, high-ranking bureaucrats found themselves in want of different jobs elsewhere, although the rank-and-file were allowed to continue their service in the Ministry of Internal Affairs (*Ministerstvo Vnutrennikh Del*, hereafter MVD).

The following section explores the Ministry of Health's failure to meet the demands of health activists and people living with HIV/AIDS (PLWHA) and constructively respond to international criticism, followed by efforts of its spokespeople to highlight the state as the referent object of security rather than the well-being of its populace.

Minzdrav: Securitization as a Gaming Strategy

In this section, I will discuss the Ministry of Health's failure to meet the demands of health activists and people living with HIV/AIDS and constructively respond to international criticism. The discussion highlights the attempts of meso-level health bureaucrats to provide value to Putin and protect the ministry from losing valuable bureaucratic powers.

In 2010, Minzdrav faced a severe crisis that would shape its approach to securitizing Russia's HIV/AIDS. Although its HIV/AIDS record was never spotless, the crisis of 2010 highlighted the systemic problems in the ministry's performance. Health officials had to deal with street politics, the dissent of the street-level health bureaucrats working for the regional AIDS centers, and international criticism. Similarly, the protest of street-level health professionals in 2015 put the ministry on the defensive.

First, public criticism of unusual intensity came from everywhere. After the demonstration erupted in the federal capital, six major provincial cities followed suit. In October, HIV activists flooded Kaliningrad and St-Petersburg's streets; in November, the protests widened to Orenburg, Tula, Kazan, and Tver. In principle, the ministry could have involved civil society organizations in its work. However, the general hostility to the AIDS service organizations foreclosed the top health professionals' ability to learn from outsiders and change policy. Little wonder, the Ministry's representatives accused the alarmists of intentionally damaging Russia's reputation while silencing the country's health achievements. Acknowledging the local and regional governments' continuing inability to underwrite antiretrovirals' purchases would have further aggravated the Ministry's corporate vulnerability and damaged the image of the agency's professional reputation.

Second, several doctors in charge of the state-run AIDS centers publicly complained that they could not deliver appropriate treatment regimens and occasionally had to stop treating their patients because of the ongoing failure to timely disburse drugs. These complaints were a direct challenge to the Ministry's top leadership. Regional AIDS centers are significant as they deliver health policy at the street level and deal with infected and vulnerable populations on a daily basis. Their ability to cover all eligible patients often depended on nonstate contingency funds, making them potential allies of civil society groups. Although regional AIDS centers seldom spoke in a unified and loud voice, they presented a serious challenge to the Minzdrav authority and reputation in the time of this crisis.

In general, the dissenters questioned how competent top-tier bureaucrats were and objected to the official claims regarding the effectiveness of the whole HIV/AIDS governance system. Among the most vocal critics of the approach described above was Vadim Pokrovsky, the head of the Federal AIDS Center, an unrelenting judge of the domestic health governance shortcomings who took the side of the protesters in the fall of 2010, Valentin Pokrovsky, the head of the Country Coordinating Mechanism (CCM), and Vladimir Mendelevich, a progressive narcologist from Kazan. They tried, albeit unsuccessfully so, to turn the issue of HIV/AIDS into a national public health emergency.

The Federal AIDS Center, a semi-autonomous agency in charge of developing policy recommendations, assessed that less than 50% of patients in need had received the requisite treatment with antiretroviral therapy. That assessment indicated that the government enforced late treatment initiation, with a 200 cell count, against the proven international recommendations and the frequent inability of Minzdrav to account for the HIV-positive patients not yet technically registered in the regional AIDS centers. Although the ministry's propensity to manipulate numbers was nothing new (Wallander 2006: 50–52), this round of debates exposed deep rifts. Despite many calling out their gaming strategies, the Ministry insisted that every HIV-positive patient is covered. Further, in November 2010, Vadim Pokrovsky faced an official investigation and almost lost his position at the Federal AIDS Center, while some regional AIDS centers that had generated the most visible public complaints, like the one in Arkhangelsk, closed down.

Third, the Ministry of Health and Social Development felt especially vulnerable when international actors highlighted similar concerns—that Russia was falling short of the necessary targets. Several hundred (480) organizations highlighted stories of the monthly delays in delivering antiretroviral therapy and asked the Global Fund to Fight AIDS, Tuberculosis, and Malaria (GFATM) to continue to finance the ARV therapy programs in Russia. In 2010, UNICEF warned of the HIV epidemic among street kids (UNICEF 2010), and a prestigious medical journal published an admonishing article on Russia's anti-narcotic policy (Rhodes et al. 2010). Further, UNAIDS and the World Health Organization (WHO) continued to publish epidemiological data on seroprevalence, significantly higher than those circulated by the Kremlin. Those in the government who were never sympathetic to transnational partners no longer concealed their intolerance to external health agencies and agents of change. The Ministry ignored all these concerns as the government decided to expel international agencies from the country, despite their impressive performance and promising health assistance prospects.

Although the Minsotszdrav was able to stifle internal dissent and ignore external criticism, the crisis remained uncontained. Health and social bureaucracies attracted harsh criticism from Putin and independent experts alike. Many legislators (Tatyana Yakovleva) and healthcare professionals (Leonid Roshal) criticized the concentration of all these powers in the Ministry of Health and exposed the Ministry's dismal performance. Calls to disband the Ministry of Health and Social Development peaked by 2011 and culminated in its radical reorganization, a bureaucratic solution consistent with Putin's governance methods. In 2012, the Ministry lost all its social security departments, passed on to the newly formed Ministry of Labor and Social Affairs. In 2013, the drug purchase system shifted from the Ministry of Health to regional governments. However, these measures have increased neither the Ministry's capacity nor the quality of health governance. Instead, they only added to the Ministry's already strong sense of corporate vulnerability.

In response, several system-level bureaucrats chose to securitize the epidemic to exculpate the Ministry from further underperformance allegations. Minzdrav enjoyed the intellectual support of conservative Moscow-based health specialists, such as Alexei Mazus, the head of the Moscow city center for AIDS prevention and then also part-time chief Russian specialist on HIV/AIDS prophylaxis and treatment, chief Russian narcologist Evgeny Bryun, Lyudmila Stebenkova, the Moscow Duma deputy in charge of the city's health affairs, and their allies from the Russian Institute for Strategic Studies (*Rossiiskii Institut Strategicheskikh Issledovanii*, hereafter RISI). This core group of individuals was interested in maintaining their professional reputation and administrative positions and aspired to transform the Russian health system in an illiberal and conservative direction.

That Mazus's interviews and media appearances consistently highlighted only the victorious side of the Russian response to HIV/AIDS speaks volumes of his hidden agenda. For more than a decade, starting in 2006, he publicly praised Moscow health authorities which achieved near-universal testing of potentially infected people and provided antiretroviral therapy free of charge. Although valid estimates of the success in HIV/AIDS prevention achieved in Moscow were unlikely, Moscow AIDS Center claimed a grandiose success in achieving complete coverage of those in need of ARVs and initiating a conservative approach to prophylaxis based on strong moral values. With the help of Evgeny Kozhokin, Mazus developed broader political claims regarding ontological menaces inherent in the "wrong" and un-Russian ways of thinking and talking about the scourge of AIDS and IV-drug use.

They did not see international cooperation against the pandemic of HIV/AIDS as an outcome of collective action involving many actors that often act on a genuine humanitarian impulse to save human lives. Instead, they contended that such cooperation was a deliberate and coordinated project to take over domestic healthcare policies and human services. International endorsement of harm reduction and condoms as essential methods of prevention, in this rendition, is equivalent to the promotion of narcotics and alternative lifestyles (Mazus and Kozhokin 2005). Domestic health activists, they argued, come from high-risk groups. They heeded their foreign funders' wishes and chased transnational corporations' money. Later on, Kozhokin and Mazus explained that Western approaches to HIV prophylaxis among high-risk groups, advocated by prominent international foundations, often contradicted the traditional values of the healthy majority, triggered serious societal confrontations, and thus quickened the spread of the infection instead of curbing it (Mazus and Kozhokin 2016).

The best-known domestic argument on AIDS securitization is the 2016 book, *Fighting the Epidemic of HIV/AIDS: Global Trends and Russian National Security* (Guzenkova et al. 2015). Penned by RISI members, it is astonishing in its inculpative glitz and catchy conspiratorial undertones. Building on Kozhokin and Mazus's articles, the book's authors made several astonishing points. First, Russia's external foes weaponized addicts, prostitutes, and men having sex with men to make political demands. These demands could destabilize political regimes at odds with Western democracies. In this view, the vulnerable populations and their advocates in Russia are not merely the patients involved in the struggle for health services and human dignity but recruited and well-compensated subversive forces that scheme to dominate the healthy majority and transplant alien cultural norms. Further, the work of several service organizations hitherto viewed as reputable, such as Transatlantic Partners against AIDS/Global Business Coalition (TPPA/GBC), was interpreted as an imposition of alien values and dangerous health laws on the Russian government.

Second, the authors claimed that international organizations, such as the Global Fund, offered harmful advice intentionally. They systematically promoted tolerance to alternative lifestyles and stimulated sexual appetites among youngsters to undermine the proven conservative strategies of HIV prevention. International organizations' programs, in this view, sought to build a tolerance to controlled substances in order to create legal domestic markets for narcotics. The international injunction to dispense first-line antiretroviral therapies to narcotic addicts was a deliberate attempt to help the immunodeficiency virus mutate since IV-drug users could not and often did not want to adhere to the regimen.

Third, the authors averred that it was profit-seeking that drove the Joint United Nations Programme on HIV/AIDS's (UNAIDS) creators from the very outset. No longer providing charitable help and giving up its rhetoric of human dignity, UNAIDS pushed developing countries to overspend their scarce resources to combat the epidemic on the terms dictated by these organizations. UNAIDS, the Global Fund, and other charities worked in transnational pharmaceutical companies' interests since low international prices on the first-line antiretroviral drugs disincentivized domestic economies to manufacture life-saving pills.

In the early stages of the epidemic, such views were on the periphery of the official health discourse, but by 2016 they had defined the mainstream articulations. Arguments of this sort effectively foreclose any discussion about the inherent problems related to the Ministry's underperformance and its constituent parts. Once evoked by health administrators, the securitization discourse made no further use of discussing policy alternatives. In this context, the Russian HIV/AIDS epidemic was insurmountable because of an international conspiracy that aggravated the domestic epidemiological situation and destroyed the population's well-being. Although Minzdrav's critics kept exposing the Ministry's pitfalls, their words had less traction than the massive effort to securitize the epidemic along the lines described above.

In summary, as the criticism and the evidence of underperformance mounted, the Ministry of Health and the Moscow AIDS Center chose to blame the Western recommendations regarding the appropriate response to the epidemic. The emerging discourse of HIV/AIDS securitization—assigning epidemiological blame to external actors beyond the control of Russian health organs—emerged as an instrumental rebuttal to the otherwise self-defeating admission that the response to the epidemic was inadequate. Thus, domestic health actors welcomed those experts and opinion leaders whose claims about the epidemic's meaning could validate their institutionalized course of collective action and protect their reputation. The following section discusses how and why the Orthodox Church, another key actor in health governance, has validated and crystallized the conservative version of health securitization.

ROC: Securitization for Rechurching

This section explores the Moscow Patriarchy's attempts to detail, crystallize, and entrench the securitizing discourse with the state as the referent object of security rather than the well-being of its constituents. Counterintuitively, the Russian Orthodox Church (ROC) faces similar problems as the state agencies involved in health.

Despite its seemingly influential position in the nominally Orthodox country, ROC's corporate vulnerability stems from the organization's limited social appeal and the believers' "churchlessness." As Freeze (2017) notes, the "religious revival in Russia has been unchurched: the high rates of self-described religiosity accompany abysmally low rates of church membership." Paradoxically, the trend of increased religiosity is dampened by the opposite trend: compared to 2005, more Russians do not consider religion to be of any import to their lives (Levada-Tsentr 2021). Notably, a recent upsurge in Russians' religiosity is attributed to the fear of coronavirus but not the attractiveness of the Church as an institution. Worse, over the last decade, the overwhelming majority of respondents think that the Church must not influence public policymaking, while only 6% of respondents consider the role of the church in public affairs insufficient (Levada-Tsentr 2017).

These trends highlight the inherent corporate vulnerability of ROC's social standing. Arguably, Patriarch Kirill I (2009–present) adopted a strategic course on expanding "rechurching" by emphasizing and popularizing ROC's mission through increased media appearances. This "megaphone" rechurching went hand in hand with the attempts of other bureaucratic agencies, discussed in two previous sections, to engulf the public in agency-complementary messages. That Kirill, despite the official rhetoric of refraining from intervening in political campaigns or supporting political leaders, directly promoted and contributed to Putin's ambitions in developing Russia-friendly geopolitical surroundings and consolidating an international conservative and illiberal coalition is well-documented (Druzenko 2011; Lamoreaux and Flake 2018; Stoeckl 2016, 2020).

ROC's inherent conservatism and illiberalism are valuable to the regime as they give credence to Putin's political skepticism of the West and legitimize multiple accusatory pronouncements that time and again resurface in the Kremlin's rhetoric. In 2021, Sergey Lavrov, leading United Russia in the upcoming Duma elections, infamously noted that liberal and progressive sexual education destroys "the genetic code of the planet's key civilizations… openly seeking to drive a wedge into the Orthodox world, whose values are viewed as a powerful spiritual obstacle for the liberal concept of boundless permissiveness" (Lavrov 2021). His claim that Western schoolchildren learn that Jesus Christ was bisexual captures the domestic elites' ability and willingness to harness illiberal religious pronouncements to substantiate political objectives.

A magisterial avenue of pushing back against corporate vulnerability appeared in the ROC's foundational document, entitled *Foundations of the Social Conceptions of the Russian Orthodox Church* (Patriarchia.ru 2000). In line with this document, Kirill I adopted the strategic course on enchurchment (*votserkovlenie*) of the rapidly growing ranks of believers by promoting the Church's so-called this-worldly mission, that is, not only to save people in this world but also to save and resurrect the world itself from sin and destructive behavior. Although the Church functionaries have been running several non-theological health-related programs for more than a decade, focusing on HIV/AIDS became attractive to the Russian Orthodox Church.

The Church functionaries tried to regain social authority by resurrecting the notion of social work (*diakonicheskoe sluzhenie*) as an essential part of Orthodox practices (Mitrokhin 2004) and organizing a variety of educational programs, ranging from health to official patriotism (Rousselet 2015). In recent times, for ordinary church-affiliated workers, providing social services has meant giving grief councils in the hospitals or introducing ailing people to the basic tenets of the Orthodox faith. In practical terms, HIV prevention services for IDUs and the reduction of demand for drugs remained elusive, if measurable at all. Only 600 people living with HIV/AIDS in Moscow received some help from the St-Dimitriy Sisterhood of medical nurses, while the nationwide capacity of the Orthodox rehabilitation centers never exceeded 800 people. Three years of educational activities (2012–2014) among youth remained limited in scope, as they reached only 1300 individuals. For the Petersburg-based charitable fund "Diaconia," it might have been an impressive result, but for the Church with its potential outreach to nourish all Orthodox Christians in the country, these numbers looked meager. Further, it would also be somewhat fiction to believe that the Patriarchy's activities included evidence-based methods: multiple reports noted that the Church promoted abstinence and forced IV-drug users to work as the main rehabilitation methods. Vsevolod Chaplin (1968–2020), then deputy head of the influential Department for External Church Relations of the Moscow Patriarchate, averred that sermons and moral values are indispensable if not sufficient for curbing the spread of HIV/AIDS.

Russian religious leaders also pursued an essential organizational goal: to enhance the Church's societal standing while forging relationships with helpful political allies. The Church seemingly established itself as a competent domestic force on the grounds of a five-year record of working to prevent HIV/AIDS and helping with palliative care of HIV-positive patients. At the very least, the Church could have learned how to provide health services from its previous experience working with the United States Agency for International Development (USAID) and the United Nations Development Programme (UNDP). This Russian-American program, entitled "Support to HIV and AIDS Prevention and Palliative Care Initiatives of Faith-Based Organizations in the Russian Federation," lasted from 2006 through 2011. The Patriarchy also approached Minzdravsotsrazvitiya for funding but unsuccessfully so.

Then, the Patriarchy turned to FSKN. The alliance between the Church and FSKN proved mutually beneficial. Gosnarkokontrol's system-level bureaucrats sought to cultivate the perception of garnering wide nonstate, grassroots support for their initiatives, while the Church hoped to receive material and logistical backing from the agency. The rapprochement began in December 2010, when Ivanov and His Holiness Patriarch Kirill signed a formal agreement. Notably, the parties agreed that the development of the 40 functional rehabilitation centers would be the main objective of their cooperation. The agreement implied that the faith-based centers would join the nationwide network. Other, less tangible forms of cooperation, such as spiritual education, patriotic enlightenment of the youth, and the country's volunteer movement, were also declared.

In general, the flurry of activities and the signed agreements show that the two corporate actors developed a mutual respect and did so not just at the top level. In 2011, for instance, the Omsk regional division of the agency and local church functionaries signed an agreement of cooperation. In January 2011, the deputy director of FSKN, Nikolay Tsvetkov, took part in the anti-narcotic section of a faith-based educational conference, where he mostly praised a partnership between the clerics and law enforcement. To demonstrate his commitment to the Church as an essential partner, Ivanov visited the Spaso-Preobrazhensky rehabilitation center in the Stavropol region and praised its activities. He also lobbied for the state sponsorship of the nationwide net of faith-based rehabilitation centers. On June 17, 2015, Putin approved that initiative at the State Council meeting.

Most importantly, the Church was instrumental in securitizing the epidemic of HIV/AIDS. The conservative wing of the Russian Orthodox Church claimed that Westerners desired to undermine Russia's population growth by spreading the human immunodeficiency virus in the country. Another key message was that the weakness in resisting external influences, not the domestic failure to deliver, prevented the authorities from stopping AIDS at home. The system-level religious authorities decided to flesh out the claim by utilizing hitherto marginal public utterances first articulated by Irina Medvedeva and Tat'yana Shishova in a prestigious newspaper, Nezavisimaya Gazeta (Medvedeva and Shishova 2000).

The two authors, art-therapists by vocation who lacked professional medical training, attacked the notions of reproductive rights, sexual education, family planning, and feminism as policy tools used by the United States to attain its strategic interests at the expense of the developing countries. The article noted that the National Security Study Memorandum 200 ("Implications of Worldwide Population Growth for U.S. Security and Overseas Interests") provided a multitude of intergovernmental and transnational organizations with the blueprint for action against Russia. In their second co-authored article ("The Country of Victorious AIDS"), published a year later, Medvedeva and Shishova averred that all too many transnational actors, including the United

Nations Educational, Scientific and Cultural Organization (UNESCO), the United Nations Population Fund (UNPF) and Médecins Sans Frontières (MSF), were interested in blowing the scope of the epidemic out of proportion (Medvedeva and Shishova 2001). In both publications, the authors stressed the impossibility of a positive relationship between foreign assistance, on the one hand, and domestic development and human well-being, on the other. They thus paved the way for the forthcoming governmental assault on the internationally funded health service and advocacy NGOs as the agents of foreign influence. They suggested that domestic authorities crack down on these organizations and push back against international recommendations and evidence-based practices in AIDS prevention.

In the years that followed, Medvedeva and Shishova's writings appeared on various faith-based Internet sites, ranging from the mainstream ones under the patronage of prominent church functionaries such as Tikhon (Shevkunov) and the Saratov bishop Longin (Korchagin) to the radical ones obsessed with exposing the evidence of global spiritual decay and the coming apocalypse. To be fair, Patriarch Kirill did not formally endorse Medvedeva's and Shishova's arguments as part of the Church's health concept. Still, both authors found a prestigious tribune at the official Christmas Educational Readings, where they moderated discussions and contributed to a special section on globalization for many years.

This approach gained further prominence when a think tank, loosely associated with the Russian Academy of Sciences but mostly known because of Vladimir Yakunin's direct patronage. Yakunin, at that time, presided over the state-run Russian Railways and belonged to Putin's inner circle. This think tank, *Tsentr problemnogo analiza i gosudarstvenno-upravlencheskogo proektirovaniya*, published a series of conference proceedings and monographs, which massively borrowed from Medveva's and Shishova's work (see, for instance, Sulakshin 2007). Yakunin also served at the Center of the National Glory of Russia and St. Andrew the First-Called Foundation, which funded Orthodox Church-related projects.

Less than a decade later, any official discussion of the AIDS policy invariably evoked the notion of demographic security. Although the "Strategy of the National Security of the Russian Federation until 2020" mentions the virus's spread as a critical challenge to public health, the notion of demographic decline receives a priority. Similarly, the public health aspect of the epidemic remains secondary in the "Concept of the Demographic Policy of the Russian Federation for the period until 2025."

In summary, the Moscow Patriarchy's impact on the securitization discourse was profound. Instead of raising public awareness about HIV/AIDS as a public health emergency and human security crisis, the Church tried to construct a justification for the government's inability to stop the epidemic. It also adopted and institutionally validated a conservative and illiberal health securitization discourse, which found its place in top bureaucrats' political musings.

Were Alternative Responses Feasible?

One part of the story here is about the desire of relevant actors to create value for their principal by speaking in unison with Putin's vision of Russia's ontological insecurity, making powerful public forays on framing the epidemic in accordance with Putin's geopolitical imagery of opposing the West and his commitment to anti-Western, illiberal, and conservative values. Another part of the story is about how these attempts turned out to be a gaming strategy that covered the agencies' failures to implement their main organizational tasks, failures that inevitably attracted much public scrutiny. In this light, securitization of HIV/AIDS is a counterproductive and reactionary ex post justification of their underperformance. Among all the actors discussed in the chapter, FSKN acted like an aggressive securitization entrepreneur; and securitizing the pandemic went hand in hand with the agency's mission creep. For the Ministry of Health, securitization of HIV/AIDS, as a gaming strategy, allowed to attribute the agency's many failures in performing its core tasks to exogenous factors. The Church tried to defend its inward-looking values and hoped to create public capital by vigorously participating in the public discussion regarding the epidemic. Its top authorities also found and gave public tribune to the obscure individuals whose views on the disease, globalization, and medicines were most reactionary and backward-looking. All these actors found it all too easy to blame the outside forces while highlighting their role in protecting the people's well-being.

Creating political value for Putin and publicly committing to self-justifying discourses instead of impartially tackling health crises has its price. Today, Russia is now entering a generalized stage of the epidemic and has fewer useful governance tools to respond to the health crisis productively. Personalism incentivized actors to protect their contracts with the principal, thereby triggering the vicious cycle of HIV/AIDS governance and generating adverse health outcomes. While this chapter takes the undeniable facts of domestic mobilization of resources as given, the evidence of the personalistic regime's disastrous impact on health outcomes is undeniable. The worse adverse consequence was that actors jointly undermined the national evidence-based response to HIV/AIDS. In general, all the discussed actors collectively contributed to the failure to stop or reverse the spread of the epidemic, which in 2017 became generalized with one million officially registered HIV-positive individuals, including 200,000 who had already died from AIDS. At this point, it would be premature to rule out the international estimates that the epidemic had claimed at least twice as many individuals as officially acknowledged by the Russian state. In the future, securitization of HIV/AIDS in Russia will continue to undermine learning from external sources and impede innovation, which is so urgently needed to place the epidemic under control.

Could the agencies perform better and differently? Accountability and the limited ability to learn best practices. The agencies of interest operate in the confines of a personalistic regime, and therefore they are accountable to their principal, not to the society. In health governance, two possible strategies were simply not on the table: agencies could neither fix their underperformance by using evidence-based strategies nor engage civil society in their work. First, the costs of pursuing evidence-based strategies and performance fixes look very high to most actors in health governance. The Kremlin never instructed agencies to follow external best practices and adopt new policy standards to fix the agencies' performance-based lapses. Had agencies chosen to overcome their underperformance's underlying reasons, they would undermine the sense of their corporate security.

FSKN understandably was equipped to deal with law enforcement tasks, not public health interventions. In the view of the system-level representatives of FSKN, the only way to stop the spread of HIV infection was to eradicate the supply of IV drugs and curtail their circulation. To change, the Ministry of Health, the second actor discussed here, would have to transform its institutional setup, which was dominated by conservative narcologists that maintained medical convictions typical for Soviet psychiatry and rejected harm reduction (Sokolova 2016). Officially endorsing and adopting harm reduction would have disrupted the routine work of the system of Minzdrav's countrywide net of narcological centers, possibly undermining narcologists' job security. Public attention to the issue would trigger the ministry's conflict with the government. In the early 2000s, the Moscow Patriarchy had little scientific and epidemiological knowledge, and it claimed that HIV/AIDS, narcotic addiction, and alcohol dependence resulted from succumbing to sin. Learning about evidence-based solutions was simply outside their range of spiritual interest. Instead, it tried to develop its public image as an exorcist of social sins while pursuing societal alliances with other domestic actors involved in health, most notably FSKN.

Second, because the Kremlin kept sending a consistent message that corporate actors should protect their autonomy from civil society, learning from nonstate actors and engaging them was antithetical to political survival. In principle, bureaucracies should protect their autonomy to act as they see fit on the grounds of technical rationality. In reality, the Kremlin strove to maintain its autonomy from society and mitigate any forms of vertical accountability "rather than creating the administrative capacity to run a well-functioning twenty-first century government" (Taylor 2007: 41). The government has been slowly shutting down nonstate entities involved in political activity and portraying activists, including health service organizations, as the source of ontological danger.

For state agencies involved in health governance, it meant disembedding themselves from those societal-level actors directly serving vulnerable populations (people living with HIV/AIDS, IV-drug users) and abstaining from training street-level implementers to do their jobs differently. In principle, a robust civil society can monitor health administration and improve the policy course. It is often noted that "Russian state institutions <...> have a vital interest in collaboration with civil society since they rely on the organizations' expertise, resources, and skills in order to effectively counter the spread of HIV/AIDS" (Pape 2014: 7). However, pursuing close ties with health activists would imply that FSKN had to learn about evidence-based methods of infection prevention and change its routine operations. Lest they endanger the Ministry of Health's unity and its public image, the system-level bureaucrats had no incentive to heed societal actors' suggestions. By not involving health activists in its work, the Church escaped the unpalatable public confession that it had little experience and capacity to deal with the epidemic of HIV/AIDS.

Conclusion

The author proposes a political perspective that highlights the incompleteness of contracts under personalistic regimes as the driving force behind the securitizing move. Over time, the securitizing discourse with the state as the referent object of security rather than its populace's wellbeing was crystalized and entrenched. Combined with the corresponding institutionalized courses of action, these discourses had little to do with a comprehensive and evidence-based response to the epidemic. Substantively, agents impugned the West for its destructive influence on Russian health, and, politically, they did so to protect their access to valuable activities and state resources that the ruler granted them in return for their loyalty. At the end of the day, health securitization exalts the Kremlin's authoritarian regime and strives to protect corporate actors from termination or alienation from valuable activities and resources.

In the preceding chapters, I have discussed several distinct survival strategies individual elites adopt. However, often it is the survival of agencies and the privileged status of corporate actors—firmly tied to the autocrat's favors—that is at stake. The strategy of bureaucratic survival in Russia's personalistic regime is similar to that of individual survival and entails challenges the top bureaucrats and meso-level administrators must jointly navigate and counter. Speaking loyalty loudly and deploying various gaming strategies is a part of bureaucratic endurance. Individual insiders could protect themselves and move to different government positions within Putin's system. Yet, it is not enough since moving to comfortable and nominally prestigious sinecures is a de-facto demotion, which entails significant losses. Thus, insiders and the agencies they lead must create political value for Putin. Doing so is quite a challenge for good governance, as the emphasis on creating political value generates negative consequences for government quality and policy effectiveness. Further, noticeable underperformance and internal conflicts aggravate agencies' positions and make them an attractive object of Putin's ire. Health securitization becomes an instrument intended to protect contracts.

Chapter 6 concludes the investigation. In addition to reiterating my main argument, it also attempts to take stock of the empirical assessment, comparing and contrasting pessimistic and optimistic views on the health governance outcomes in the country. The final chapter also discusses three prevalent explanatory perspectives, including the exposition of kleptocracy as the chief motivation of contemporary authoritarian regimes, the spreading of neoliberal reason as the primary driver of failures in health provisions, the securitization approach, and the tendency to investigate the Russian case through the lens of numerous microscale strategies.

References

Agadjanian, A. 2017. Tradition, Morality and Community: Elaborating Orthodox Identity in Putin's Russia. *Religion, State and Society* 45 (1): 39–60.

Ananyev, M. 2018. Inside the Kremlin: The Presidency and Executive Branch. In *The New Autocracy: Information, Politics, and Policy in Putin's Russia*, ed. D. Treisman. Washington, DC: Brookings Institution.

Baev, P. 2017. Tenth Anniversary of Putin's Munich Speech: A Commitment to Failure. *Eurasia Daily Monitor* 14 (17).

Belton, C. 2020. *Putin's People: How the KGB Took Back Russia and Then Took on the West*. New York: Farrar, Straus and Giroux.

Bogdanov, V. 2017a. MVD: Ukraina stala glavnym tranziterom narkotikov v RF. *Rossiiskaya Gazeta*, 12 April.

Bogdanov, V. 2017b. MVD: Protiv Rossii osushchestvlyaetsya narkoagressiya. *Rossiiskaya Gazeta*, 14 April.

Bogomolov, K. 2021. Pokhishchenie Evropy 2.0. *Novaya Gazeta*, 10 February.

Druzenko, G. 2011. Geopolitics from the Patriarch. *Russian Politics & Law* 49 (1): 65–73.

Edenborg, E. 2020. Russia's Spectacle of "Traditional Values": Rethinking the Politics of Visibility. *International Feminist Journal of Politics* 22 (1): 106–126.

Freeze, G.L. 2017. Russian Orthodoxy and Politics in the Putin Era. *Carnegie Endowment for International Peace*, 2 September.

Gel'man, V. 2017. Political Foundations of Bad Governance in Post-soviet Eurasia: Towards a Research Agenda. *East European Politics* 33 (4): 496–516.

George, A., and A. Bennett. 2005. *Case Studies and Theory Development in the Social Sciences*. Cambridge, MA: MIT Press.

Grube, D. 2019. *Megaphone Bureaucracy: Speaking Truth to Power in the Age of the New Normal*. Princeton: Princeton University Press.

Guriev, S., and D. Treisman. 2019. Informational Autocrats. *Journal of Economic Perspectives* 33 (4): 100–127.

Guzenkova, T., O. Petrovskaya, and I. Nikolaychuk. 2015. *Protivodeistvie Epidemii VICh/SPID: Global'nye Trendy i Natsional'naya Bezopasnost' Rossii*. Moskva: RISI.

Hale, H.E. 2015. *Patronal Politics: Eurasian Regime Dynamics in Comparative Perspective*. New York: Cambridge University Press.
Hashim, S.M. 2017. High-Modernism and Its Limits—Assessing the Sources of State Incapacity in Russia. *Communist and Post-Communist Studies* 50 (3): 195–205.
Horvath, R. 2016. The Reinvention of 'Traditional Values': Nataliya Narochnitskaya and Russia's Assault on Universal Human Rights. *Europe-Asia Studies* 68 (5): 868–892.
Ivanov, V. 2016. Zapusk sistemy reabilitatsii narkomanov ostanovit epidemiyu VICh. *Ria Novosti*, 23 March.
Kiselev, D. 2014. Kogda nichto ne svyato, kogda nichto ne sderzhivaet. *Tetradi po Konservatizmu* 1 (1): 19–27.
Klotz, A., and C. Lynch. 2007. *Strategies for Research in Constructivist International Relations*. Armonk: M.E. Sharpe.
Kosachev, K. 2006. Diktat nekompetentnosti. *Rossiya v Global'noi Politike* No. 1, January–February.
Kosachev, K. 2007. Rossiya i Zapad: nashi raznoglasiya. *Rossiya v Global'noi Politike* No. 4, July–August.
Kravtsov, V. 2015. *HIV/AIDS and Norm Diffusion in Putin's Russia and Mbeki's South Africa*. Athens: University of Georgia Press.
Lamoreaux, J.W., and L. Flake. 2018. The Russian Orthodox Church, the Kremlin, and Religious (Il)Liberalism in Russia. *Palgrave Communications* 4 (1): 115.
Laruelle, M. 2015. Patriotic Youth Clubs in Russia. Professional Niches, Cultural Capital and Narratives of Social Engagement. *Europe-Asia Studies* 67 (1): 8–27.
Laruelle, M. 2016. The Izborsky Club, or the New Conservative Avant-Garde in Russia. *The Russian Review* 75 (4): 626–644.
Laruelle, M. 2020. Making Sense of Russia's Illiberalism. *Journal of Democracy* 31 (3): 115–129.
Lavrov, S. 2021. O Prave, Pravakh i Pravilakh. *Rossiya v Global'noi Politike* No. 4, 28 June.
Levada-Tsentr. 2017. Religioznost'. *Press-vypusk*, 18 July.
Levada-Tsentr. 2021. Religioznost' v period pandemii. *Press-vypusk*, 14 April.
Luzhkov, Yu. 2006. My i zapad. *Strategiya Rossii* No. 6, June.
Matvienko, V. 2020. Vstrecha s senatorami Rossiiskoi Federatsii. *Kremlin.ru*, 23 September. http://www.kremlin.ru/events/president/news/64076.
Mazus, A., and E. Kozhokin. 2005. SPID i demograficheskaya pustynya. *Rossiiskaya Gazeta*, 12 July.
Mazus, A., and E. Kozhokin. 2016. V zashchitu chelovecheskogo zdorov'ya, Freyda i OON. *Nezavisimaya Gazeta*, 17 November.

Medvedev, S. 2004. Juicy Morsels: Putin's Beslan Address and the Construction of the New Russian Identity. PONARS Policy Memo 334.
Medvedeva, I., and T. Shishova. 2000. Demograficheskaya voyna protiv Rossii. *Nezavisimaya Gazeta*, 12 January.
Medvedeva, I., and T. Shishova. 2001. Strana pobedivshego SPIDa. *Pravoslavie.ru*, 25 June.
Melville, A. 2017. Neo-conservatism as National Idea for Russia? In *State and Political Discourse in Russia*, ed. P.M. Cucciolla, 147–160. Rome: Reset-Dialogues on Civilizations.
Melville, A. 2018. Russian Political Ideology. In *Russia: Strategy, Policy and Administration*, ed. I. Studin, 31–41. London: Palgrave Macmillan.
Mikhalkov, N. 2010. Pravo i Pravda. Manifest Prosveshchennogo Konservatizma. *Polit.ru*, 10 October. https://polit.ru/article/2010/10/26/manifest/.
Mitrokhin, N. 2004. *Russkaya Pravoslavnaya Tserkov': Sovremennoe Sostoyanie i Aktual'nye Problemy*. Moskva: Novoe Literaturnoe Obozrenie.
Moe, T. 1989. The Politics of Bureaucratic Culture. In *Can the Government Govern?*, ed. J. Chubb and P. Peterson, 267–329. Washington, DC: The Brooking Institution.
Morozov, O. 2014. Osnovnye Polozhenyya Sotsial'no-konservativnoi Ideologii. *Tetradi po Konservatizmu* 1 (1): 9–16.
Ostbo, J. 2017. Securitizing "Spiritual-Moral Values" in Russia. *Post-Soviet Affairs* 33 (3): 200–216.
Paget, D. 2020. Again, Making Tanzania Great: Magufuli's Restorationist Developmental Nationalism. *Democratization* 27 (7): 1240–1260.
Pape, U. 2014. *The Politics of HIV/AIDS in Russia*. London: Routledge.
Papkova, I. 2011. Russian Orthodox Concordat? Church and State Under Medvedev. *Nationalities Papers* 39 (5): 667–683.
Patriarchia.ru. 2000. Osnovy Sotsial'noi Kontseptsii Russkoi Pravoslavnoi Tserkvi. http://www.patriarchia.ru/db/text/419128.html.
Petrov, I. 2015. FSKN: Spaysy mogut ispol'zovat' dlya organizatsii tsvetnykh revolyutsii. *Rossiiskaya Gazeta*, 21 April.
Pomerantsev, P. 2014. The Hidden Author of Putinism: How Vladislav Surkov Invented the New Russia. *The Atlantic*, 07 November.
Putin, V. 2009a. V.V. Putin provel v Zelenograde soveshchanie "O strategii razvitiya farmatsevticheskoi promyshlennosti", 9 October. http://archive.government.ru/docs/7859/.
Putin, V. 2009b. Pochemu trudno uvolit' cheloveka. *Russkii Pioner*, 22 August. http://ruspioner.ru/ptu/single/1195/.
Putin, V. 2020. Vystuplenie na final'noi sessii diskussionnogo kluba Valdai, 22 October. http://kremlin.ru/events/president/news/64261.
Rhodes, T., et al. 2010. Policy Resistance to Harm Reduction for Drug Users and Potential Effect of Change. *British Medical Journal* 341: c3439.

Robinson, N. 2017. Russian Neo-patrimonialism and Putin's Cultural Turn. *Europe-Asia Studies* 69 (2): 348–366.
Robinson, N. 2020. Putin and the Incompleteness of Putinism. *Russian Politics* 5 (3): 283–300.
Romanova, I. 2016. Onishchenko: Na mirovoy arene tol'ko Rossiya sposobna effektivno protivodeystvovat' narashchivaniyu voenno-biologicheskogo potentsiala. *Rossiiskaya Gazeta*, 20 May.
Rousselet, K. 2015. The Church in the Service of the Fatherland. *Europe-Asia Studies* 67 (1): 49–67.
Sharafutdinova, G. 2014. The Pussy Riot Affair and Putin's Démarche from Sovereign Democracy to Sovereign Morality. *Nationalities Papers* 42 (4): 615–621.
Snyder, T. 2018. *The Road to Unfreedom: Russia, Europe, America*. New York: Tim Duggan Books.
Sokolova, E. 2016. State Response to the HIV/AIDS Epidemic in Russia: Institutional Factors. PhD diss., Temple University.
Stenin, A. 2004. Veterinaram otpustili grekhi. *Rossiiskaya Gazeta*, 25 September.
Stepanova, E. 2015. The Spiritual and Moral Foundation of Civilization in Every Nation for Thousands of Years: The Traditional Values Discourse in Russia. *Politics, Religion & Ideology* 16 (2–3): 119–136.
Stoeckl, K. 2016. The Russian Orthodox Church as Moral Norm Entrepreneur. *Religion, State and Society* 44 (2): 132–151.
Stoeckl, K. 2020. The Rise of the Russian Christian Right: The Case of the World Congress of Families. *Religion, State and Society* 48 (4): 223–238.
Sulakshin, S., ed. 2007. *Natsional'naya Identichnost' Rossii i Demograficheskii Krizis*. Moskva: Nauchnyi Ekspert.
Surkov, V. 2005. My real'no schitaem, chto davat' vlast' liberal'nym druz'yam opasno i vredno dlya strany. Vystuplenie na zakrytom zasedanii General'nogo soveta obedineniya Delovoi Rossii, 17 May. *Polit.ru*, 12 July. https://polit.ru/article/2005/07/12/surk/ .
Talleh Nkobou, A., and A. Ainslie. 2021. Developmental Nationalism? Political Trust and the Politics of Large-Scale Land Investment in Magufuli's Tanzania. *Journal of Eastern African Studies* 15 (3): 378–399.
Taylor, B.D. 2007. *Russia's Power Ministries: Coercion and Commerce*. Syracuse: Institute for National Security and Counterterrorism, Syracuse University.
Taylor, B.D. 2018. *The Code of Putinism*. New York: Oxford University Press.
Ting, M. 2003. A Strategic Theory of Bureaucratic Redundancy. *American Journal of Political Science* 47 (2): 274–292.
Titov, S. 2011. U narkopolitseyskikh okazalos' slishkom mnogo del. *Kommersant-Online*, 06 October.
Tsygankov, A. 2016. Crafting the State-Civilization Vladimir Putin's Turn to Distinct Values. *Problems of Post-Communism* 63 (3): 146–158.

UNICEF. 2010. *Blame and Banishment: The Underground HIV Epidemic Affecting Children in Eastern Europe and Central Asia*. Geneva: UNICEF.

Vinnik, S. 2015. Tabletki s igloy. *Rossiiskaya Gazeta*, 15 October.

Vladykin, O. 2016. Polchishcha boevykh virusov podgotovleny dlya nastupleniya. *Nezavisimoe Voennoe Obozrenie*, 25 March.

Wallander, C. 2006. Russian Politics and HIV/AIDS: The Institutional and Leadership Sources of an Inadequate Policy. In *HIV/AIDS in Russia and Eurasia*, vol. I, ed. J. Twigg, 33–56. New York: Palgrave Macmillan.

Waller, J. 2021. Elites and Institutions in the Russian Thermidor: Regime Instrumentalism, Entrepreneurial Signaling, and Inherent Illiberalism. *Journal of Illiberalism Studies* 1 (1): 1–23.

Wendt, A. 1999. *Social Theory of International Politics*. Cambridge: Cambridge University Press.

Wilkinson, C. 2014. Putting "Traditional Values" into Practice: The Rise and Contestation of Anti-Homopropaganda Laws in Russia. *Journal of Human Rights* 13 (3): 363–379.

CHAPTER 6

Conclusions, Implications, and Dashed Hopes

Considering that our population decline [is] 260 thousand per year, everything that is associated with a decrease in mortality from external and internal factors, everything related to the development of medicine is one of the priorities in the Russian Federation, and I think that this work should only be welcomed.

—Vladimir Putin, answering a question about Maria Vorontsova's involvement, Putin's presumed eldest daughter, in the Nomeko medical project, December 2019.

So just live. The infection will take its toll. We will all get through the sickness all the same. Who's supposed to die will die.

—Alexander Myasnikov, Head of the Information Center for Monitoring the Coronavirus Situation on the air of the Russian propaganda YouTube channel Soloviev Live, May 19, 2020.

INTRODUCTION

This book investigates the effects of personalistic regimes, of which Russia is an example, on the process of health governance. Although many scholars claim that the notion of "governance" is both ubiquitous and elusive, it refers to the systematic, patterned ways political actors make their decisions and implement them. The insights linking bad governance with limited political competition and the arguments connecting inefficient policies with politicians' narrow interests (Acemoglu 2003; Acemoglu and Robinson 2006) provide a good point of intellectual departure. Still, there is a need to probe the pitfalls of health governance further. The book argues that personalistic regimes possess inherent features that lessen governance effectiveness. In abstract terms, endogenous, optimizing responses to the institutional setting shape the manner in which principals and agents deliver fundamental goods and services. To repurpose Margaret Levi's definition (1989: 11), governance practices reflect "the outcome of an exchange between the ruler and the various groups who compose the polity."

I contend that the regime triggers optimizing responses and adaptations, but they could not contribute to good health governance in the country. Personalistic regimes assign roles, guide interactions between the occupants of these roles, and develop a unique system of incentives and constraints for all actors involved in governance practices. Rulers play the role of competent and beneficial leaders when they deliver public goods and services to the citizens. Rulers are patrons for elites, while elites and intermediaries assume the roles of clients and vassals, and the former also implement mandates in order to satisfy their boss, not the common people. Rulers also expect citizens' electoral support and approval in return for services provided. This description is consistent with one of the best definitions of social institutions (see Young 1994: 26).

The political and strategic nature of tacit contracts, interactions, and interdependencies among major participants involved in governance presents them with explicit constraints and incentives which they must carefully navigate. The principal, bureaucracies, intermediaries, and average citizens make a collective choice that supports Russia's personalistic regime and bad governance practices. When we describe Russian personalism as a regime, we must keep in mind that neither principals nor their subordinates can forgo interdependent decision-making because none can obtain the most preferred outcome by independent decision-making. In a nutshell, Russia's personalistic arrangement is detrimental to health governance, and it is likely to persist as long as actors' plans are consistent with each other.

Highlighting interdependencies that inhere in a weakly institutionalized setting—the electoral authoritarianism under personalistic rule is devoid of any impersonal forms of institutionalization—reveals an analytical engine that drives the machinery of bad governance. Personalism generates patterns of behavior (valued in as much as they allow elites to attain their parochial interests) and regularized governance practices, but it fails to impose fair and robust governance practices in the interests of people's welfare. Enduring patterns of behavior among relevant political actors are ensconced in calculations of cost and benefits imposed by personalistic rule and, to a lesser degree, supported by various intra-elite norms (such as the verbal public subservience), which expedite communication between a personalistic leader and his subordinates.

Ultimately, because Putin's regime relies on personalized contracts and not on strong formal organizations, the leaders are the source of bad governance. Contrary to the musings of Putin's prominent operatives (Vyacheslav Volodin insisted that without Putin, there would be no Russia), the Russian president does not embody the country's comparative advantage. It surely would be a mistake to assert that leaders do not matter, but we should discount the widespread idea that "[w]ith the right leadership, authoritarian regimes can implement the tough policies required for long-term economic prosperity" (Ezrow and Frantz 2011: 131). Absent a personalistic environment, key actors would have behaved differently; but today, their behavioral calculation is submitted to the institutional logic of personalism but not to any conditions outside the regime.

In this context, good governance—understood as maximizing people's wealth and "working for the public good in a fair way, rather than pursuing primarily personal or elite interests"—is severely compromised. Although I have preferred to refrain from using the term spoliation, given plunder is its strict meaning, it could be illustrative in the broad sense to describe the process wherein elites prioritize personal gains over and at the expense of the general welfare. The "good" in the observable governance practices is likely to be jeopardized when optimizing responses crowd out political responsiveness and professionalism. As much as striving for "good" choices in extant governance practices undermines their position, health participants are likely to avoid them. In personalistic regimes, an unbridgeable gap lies between the ideal of "good" governance and the "real" practices. Good governance is not consistent with the regime's setup, which is likely to undermine its developmental goals in the long-term perspective and preclude solving the emerging problems.

This chapter concludes my investigation. In addition to reiterating the main argument, the first section takes stock of the empirical assessment, comparing and contrasting pessimistic and optimistic views on the health governance outcomes in the country. The second section discusses four prevalent explanatory perspectives, including the exposition of kleptocracy as the primary motivation of contemporary authoritarian regimes, the spreading neoliberal reason as the driver of failures in health provisions, the securitization approach, and the propensity to anchor explanations in multiple peripheral or context-specific variables. Thirdly and finally, I discuss whether Russian governance will improve should democracy prevail.

Is (Moderately) Optimistic Assessment Warranted?

As many Russian citizens become concerned about the quality of and access to health care, it is not surprising that the Kremlin's commitment to improve health outcomes and distribute resources to the populace has increased over time. At the very least, the Kremlin wants to communicate a positive impression of its governance efforts. The failure to do so would be costly as it could accelerate people's disillusionment with the regime and weaken the principal's claim to power during electoral cycles. At first glance, the Russian health system, like any other, has its problems, but these problems do not make surplus and social betterment meaningless. The very fact of clearly defined and pursued developmental efforts and even modest, but real nonetheless, improvements in terms of people's access to fundamental goods and services is well-documented. After all, most Russian strategic programs (National Priority Projects, Strategy-2010, Strategy-2020, Pharma 2020) appear genuine at targeting real issues and improving citizens' welfare.

Although it is tempting to view Russian health governance from this angle, such an approach is misleading. One obvious objection concerns the failure to bracket exogenously existing favorable circumstances. It would be surprising not to find at least moderate evidence of social betterment, given the sheer length of Putin's rule. There is a tendency to overlook the impact of exogenous factors, including the general advancement of medicines and the ability to provide goods and services when the global prices on primary commodities are exorbitantly high. In other words, positive outcomes (improvements in some generic sense as attaining some goals over an extended period of time) could be generated by structural, macroeconomic factors. For instance, mineral rents could be determinants of growth, and the constituents could misinterpret windfall rents as a sign of the regime's effectiveness. As the saying has it, a rising tide lifts all the boats. Predictably, Russians enjoyed the benefits of overall economic growth, ignored the lack of deep institutional reforms, and dismissed the persistence of bad governance practices.

Further, the validity of the positive assessment of Putin's approach to health is linked to the definition of success. The measurement of positive outcomes could be utterly subjective when an analyst focuses solely on goal attainment as the main criterion for the regime's effectiveness. The authorities could achieve some goals in neither a fair nor efficient manner. An analysis then must pay attention to the crucial distinction between a regime's ability to attain specific goals and its ability to enforce efficient and fair practices in attaining these goals. Covering many people with antiretroviral medicines and making facial coverings available for the citizens are examples of the former. Giving public contracts to the most competitive instead of well-connected firms linked to political insiders is an example of the latter. Undeniable but modest improvements in health outcomes did not translate into a convincing story of health governance success. For instance, the government kept purchasing magnetic resonance imaging (MRI) scan machines and ambulance cars but failed to distribute them across regions based on real and concrete local needs.

Another problem in an optimistic assessment of the outcomes of the provision of fundamental goods in Putin's Russia is the normative notion that the state must not retreat from the provision of public goods and, instead, increase the scope of public obligations and assume wide-reaching activist functions. The Kremlin surely did not leave the health sector alone. According to an optimistic view, the Russian government is seemingly on track to improve health outcomes by entirely modernizing the country's outworn health system. The literature notes that in the early 2000s, President Putin brought the state back in, significantly improved both health outcomes and the performance of the healthcare system (Cook 2015; Manning and Tikhonova 2009), and arguably broke free from the pathologies that characterized the state of Russian health care in the 1990s (Twigg 2002).

However, in Russia, the return of the state in health regulation was part and parcel of creating partially noncompetitive markets that would privilege particular groups, firms, and individuals, for whom access to the state resources became the source of rents. Critics of neoliberalism might be correct in challenging the assumption that "the neoliberal belief that markets and private initiative are the only efficient means of providing services to people—with governments simply playing an enabling role" (Keshavjee 2014: 140). Worse, state intervention—in substance and quality—will, too, depend on the nature of the extant political regime and thus not necessarily lead to nullifying the most pernicious effects of neoliberalism, such as "the shriveling of public provision, a rise in socioeconomic inequality, and an increase in general insecurity" (Sewell 2009: 254). Unwarranted is an uncritical faith in the state's ability to properly manage and allocate health goods.

It is not overly surprising that on the eve of the Putin regime's twentieth anniversary, the health balance sheet is not in Putin's favor. Below I highlight significant problems discussed in the preceding chapters, but the list of the Kremlin's failure to deal with routine and extraordinary health governance tasks could go on.

1. Restricting access to the trial protocol and raw data on the phase 3 trial of the Sputnik V vaccine, combined with errors in the official statistics and results, make the breakthrough achievement less credible according to the international standards (Bucci et al. 2020; Bucci et al. 2021).
2. The head of a domestic health surveillance agency co-owned a patent on another original Russian-made vaccine, which turned out to be a dud. But the government kept distributing it for the mass vaccination campaign for nearly half a year after the media pulled fire alarms on it, and nobody got punished for this disaster.
3. Costs of essential life-saving medicines soar, while massive shortages disrupt a steady supply of primary medical products. The government continues imposing severe restrictions on the purchase and use of foreign pharmaceutical products despite domestic firms failing to supply analogs. These restrictions include the de facto domestic ban on safe and effective foreign vaccines.
4. Well-connected private actors acquire monopolistic rights to produce and distribute goods and services for the public sector, but they do not supply citizens with necessary medicines. Inefficiencies in the distribution of public resources snowball, and the government continues to underfund healthcare.
5. It is shocking that an industrialized country with a decent state capacity still lacks an adequate supply of medical oxygen for two

years in the COVID-19 pandemic. Terrifying is the lack of hospital beds, which disappeared as a result of healthcare optimization. Some populous but hard-to-reach cities no longer have morgues, and the citizens have to transport their deceased relatives elsewhere using private vehicles.
6. The medical community complains about the insensitivity of the state officials to its vital needs, and overworked physicians and nurses simply burn out, while some commit suicide out of desperation. External oversight actors bumped into widespread resistance at the regional level when trying to establish good working relationships with local health bureaucracies and make decision-making—especially in regard to massive healthcare reductions under the banner of optimization—accountable and transparent.
7. The most glaring failure is the intensifying spread of HIV/AIDS, while the pandemic has been curbed in most countries by now. Hardly positive is the mission creep of state and nonstate agencies, including the law enforcement agencies, which stoke the fire of the health security narrative but neglect to address public health issues adequately.

Broadly speaking, it is essential to distinguish between different sources of health governance deficiencies: one comes as a result of the limited existing state capacity (understood as the availability of material resources); another one stems from the lack of administrative competence to perform routine tasks in the health sector; the third one develops out of the very nature of tacit contracts and personalized exchanges that inhere in personalistic regimes. In personalistic regimes like Russia, the availability of (limited but sufficient) material resources and reasonably decent quality and competence of individual state administrators matter less than the pressures to satisfy their tacit contracts with the principal in order to protect access to valuable activities and resources.

None of the actors involved in health governance are free to regulate health as they see fit without mirroring Putin's injunctions or learning best governance practices from external actors, civil society, and the business community. Acting on their professional judgment and ethos would make state actors worse off as Putin can dismiss those who disobey his directives and terminate the entire agency if he finds it necessary. In this context, those actors who wish to influence and change how things are getting done will find themselves worse off. Therefore, for all state actors, to remain personally loyal to Putin and create value for him is more important than being committed to professional norms and working for the people's welfare. Alternative ideas and approaches disappear from the governance practices, and individuals and agencies' ability to govern competently diminishes.

Yet another underlying problem is that the elite's loyalty is not just for sale—it is on sale. The greater the number of people willing to be involved in the patronal system and compete with each other to enjoy its spoils, the less is the price tag of loyalty and obedience, and so the fewer elites can encumber the dictator by meaningful checks on his governance arrangements. Because a supply of individuals who desire to stay in top administrative positions is ample, but privileges and personalized contracts are rivalrous (elites are sensitive to the perceived dissipation of rents), the regime's elites turn into sycophants, whose creepy subservience is on the public display. In these circumstances, the principal cannot select more competent agents and intermediaries, even hypothetically, only loyal and subservient ones. Importantly, personalistic leaders must uphold their part of the bargain. For the regime's principals, punishing mediocre performers, careerists, and rent-seekers is hardly an option because top bureaucrats might decide to hold back their loyalty and seek to join the rival coalitions.

It is not a mere cultural ornament that Russian elites are quick to speak loyalty and thank Putin for his wise guidance, a behavior that resembles worse instances of kowtowing typical to dictatorships but is laughable and asinine in the modern democracies. Russian experts cognize this subservience as an essential element of personal and bureaucratic survival (Rykovtseva 2020). As the regime matures, new rituals emerge: on September 25, 2020, twenty newly elected governors met their principal at a televised event, wherein some of them were able to express their deep gratitude to Putin up to seven times in a single short communication. This vignette gives the sense of deeply internalized subservience among top individuals. Although the willingness to obey blindly does not rule out the individual elite's obsequiousness, subservience becomes a norm, a standard of appropriate behavior for actors who wish to signal their faithfulness to the Kremlin. "I would like to say one thing. < ... > We are all gathered to express our love for you, Vladimir Vladimirovich," exclaimed Ilya Glazunov, a famous artist and an opponent of democracy and civil rights, speaking at the ONF conference on December 5, 2013. It is only logical that if those individuals who comprise the country's elite circles want to survive and protect their privileged position in the regime, they must heed Putin's demands of loyalty without delay or hesitation.

Finally, as this investigation demonstrates, although Putin has been highlighting the goals of industrial modernization and social betterment as central to his presidency, the regime's ability to deliver tangible, not phantom-like, breakthroughs is heavily circumscribed by the very nature of his rule (Taylor 2019). Numerous gaming strategies, including policy outcomes misrepresentation, misuse of resources, misinformation of the public, and self-serving issue-framings, ensue. These strategies could satisfy principals and protect their subordinates if deployed skillfully. The problem is that gaming strategies further damage the provision of public services. Much as Putin is satisfied with imitating health improvements, so are the rest of the actors involved in health governance. Still, that Russia by and large failed at governing health effectively is not a matter of dispute and opinion.

Additional Perspectives on Bad Governance

In the preceding chapters, I have argued that the main features of Russia's personalistic regime trigger the Kremlin's inability to initiate good governance. This section probes four additional perspectives on the underlying currents in Russian health governance. First, without denying the importance of arguments highlighting the role of kleptocracy in Russia's bad health management, I seek to show their limited explanatory utility. Second, because statements regarding neoliberalism dominate health governance literature, I strive to evaluate whether evoking the concept provides a straightforward explanation of health governance in the country and whether the Russian case allows for a fresh perspective on the matter. Third, given the dire health situation and the objective need to escalate the response to the epidemic in the country, Russia can be viewed as a case in which epidemiological securitization arguments are likely to hold. But such a view must be scrutinized. Fourth, I take stock of an approach that tends to interpret Russian governance practices in a highly contextualized and particularistic fashion. On balance, I argue that these four perspectives provide valuable insights, but they are not so much umbrella explanations of health governance as necessary thinking tools that sharpen our analysis. None of the four perspectives described here could capture the overall pattern of health governance practices in the country.

Kleptocracy and Governance in Russia

Thinking of Russia's government's limited ability to conduct good health governance and provide fundamental goods is often connected to the notion of kleptocracy. Academic studies of kleptocracy pinpointed the phenomenon as an underlying motive of the ruler and elites and the predominant driver of governance spoliation in the country (key academic arguments are in Markus 2015; Dawisha 2016; Aslund 2019; Gel'man 2019;Belton 2020). Striking is that most of Putin's ministers and many legislators operated medium-to-large businesses (Lamberova and Sonin 2018: 139). Investigative journalists, too, expose Putin's entourage malversations and thereby incriminate Putin's regime as predatory and extractive. Alexey Navalny's films, "Putin's Palace. History of World's Largest Bribe" and "He Is Not Dimon to You" are prime examples of jaw-dropping anti-corruption investigations. In this approach, the desire to loot the nation's resources is the ruler and elites' primary preference, if not *raison d'etre*. In addition, although this relationship is too complex to be explored to the degree it deserves, many authors highlight capital liberalization across the globe and capital legalization in safe havens as facilitating instruments of predatory rule (Piketty 2020; Klein 2007), thereby interpreting kleptocracy as a systemic condition.

That Putin's group of cronies and their friends loot state assets is well-documented (Aslund 2019: 132–153, 227–228). "Cronies" is not a coherent group of individuals: their backgrounds and the nature of their connections to Putin differ, but all of them enjoy political protection as long as they perform essential tasks to the principal. Some of these tasks are shady, if not borderline criminal, but they are known to the general audience only because of anti-corruption investigations, both domestic and international. Most of these individuals consistently receive lucrative public contracts and enjoy privileged access to public resources and valuable activities. For instance, one of the exceedingly wealthy Rotenberg brothers, both of whom could be considered Putin's long-time personal friends, took the heat of Alexey Navalny's anti-corruption investigation, which accused Putin of possessing a billion-dollar palace in the middle of the picturesque hills and forests of the Russian south. Like Sergey Roldugin (a cellist allegedly implicated in a nearly $9 billion global money-laundering scheme, see Novaya Gazeta 2016), others were believed to serve Putin as his informal "purse." Others, like Yevgeny Prigozhin—an oligarch and convicted criminal who spent much of the

1980s in jail (Zhegulev 2016)—seem to be in charge of carrying out Putin's clandestine foreign policy agenda in Libya and meddling in the American elections in 2016. While all the aforementioned individuals are Putin's clients, who perform specific tasks for their patron in return for favors and protection, they are not the regime's agents in the strict sense because they are not directly involved in performing public governance tasks set by the Kremlin.

I tend to think that kleptocracy is not the sole purpose of Putin's presidency. Rather, the regime tolerates and uses rent-seeking as a tool to maintain a personalistic system of rule and governance. Kleptocracy and the spread of moral hazard is also a negative externality that emerges out of the way Putin thinks he could stay in control of achieving his substantive policy objectives. Putin pursues presidency-for-life and tacitly promises that loyalists could reasonably expect to enjoy continuous and uncompetitive access to valuable resources and activities in the foreseeable future. Excessive rent-seeking is a negative externality that emerges out of the Kremlin's governance style. Putin seems to have internalized the view that proper organization of public affairs and administration of social goods and services is best achieved by hand-picking the right firms for public tenders and appointing a single operator responsible for producing and delivering a particular product or service in the public sector. Regrettably, Putin's associates follow suit by hand-picking firms that members of their families own or have some kind of vested interest in. This approach creates massive state monopolies, which often fail to deliver, but leaves Putin with a comfortable feeling of total control over the distribution of fundamental goods and services. It also makes the state vulnerable to capture or indirect takeover of the industries by political insiders seeking and receiving rents. This type of relationship suppresses competitiveness in the private sector and dampens the need to deliver health goods efficiently and promptly while allowing to extract rents.

On the one hand, there are limits to kleptocracy; and governance mechanisms are not designed to promote theft and personal enrichment alone. Core objection—"what the Russian state does when it's not stealing" (Taylor 2018: 137)—cautions against taking kleptocracy out of the broader politico-economic context. As Margaret Levi (1989) reminds us, all rulers are predatory, but they could also prioritize social objectives. Modest improvements in health outcomes are undeniable: ordinary patients gained reasonable access to modern medical devices, benefited from federally backed funding for antiretrovirals, and received medicines targeting orphan diseases. Without restrictions on looting, these improvements would have never materialized.

Pure theft is not consistent with the regime's long-term survival. It could be in Putin's interest to limit the appetites of rent-seekers in order to increase the delivery of social services and economic goods to the people, thereby sustaining or increasing his popularity. The regime is interested in constraining fraudulent enrichment because rampant rent-seeking is antithetical to delivering social goods and services and pursuing an ambitious developmental agenda. It is also not by chance that the Kremlin took pains to develop the external system of health governance monitoring and oversight to create the impression that street-level corruption and misappropriation of public resources were under control. Putin's third presidential term started a trend wherein large numbers of arrests curbed the rent-seeking appetites and the widespread corruption among the meso-level bureaucrats. Notably, some high-profile corruption cases reached Putin's attention (Pisano 2014), while most egregious perpetrators of theft in the health sector received decades-long prison sentences. Still, even the progress toward rooting out street-level corruption and individual cases of rent-seeking will hardly improve governance quality.

It appears that further extractions tend to prop up the regime, not individual appetites. Although the textbook recommendation is not to increase taxes during the hard times of economic recession and stagnation, the increasing tax burden comes in multiple indirect forms, including dramatic increases in payroll tax and pension reform that effectively extracted five years of pensions from all those who no longer qualified to retire. Arguably, it was the administrative prowess of the Federal Taxation Service's long-term director, Mikhail Mishustin (2010–2020), that convinced Putin to replace Dmitry Medvedev as Russia's Prime Minister. As inefficiencies accumulate and performance-based legitimacy erodes, Putin is on the path of cannibalizing Russia's economy.

On the other hand, there is no reason to believe that the use of public resources inconsistent with wealth-maximization and welfare promotion will stop any time soon. If Russian criminal culture has indeed corrupted not just the ordinary Russians ability to express thoughts without a criminal slang (Putin, too, shocks journalists with his habitual use of criminal idioms) but political norms and social morality as well (Galeotti 2018: 256–257), then Karen Dawisha and Vladimir Gel'man's arguments may be considered an understatement. The findings from other regions indicate that kleptocratic practices are not necessarily detrimental to the regime. People are willing to support corrupt governments when they expect tangible benefits in return (Manzetti and Wilson 2007; Han 2020) and have low expectations for state provision of healthcare (Ratigan 2020). Similarly, many Russian citizens continue to support the regime and its autocratic leader despite the numerous exposures of corruption in the Kremlin and the dire state of affairs in the national health system, especially troublesome in the country's impoverished periphery.

In summary, the foregoing considerations destabilize the cohesiveness of the idea that kleptocracy, no matter how prevalent in the country, is the core purpose of Putin's rule, on which the regime hinges. Kleptocracy is curiously imbricated in the regime's pursuit of social objectives and development. We cannot settle this debate here. On balance, kleptocracy is both an instrument of personalistic power and a negative externality that flows from the Russian governance system's general principles.

Neoliberalism and Russian Health

Taming neoliberalism is necessary to ensure that the public sector can deliver affordable, high-quality services, and governmental efforts in that direction are laudable. The question is whether invoking the concept of neoliberalism could offer a better, more cohesive explanation of the Kremlin's approach to health governance.

Scholars describe neoliberalism as a global ideological project which either erodes the state obligation to carry out its essential tasks or creates massive negative externalities, affecting public health in undesired ways (Homedes and Ugalde 2005). There is a reasonably broad consensus that neoliberalism has become a key component of public policies in many issue areas and many countries across the globe (Simmons and Elkins 2004; Appel and Orenstein 2016). People's well-being seemingly is under threat from what is often defined "as a peculiar form of reason that configures all aspects of existence in economic terms" (Brown 2015: 17) and minimizes social protection. Following Ted Schrecker and Clare Bambra, "neoliberalism is returning us to an environment in which (chronic) disease can flourish," and it increased susceptibility to acquiring cancers and heart diseases (Schrecker and Bambra 2015: 20). The state tends to roll back its commitments to provide medicines as a fundamental public good (O'Manique 2004).Neoliberalism, therefore, can be seen as an effective plan of reprogramming state functions, a plan that seeks to protect markets and places primary responsibility, if not blame, for health outcomes on individuals rather than structural factors outside of individuals' control.

In Russia, the search for nonmarket solutions to improve social outcomes is submitted to the principals' awareness that concentrating material resources in their hands means consolidating their power vis-a-vis elites and society alike. Consistent with the system of personalistic incentives and constraints, creating noncompetitive markets is a conscious strategy to grant privileges to particular groups, firms, and individuals in return for political loyalty. Nonmarket solutions induce fidelity in agents and elites as long as they benefit from privileged access to state resources. Episodes of governance illustrated in the previous chapters (mainly in Chapter 2) might imply that many critical decisions in health resisted the neoliberal reason. Indeed, the authoritarian Kremlin restored control over social life and acquired a taste for thoroughgoing regulation. Steps to decommodify medicines, replace foreign medicines and medical devices with domestic products, and commit resources to several megaprojects seemingly challenge neoliberal health strategies. However, there are reasons to doubt the validity of this interpretation.

First, the commodification of pharmaceutical knowledge and life-saving products is a central feature of the neoliberal approach to health. In theory, governmental intervention in markets to make medicines affordable goes against the neoliberal idea that the private market should not be subject to government interference (Keshavjee 2014: 122). Moscow's official rhetoric highlighted the desire to ensure pharmaceutical accessibility for the low-income population and acknowledged the necessity to save on budgetary expenditures. However, Putin's mandate instructed agents to save money more than it prioritized uninterrupted access to drugs. Agents deployed many disruptive and contradictory strategies to have prices under control, and they cared more about positive impressions than the objective needs of the Russian patients.

Second, although the liberalization of trade, services, and products is supposed to stimulate economic growth, the keen observers of global health are not thoroughly convinced that open markets are decidedly beneficial for domestic development (Labonte and Ruckert 2019: 132–133). The dominance of foreign goods in domestic health systems could undermine human and pharmaceutical security. Instead, ramping up domestic capacity to manufacture both ready-to-use pharmaceutical forms and medical devices alleviates national dependence on imports, helps preempt possible shortages of internationally produced active pharmaceutical ingredients (APIs) and pharmaceutical forms, and gives credence to bargaining leverage against the vendors of brand-name medications. Although working toward these objectives is commendable, Putin's lopsided mandate deprioritized healthcare needs compared to his political objectives. Agents obeyed Putin's mandate blindly, and they worked to reach shallow metrics while hardly caring about benefits for ordinary Russians.

Third, sharp critics of neoliberalism might succumb to the illusion that the state-led investments in health programs challenge the idea of austerity, commonly viewed as a cardinal means of furthering the neoliberal agenda (Blyth 2013). The Kremlin's critics, this author included, offer a different rendition of the government's approach to health governance: autocratic profligacy is not a credible challenge to the neoliberal reason. The literature suggests a traceable dynamic wherein the infusion of substantial financial resources in politically motivated and attractive projects accompanies welfare retrenchment (Matveev 2020; Matveev and Novkunskaya 2020) and coincides with slashed funding for routine necessities, such as hospital beds in the public sector. This approach has nothing to do with creating equality and equity in health. As it appears, the Kremlin's governing wisdom is that every ruble of increased government spending for priority projects must correspond to one less ruble in health spending elsewhere, while goods and services created by stimulus spending must be offset by the decline in public spending on day-to-day operations and the increase in tax burden.

Let us consider the Kremlin's ideological posturing vis-a-vis neoliberalism. Misleadingly, during the early years of Putin's rule, several prominent individuals trained attention to the need to develop a socially responsible state in Russia (Luzhkov 2004a, b; Luzhkov 2004a; Gryzlov 2005, 2007; Mironov 2007). "Russia may be threatened with severe negative consequences if < … > neoliberal policy is not opposed. According to another neoliberal principle, free interaction of economic forces rather than state planning ensures social justice. However, this principle failed in capitalist countries," says Evgeny Primakov (1929–2015), former prime minister, speaking at the Valdai Club meeting, January 27, 2014. Rhetoric aside, the problem is that the nature of electoral authoritarianism under personalistic rule suppresses genuine ideological commitments. Over Putin's two decades in power, notable political insiders tended to interpret any universalizing ideology as a force undermining effective and responsible policymaking. As early as 2003, Boris Gryzlov, contributing to the building of personalism, noted that "Our ideology is common sense. The authorities should do what is good for most of our citizens. Centrism is pragmatism. This is the desire to set the task correctly and find an effective solution for it" (Gryzlov 2003). Being either centrist or pragmatist is politically expedient, and it allows principals and agents to evade credible commitments. Little wonder, Putin's presidential addresses to the Federal Assembly had no common ideological denominator and never featured an ideologically coherent or uncontradictory set of governance ideas.

It is not by chance that in the first decade of Putin's rule, the official concept papers and articles, penned by a multitude of high-powered individuals, embraced contradictory views. Based on Russia's comparative advantage and free trade, the ideas of global economic competitiveness appeared in the documents. However, these documents also lionized protectionism, import substitution industrialization, and state-led development. These papers refused to acknowledge that state interventionism impeded economic freedoms and hurt domestic competitiveness. In making decisions, Putin habitually relied on a motley crew of advisers drawn from both liberal and statist camps. Although positive references to neoliberal policies became a political anathema, several core participants in Russian health governance stayed true to fiscal conservatism. That Tatyana Golikova, a long-term "curator" of health, preoccupied with austerity, came from the Ministry of Finance attests to the lingering power of neoliberal thinking. However, Putin also relies on the proponents of economic interventionism, such as Andrey Belousov, his long-serving economic assistant (2013–2020).

Thus, the official rejection of neoliberalism as antithetical to the national interest and social betterment (Medvedev 2009; Luzhkov and Popov 2010; Primakov 2014a; Primakov 2014b; Putin 2019a) was unambiguously self-serving as it attempted to harvest the popularity and lionize the regime in the media. The Kremlin's propaganda machinery has been working hard to convince its audience that people will be worse off without Putin's strategic directives in health and state domination in the economy. Although that public consensus has been slightly attenuating (see Kolesnikov and Volkov 2019), anti-neoliberal and populist rhetoric remained essential to sustaining Putin's popularity. It seems to be working its deceptive magic on the domestic constituency as many

Russians continue to vest their trust in Putin. Pronouncements on the need to increase social welfare were not so much a genuine attempt to formulate the foundational principles of the welfare state as they were an expression of the authoritarian contract between the regime and its constituents.

It is hard to disagree with Thomas Piketty, who concludes that it was a deep ideological freeze that stunned the Kremlin's commitment to a more equal and just society (Piketty 2020: 604). In the absence of an ideology oriented to upholding the ideals of equality and social justice, no long-term improvement in the provision of fundamental goods is likely. That the lack of explicit ideology highlighting social justice as a central purpose of the state is an essential feature of personalism is true, but, contrary to Piketty's analysis, Russian leaders hardly envision an inegalitarian and unjust society as a normative model either. On a side note, Russia is hardly a clean case of hypercapitalism in the sense that many features positively associated with well-functioning market economies, including the rule of law and deep respect for private property, are missing (Rutland 2013; Markus 2015; Aslund 2019).

What can we learn in terms of personalistic regimes' relations with neoliberal health practices? To usher in improvements in health, academics and activists call for radical changes and welcome a more prominent administrative and regulative presence of the state apparatus in health affairs. The assumption, often unspoken, behind this call is that the increase in state involvement and dirigisme compensates for the neoliberal obsession with cutting waste while being satisfied with public goods' under-provision. In the Russian case, state intervention was informed and shaped by the main features of electoral personalism and thus did not usher in a better health governance system. Russia's statism and over-regulation, which seem to be antithetical to the neoliberal reason, did not reflect anti-neoliberal normative consensus, and thus nominally anti-neoliberal measures did not preclude Russian officials from pursuing short-term and self-interested behavior. An important implication is that the state and its methods of political control might be the root problem of poor health governance. Administrative domination is not tantamount to impersonal institutions that sustain a strong sense of mission to serve impartially in the citizens' interests. Countries with no strong impersonal institutions could hardly tame neoliberalism and achieve an acceptable level of equality in health, while assertive state interventionism will generate governance failures.

Implications for the Securitization Debate

Securitization is a curious phenomenon. The first approach is concerned with the natural outbreaks of newly emerging and reemerging infectious diseases, like a human influenza pandemic, threats of weaponizing pathogens, and biological attacks. It aims to generate strategic frameworks of preparedness and epidemic intelligence (Boin et al. 2003; Cecchine 2006) or analyze unanticipated consequences of the enacted policies at the international level (Elbe 2010; Roemer-Mahler and Elbe 2016). This approach shies away from articulating a broad analytical framework. The second approach explores how a mixture of factors exposes vulnerable populations to health risks (Ostergard 2002; Seckinelgin et al. 2010; Baringer and Heitkamp 2011). It seeks to raise awareness of the importance of individual well-being and inject its deontological commitments to human security into a positive research agenda, although it falls short of developing a full-fledged normative theory. The third approach, "epidemiological securitization," is inspired by the Copenhagen School. It is the prevailing analytical method in the literature on securitization and health, and it generally holds that domestic actors intentionally construct select issues as an existential threat to human wellbeing to escalate the response against non-military threats. European constructivists are obsessed with exploring the nuanced ways local intervening variables affect the content and efficacy of securitizing speech acts (Herington 2010; Vieira 2011; McInnes and Rushton 2011; Lo Yukping and Thomas 2010). Finally, the growing body of literature links Russian securitization of sexuality, fertility, and family planning to the multitude of factors, including international identity construction as a great power (Sjostedt 2008) to the consolidation of Putin's authoritarian regime (Makarychev and Medvedev 2015).

The studies in this vein remain relatively thin on theorizing the state's incentives to securitize particular health issues and thus fall prey to confirmation bias, wherein selective empirical observations from different cases just flesh out the general theoretical intuition. Further, securitization is neither necessary nor sufficient for governments to mobilize resources and raise awareness. The main shortcoming is then that the "epidemiological securitization" approach fails to identify causal mechanisms that would explain how and why the substantive framing of the crisis comes into being. Arguably, HIV/AIDS is simultaneously a problem linked to the issues of human rights and intellectual property and, therefore, could be securitized and responded to in disparate ways. Thus, it cannot explain why the authorities chose to portray HIV/AIDS as a public health crisis that undermines people's well-being and as an external attack on the Russian state. Still, the meaning of securitization moves remains ambiguous unless an analyst starts treating security discourses as part and parcel of governance practices inherently linked with the political regime's essential features.

That the Kremlin might securitize selected health issues and treat them as a matter of political priority is not overly surprising, given the multi-faceted and largely unmitigated health crisis in the country that suffers from low life expectancy, especially among males, linked to the high levels of alcohol and tobacco consumption, as well as the inadequate capacity of the country's health system (Marquez et al. 2007). Historical examples are plenty. The last General Secretary of the Communist Party of the Soviet Union from 1985 until 1991, Mikhail Gorbachev, initiated a massive anti-alcohol campaign of 1985–1987, extraordinary even by the standards of nondemocratic states such as the USSR, is a well-known but poorly implemented initiative to improve public health by linking it to the survival of the state and the economy (Tarschys 1993).

Chapter 5 challenges the typical portrayal of health securitization as a strategy to escalate domestic responses to an objective epidemiological threat. Instead, it proposes a political perspective that highlights the incompleteness of contracts that inhere in personalistic regimes as the driving force behind the securitizing move. Although few would reject the notion that HIV/AIDS is an issue of human security, the securitization of narcotic addiction, HIV/AIDS, and alternative lifestyles is quite different in Russia. In Chapter 5, I traced the process of how core domestic actors, most importantly the Federal Drug Control Service (FSKN), the Ministry of Health, and the Moscow Patriarchy, unfolded the discourse of HIV/AIDS as an ontological threat to the regime.

The problem is that personalistic contracts are never complete, and elites actively seek useful instruments of securing personalized contracts with Putin. Agents and corporate actors that exhibit glaring incompetence, trigger public protests, or simply air dirty laundry in public live under the credible threat of agency termination. Agents found it in their best interest to securitize HIV/AIDS as reactionary justification for their underperformance. Bad performance notwithstanding, personalistic the ruler will grant agents access to valuable activities and resources if they provide value to him. One, agents simply adopt bureaucratic gaming strategies, which create an impression of the Kremlin's benevolence and competence. This behavior is not surprising given that present-day Russia is an "informational autocracy." Securitization is such a gaming technique. It allows elites to broadcast their corporate fealty to Putin's agenda at the national level. It looks like agents govern in public (they give multiple interviews, write essays, and so on), but the recipient of their public communication is their boss.

Two, agents and their organizations tap into Putin's illiberal ideological posturing, creating value-added for the regime. Although personalistic regimes inhibit genuine ideological commitments, rulers and elites might find ideological frameworks valuable for domination over non-elites. In this light, agents and corporate actors securitize health issues as an optimizing response to the personalism's institutional setting. The securitization move went hand in hand with the broader discourse of Russian civilizational insecurity (or the need to defend its identity and uniqueness, distinctiveness for the West), which went hand in hand with the notion of Russia as a carrier of essentialized code and unique spiritual-moral values, antithetical to those of the West.

To conclude, the main findings speak to Stephan Elbe's (2006) insights regarding the inherent deficiencies of securitization and possible negative externalities that are likely to arise when public health becomes a security issue. The future of an effective response to HIV/AIDS in Russia will depend on the civil society's power to take control over the construction of threats, including their ability to impose external monitoring and vertical accountability on hitherto autonomous and underperforming health bureaucracies. But Putin's regime blocked possible learning from outside actors, thus precluding any correction of the embraced securitization strategies.

Looking for a Bigger Picture

The preceding chapters have traced distinct, but interwoven, stories wherein the main actors in the multi-level architecture that connects participants in health affairs to the regime's principals respond to the demands, incentives, and management styles of the Kremlin's authoritarian regime. Zooming in on distinct episodes of governance allowed for solid empirical grounding and anchored analytical thinking about personalistic orders to the set of specific governance practices as they occurred in Russia. Policy entrepreneurs need this perspective to understand the underlying political determinants of health, redress their strategies accordingly, and deploy their advocacy tactics more effectively (Ljubownikow and Crotty 2016). For the specialists in Russian affairs, the book offers an analytical framework of bad governance rooted in the rational institutionalist tradition and connected to competence-control theory. There are reasons why such an approach is needed.

First, there is a relatively well-developed body of literature that seeks to explain how Russian authoritarianism shapes the policy process in Russia (e.g., Taylor 2014; Remington 2019) and enumerate the internal obstacles to reforms and institutional improvement (e.g., Khmelnitskaya 2020; Matveev and Novkunskaya 2020) that preclude or significantly complicate authoritarian modernization in the country. But to date, the previous books on Russian health typically looked at specific issues (such as HIV/AIDS, see Twigg 2006; Manning and Tikhonova 2009; Pape 2014) and were not engaging broader analytical literatures on personalistic regimes this book draws on and advances.

Second, the Tetris of interpretations of Russian health governance leaves us without a bigger picture. The literature is shattered into a set of ad hoc investigations of corruption, Soviet legacies of window-dressing (e.g., Pisano 2014), the insufficient level of health expenditures and administrative bottlenecks, and neoliberal austerity reforms in the hospital sector. Some scholars tend to assign too much value to secondary political factors and concepts. Rehashing concepts with limited explanatory power is not enough to come to grips with the underlying mechanisms of governance. But scholars, time and again, do so (Gómez 2015; Poku and Sundewall 2018; Gómez and Kucheryavenko 2020). It is all too easy to be blinded to the broad political context and, therefore, decontextualize, misinterpret, and skate over the common reasons why certain instances of bad health governance occur and persist.

Third, my analysis also challenges explanatory strategies that rigidly connect governance pitfalls to Putin's predilections and idiosyncratic behavior. Further, by exposing the patterned actions of the main actors in health administration, the book challenges the idea that Putin's traits as a leader are central to sustaining bad governance. Although we must not discard the personalistic leader's outsized importance in the health governance process and his influence on it, the Russian case lends itself to building fruitful inferences about personalism's internal logic without resorting to yet another argument about "bad Putin." Such flawed arguments range from a multitude of journalistic exposures of Putin's unscrupulousness and lust for power (Gessen 2013; Satter 2016; Belton 2020) to personal insights about Putin's ideological predilections (Aleksashenko 2019: 375), which are difficult to corroborate. In short, without denying the role that the power-maximizing autocrat plays in constructing and maintaining governance practices, explaining Putin's individuality, idiosyncrasies, career path, and so on is not the right path to analyze and explain what is going on in the country in terms of health governance. The caveat is that a leader with a "code" or mentality—a set of ideas, habits, and emotions—that does not resonate with the requirements of a personalistic rule would have had a hard time establishing his rule so firmly that all the extant pathologies of personalistic governance practices would endure. For instance, a leader without a strong impulse to control and without habits to demand loyalty from subordinates would have been more likely to issue general bureaucratic grants and not expect agents to over-comply, reifying his ideas and values.

This book takes a different approach by linking health governance complexities in Russia with its personalistic regime as an underlying factor. Specifically, this investigation intended to unveil the array of factors that undermine the government's ability to improve the population's well-being. In a nutshell, personalistic regimes, of which Russia is an example, prompt a perverse system of incentives and constraints for all health governance participants and thus increase the instances of governance flubs that could not be easily corrected. Health governance, in other words, is flawed because of the distinct modalities in which the personalistic regime operates. The author argues, most importantly, that the Russian state is not a carrier of collective (societal) interests and could not become one as long as the control over the state is firmly in the hands of few individuals and as long as the regime's principals enjoy the acquiescence of their clients. In contrast to the previous empirically valuable attempts to explain why Russia fails that rely on factors specific to the Russian political trajectory and broader historical, post-communist context, my analysis presents governance failures in Russia as genetically connected to the authoritarian way of running politics. This perspective should compel area studies specialists to abandon the entrenched vision of Russia being so unique that only country-specific analytical models and ad hoc explanatory variables are applicable.

CONCLUSION: WILL IT GET BETTER?

This book's central question was: Why and how did Moscow fail at health governance? This investigation provides a coherent and nuanced level of understanding of how Putin's system operates, its main governance motivations and constraints, and why it cannot provide collective goods efficiently, dispensing the common propensity to construct fine-grained explanations or delve into isolated episodes of governance. The overall benefit of my perspective is that it links foundational features of autocratic regimes to the deep-seated mechanisms of governance and then helps structure new conversations about political determinants of health.

Metaphorically, the regime is the Bear that claims to act in the interests of the Russian patient, and the Russian patient is the Gardener who absorbs the costs of the Kremlin's ineffective and sometimes harmful health governance. The investigation shows that because of the distinct ways personalistic regimes operate, the effectiveness of governance attenuates, perhaps fatally. In this system, no individual actor is interested in putting brakes on the machinery of governance with its perverse system of constraints and incentives, as described in the following section. Relevant political actors lack incentives to break free from the rules of the game as imposed by the autocrat and fail to pursue an alternative course of action. Thus, the radical and definitive improvement in the state administration could be achieved only at the expense of dismantling the regime and reconstructing the entire state apparatus; and that is not something Russian elites are likely to do. The only reason to remain optimistic is to believe that absent personalist rule health actors would not behave the same way as they do now.

A major obstacle on the road to improvement is that elites are unwilling to acknowledge the simple fact that the political system they had built prevented them from increasing state efficiency. Although the epidemic of COVID-19 exposed the faulty optimization strategy, the government seemed not to worry that the healthcare sector failed at performing its routine tasks. In a dark twist of fate, the full-blown phase of the Covid epidemic was a blessing for the regime, as it can conveniently blame its failures and inadequacies of health governance on the extraordinary circumstances and exceptional challenges.

In contrast to the last generation of the Soviet leaders (Kotkin 2001: 59), Putin and his entourage are unlikely to pour over the reformist dilemma: they can bridge the gap between the promises of social betterment, expressed in the series of Putin's May decrees, and disappointing realities, not through deep institutional reforms, but by making bureaucratic gaming techniques more sophisticated. Although Putin's Russia has been stagnant and not developed as planned at the outset of Putin's rule, it is also unlikely to find itself in a nose-dive, reminiscent of the last Soviet decade. Nor does the officialdom possess any normative ideals that can animate the desire to change. Further, there is considerable anecdotal evidence that autocrats' lust for personal power makes them prefer to see their countries fail instead of taking a path of uncomfortable and decisive reforms. In his memoirs, Mikhail Gorbachev (1995) claimed that he had resisted deep institutional reforms in the late 1980s because he had not been willing to break out of the deeply internalized ideological commitment to socialism. Andrey Grachev (2001), his biographer and last press secretary, confirms that statement. But, more plausibly, Gorbachev knew that deep reforms would beget the loss of his personal power. Collapse ensued.

The difficult question is whether Russia will fare better under democratic rule. True, democracies are likely to ensure better health outcomes than nondemocracies (Wigley and Akkoyunlu-Wigley 2011; Wang, Mechkova, and Andersson 2018; McGuire 2020; Cronert and Hadenius 2020). In democracies, good governance—the crucial "pro-health" factor—is undermined by a large number of veto players and electoral business cycles but is secured by strong formal institutions, a high level of transparency and political accountability of state officials, and self-enforcing professional ethos of civil servants bound by the rule of law. Still, democracies are better at governing.

What do prominent Russians think about that? Alexey Navalny and Vladimir Milov, two noteworthy opponents of authoritarianism, who act in dual roles of opposition leaders and experts in corruption and economic matters, argue that democratic transition is a prerequisite for good governance. As experts, they propose magisterial ideas on making the political and administrative systems work for the people in the "beautiful Russia of the future." As political leaders, they must project optimism lest their supporters succumb to a dark sense of disempowerment and nihilism. Others, like Viktor Erofeev, an acclaimed but controversial writer, think not so much about the institutional constraints that shape agents' behavior as the inherently dark nature of Man, building on the pessimistic tradition of William Golding. Erofeev places the onus of change on the ordinary people, who, in his view, lack a discernible set of democratic and liberal commitments (Velekhov 2020). Lack of norms and decency at the street level will beget and perpetuate bad governance, irrespective of the nature of the political regime. Perhaps, he overstates things, but the anomie that engulfed the country might not be reversible.

Regardless, the scenario of democratic transition is a long shot; when and how it will happen is not easy to predict at this juncture in time. Building and spreading democratic norms and values is an onerous and time-consuming task, and the unambiguously positive outcome cannot be guaranteed. The most realistic scenario for Russia is to become a sort of political regime, which Lucan Way describes as a "pluralism by default," wherein no would-be personalistic leader is capable of establishing the system of his/her own personalistic rule (Way 2015), but the rule of law necessary for modern liberal democracy are missing. The features of health governance under "pluralism by default" could be extrapolated by examining Ukrainian and Moldovan cases. This promising research program is yet to be pursued.

Given the vast literature on good governance, fairly straightforward are the institutional features of a regime capable of effective governance. The subject of further refinements, effective governance is tentatively conceptualized as the presence of a system of depersonalized authoritative rules which (a) all social actors must follow in order to gain promotion and have access to valuable activities and resources; (b) are entrenched in permanent formal organizations which bind the elite and top executive alike but are not the pure expression of their interests; (c) are valued and followed on their own terms (i.e., they must be separate from the immediate rational calculation of cost and benefits, and therefore limit predation and blatant rent-seeking); (d) are autonomous from the outsized influence of top executives and veto players and are capable of surviving their natural or political lifespan; (e) cannot be easily manipulated to the incumbent's or elites' situational advantage; (f) are adaptable in the sense that they allow altering a pattern of behavior to deal effectively with novel circumstances and challenges.

The preceding analysis does not license an optimistic prognosis. On the one hand, it is likely that health governance deteriorates, but no major social calamity ensues. The governance practices continue to reflect elites' self-interest, while agents continue to imitate progress and deploy gaming strategies. Simultaneously, the regime's sensitivity to the adverse public reaction diminishes. The warning comes from the fact that Putin pressed on with the hugely unpopular confiscation-like pension reform while he found it best to reverse equally unpopular monetization reform in his earlier years in power. Contracts are always incomplete, and the most vulnerable parties, including patients and health intermediaries, are less important to the regime's survival than the elites. Putin can sacrifice his dwindling popular appeal, but he must tightly control his subordinates and fulfill patronal obligations to his clients. Health goods and services are fewer and of inferior quality, while loyal monopolists enjoy the spoils.

On the other hand, recent events license a direful forecast also. No matter how much spin-doctors lie, there is a growing awareness that the regime is responsible for governance failures. One thing is clear: amid the Covid pandemic, the spectacle of effective governance is not as convincing as several years back. Medical professionals join protests and work to rule while patients scrap their political loyalty to the disinterested president. The deficit of genuine popularity incentivizes Putin to rig or ignore unfavorable electoral outcomes and use threats. The received wisdom is that rule by violence is costly, but there are telltale signs that Putin will not shy away from choosing that path (Gel'man 2020a).

Once the public euphoria sustained by the regime's militaristic exploits and by gendered stereotypes of the ruler as a real macho evaporates, once well-liked and charismatic Putin faces an apparent prospect of becoming a liability for the elites whose own survival, given the constraints of the electoral authoritarianism, depends on the autocrat's ability to remain popular. Once elites' fidelity to the unpopular leader vanishes, the regime will likely reach a point that could jeopardize Putin personally. Consequently, he might proceed with repressions and tightening the circle of loyal elites or, less likely, opening the regime up for a limited competition (Meng 2020). It would not be too hasty to see Russian saber-rattling and military escalation along the Ukrainian border to deflect negative attention from faulty governance practices and undesirable social outcomes.

In short, when personalistic legitimacy attenuates, institutions are hollowed out, and the social promises remain unfulfilled, coercion ensues. Contrary to wishful expectations of improvements in governance, the regime will mutate into a strictly predatory and coercive one.

REFERENCES

Acemoglu, D. 2003. Why Not a Political Coase Theorem? Social Conflict, Commitment, and Politics. *Journal of Comparative Economics* 31: 620–652.
Acemoglu, D., and J. Robinson. 2006. Economic Backwardness in Political Perspective. *American Political Science Review* 100 (1): 115–131.
Aleksashenko, S. 2019. *Kontrrevolyutsiya: Kak Stroilas' Vertikal' Vlasti v Sovremennoi Rossii i kak eto Vliyaet na Ekonomiku*. Moskva: Al'pina Publisher.
Appel, H., and M.A. Orenstein. 2016. Why did Neoliberalism Triumph and Endure in the Post-Communist World? *Comparative Politics* 48 (3): 313–333.
Aslund, A. 2019. *Russia's Crony Capitalism: The Path from Market Economy to Kleptocracy*. New Haven: Yale University Press.
Baringer, L., and S. Heitkamp. 2011. Securitizing Global Health: A View from Maternal Health. *Global Health Governance* 4 (2): 1–21.
Belton, C. 2020. *Putin's People: How the KGB Took Back Russia and Then Took On the West*. New York: Farrar, Straus and Giroux.
Blyth, M. 2013. *Austerity: The History of a Dangerous Idea*. New York: Oxford University Press.
Boin, A., P. Lagadec, E. Michel-Kerjan, and W. Overdijk. 2003. Critical Infrastructures under Threat: Learning from the Anthrax Scare. *Journal of Contingencies and Crisis Management* 11 (3): 99–104.
Brown, W. 2015. *Undoing the Demos: Neoliberalism's Stealth Revolution*. New York: Zone Books.
Bucci, E., et al. 2020. Safety and Efficacy of the Russian COVID-19 Vaccine: More Information Needed. *The Lancet* 396 (10256): e53.
Bucci, E., et al. 2021. Data Discrepancies and Substandard Reporting of Interim Data of Sputnik V Phase 3 Trial. *The Lancet* 397 (10288): 1881–1883.
Cecchine, G. 2006. *Infectious Disease and National Security: Strategic Information Needs*. Santa Monica, CA; Arlington, VA; Pittsburgh, PA: RAND Corporation.
Cook, L. 2015. *Constraints on Universal Health Care in the Russian Federation: Inequality, Informality and the Failures of Mandatory Health Insurance Reforms*. UNRISD Working Paper 2015–5.
Cronert, A., and A. Hadenius. 2020. Institutional Foundations of Global Well-being: Democracy, State Capacity and Social Protection. *International Political Science Review* 42 (5): 705–724.
Elbe, S. 2006. Should HIV/AIDS be Securitized? The Ethical Dilemmas of Linking HIV/AIDS and Security. *International Studies Quarterly* 50 (1): 119–144.
Elbe, S. 2010. Haggling Over Viruses: The Downside Risks of Securitizing Infectious Disease. *Health Policy and Planning* 25 (6): 476–485.

Ezrow, N., and E. Frantz. 2011. *Dictators and Dictatorships: Understanding Authoritarian Regimes and Their Leaders*. New York: The Continuum Publishing Group.

Galeotti, M. 2018. *The Vory: Russia's Super Mafia*. New Haven: Yale University Press.

Gessen, M. 2013. *The Man Without a Face: The Unlikely Rise of Vladimir Putin*. New York: Riverhead Books.

Gel'man, V. 2019. *Nedostoinoe Pravlenie: Politika v Sovremennoi Rossii*. Sankt-Peterburg: Izdatel'stvo Evropeiskogo Universiteta v Sankt-Peterburge.

Gel'man, V. 2020a. The Politics of Fear: How the Russian Regime Confronts its Opponents. *Russian Social Science Review* 61 (6): 467–482.

Gel'man, V. 2020b. Porazhenie bez Srazheniya: Rossiiskaya Oppozitsiya i Predely Mobilizatsii. In *Novaya (Ne)legitimnost': Kak Prokhodilo i Chto Prineslo Rossii Perepisyvanie Konstitutsii*, ed. K. Rogov, 63–69. Moskva: Fond Liberal'naya Missiya.

Gómez, E. J. 2015. Understanding the BRIC Response to AIDS: Political Institutions, Civil Society, and Historical Policy Backlash in Comparative Perspective. *Commonwealth & Comparative Politics* 53 (3): 315–340.

Gómez, E. J., and O. Kucheryavenko. 2020. Explaining Russia's Struggle to Eradicate HIV/AIDS: Institutions, Agenda Setting and the Limits to Multiple-Streams Processes. *Journal of Comparative Policy Analysis: Research and Practice* 23 (3): 372–388.

Gorbachev, M. 1995. *Zhizn' i Reformy*. 2 Vol. Moskva: Novosti.

Grachev, A. 2001. *Gorbachev: Chelovek, Kotoryi Khotel kak Luchshe*. Moskva: Vagrius.

Gryzlov, B. 2003. Politicheskii doklad Predsedatelya Vysshego Soveta politicheskoi partii Edinaya Rossiya B. V. Gryzlova pered delegatami III Sezda partii Edinaya Rossiya, 22 September.

Gryzlov, B. 2005. Ot stabilizatsii k razvitiyu: politicheskie prioritety Partii Edinaya Rossiya, VI Sezd Partii Edinaya Rossiya, Krasnoyarsk, 26 November.

Gryzlov, B. 2007. Politicheskie zadachi razvitiya strany. In *Vektor Rossii: Razmyshleniya o Puti Razvitiya Rossii*. SPb: Tsentr sotsial'no-konservativnoi politiki.

Han, K. 2020. Autocratic Welfare Programs, Economic Perceptions, and Support for the Dictator: Evidence from African Autocracies. *International Political Science Review* 42 (3): 416–429.

Herington, J. 2010. Securitization of Infectious Diseases in Vietnam: The Cases of HIV and Avian Influenza. *Health Policy and Planning* 25 (6): 467–475.

Homedes, N., and A. Ugalde. 2005. Why Neoliberal Health Reforms Have Failed in Latin America. *Health Policy* 71 (1): 83–96.

Keshavjee, S. 2014. *Blind Spot. How Neoliberalism Infiltrated Global Health*. Oakland, California: University of California Press.

Khmelnitskaya, M. 2020. Socio-economic Development and the Politics of Expertise in Putin's Russia: The 'Hollow Paradigm Perspective.' *Europe-Asia Studies* 73 (4): 625–646.

Klein, N. 2007. *The Shock Doctrine: The Rise of Disaster Capitalism*. New York: Metropolitan Books.

Kolesnikov, A., and D. Volkov. 2019. Pragmatic Paternalism: The Russian Public and the Private Sector. *Carnegie.ru*, 18 January.

Kotkin, S. 2001. *Armageddon Averted: The Soviet Collapse, 1970–2000: Soviet Collapse Since 1970*. New York: Oxford University Press.

Labonté, R., and A. Ruckert. 2019. *Health Equity in a Globalizing Era: Past Challenges, Future Prospects*. Oxford, UK: Oxford University Press.

Lamberova, N., and K. Sonin. 2018. The Role of Business in Shaping Economic Policy. In *The New Autocracy: Information, Politics, and Policy in Putin's Russia*, ed. D. Treisman, 137–158. Washington, D.C.: Brookings Institution Press.

Levi, M. 1989. *Of Rule and Revenue*. Berkeley and Los Angeles: University of California Press.

Ljubownikow, S., and J. Crotty. 2016. Nonprofit Influence on Public Policy: Exploring Nonprofit Advocacy in Russia. *Nonprofit and Voluntary Sector Quarterly* 45 (2): 314–332.

Lo Yuk-ping, C., and N. Thomas. 2010. How is Health a Security Issue? Politics, Responses and Issues. *Health Policy and Planning* 25 (6): 447–453.

Luzhkov, Yu. 2004a. Liberal'noe i sotsial'noe. *Strategiya Rossii* No. 1, January.

Luzhkov, Yu. 2004b. Sotsial'nost' vmesto oligarkhizma. *Strategiya Rossii* No. 10–11, October–November.

Luzhkov, Yu., and G. Popov. 2010. Eshche odno slovo o Gaidare. *Moskovskii Komsomolets*, 21 January.

Makarychev, A., and S. Medvedev. 2015. Biopolitics and Power in Putin's Russia. *Problems of Post-Communism* 62 (1): 45–54.

Manning, N., and N. Tikhonova. eds. 2009. *Health and Health Care in the New Russia*. Farnham & Burlington: Ashgate Publishing.

Manzetti, L., and C.J. Wilson. 2007. Why Do Corrupt Governments Maintain Public Support? *Comparative Political Studies* 40 (8): 949–970.

Markus, S. 2015. *Property, Predation, and Protection: Piranha Capitalism in Russia and Ukraine*. Cambridge: Cambridge University Press.

Marquez, P.V., et al. 2007. Adult Health in the Russian Federation: More than just a Health Problem. *Health Affairs* 26 (4): 1040–1051.

Matveev, I. 2020. Benefits or Services? Politics of Welfare Retrenchment in Russia, 2014–2017. *East European Politics* 37 (3): 534–551.

Matveev, I., and A. Novkunskaya. 2020. Welfare Restructuring in Russia since 2012: National Trends and Evidence from the Regions. *Europe-Asia Studies* 74 (1): 50–71.

McGuire, J. 2020. *Democracy and Population Health* (Elements in the Politics of Development). New York: Cambridge University Press.

McInnes, C., and S. Rushton. 2011. HIV/AIDS and Securitization Theory. *European Journal of International Relations* 19 (1): 115–138.

Medvedev, D. 2009. Rossiya, vpered! *Gazeta.ru*, 10 September.

Meng, A. 2020. *Constraining Dictatorship: From Personalized Rule to Institutionalized Regimes*. Cambridge: Cambridge University Press.

Mironov, S. 2007. Sotsial'nyi ideal v sovremennoi politike: O smyslovykh osnovaniyakh spravedlivogo obshchestvennogo ustroistva. *Politicheskii Klass* No. 25, January.

Ostergard, R. 2002. Politics in the Hot Zone: AIDS and National Security in Africa. *Third World Quarterly* 23 (2): 333–350.

O'Manique, C. 2004. *Neoliberalism and AIDS Crisis in Sub-Saharan Africa: Globalization's Pandemic*. Houndmills, Basingtoke: Palgrave Macmillan.

Pape, U. 2014. *The Politics of HIV/AIDS in Russia*. London: Routledge.

Piketty, T. 2020. *Capital and Ideology*. Cambridge and London: Belknap Press: An Imprint of Harvard University Press.

Pisano, J. 2014. Pokazukha and Cardiologist Khrenov. In *Historical Legacies of Communism in Russia and Eastern Europe*, eds. M. Beissinger and S. Kotkin, 222–242. New York: Cambridge University Press.

Poku, N., and J. Sundewall. 2018. Political Responsibility and Global Health. *Third World Quarterly* 39 (3): 471–486.

Primakov, E. 2014a. 2013. Hard Problems of Russia: Why Neoliberal Policy Cannot Be Accepted Today. *Nezavisimaya Gazeta*, 14 January.

Primakov, E. 2014b. Russia's Problems: Why Neoliberal Policy is Unacceptable Today. Valdai Discussion Club, 27 January. https://valdaiclub.com/a/highlights/russia_s_problems_why_neoliberal_policy_is_unacceptable_today/.

Putin, V. 2019a. Pryamaya liniya s Vladimirom Putinym, 20 June. http://www.kremlin.ru/events/president/news/page/91.

Putin, V. 2019b. Zasedanie Soveta po razvitiyu grazhdanskogo obshchestva i pravam cheloveka, 10 December. http://kremlin.ru/events/president/news/62285.

Ratigan, K. 2022. Riding the Tiger of Performance Legitimacy? Chinese Villagers' Satisfaction with State Healthcare Provision. *International Political Science Review* 43 (2): 259–278.

Remington, T.F. 2019. Institutional Change in Authoritarian Regimes: Pension Reform in Russia and China. *Problems of Post-Communism* 66 (5): 301–314.

Roemer-Mahler, A., and S. Elbe. 2016. The Race for Ebola Drugs: Pharmaceuticals, Security and Global Health Governance. *Third World Quarterly* 37 (3): 487–506.

Rutland, P. 2013. Neoliberalism and the Russian Transition. *Review of International Political Economy* 20 (2): 332–362.

Rykovtseva, E. 2020. Kholuistvo ne trebuet soglasovanii. *RFE/RL*, 24 September.
Satter, D. 2016. *The Less You Know, the Better You Sleep: Russia's Road to Terror and Dictatorship under Yeltsin and Putin*. New Haven and London: Yale University Press.
Schrecker, T., and C. Bambra. 2015. *How Politics Makes Us Sick: Neoliberal Epidemics* Houndmills, Basingstoke: Palgrave Macmillan UK.
Seckinelgin, H., J. Bigirumwami, and J. Morris. 2010. Securitization of HIV/AIDS in Context: Gendered Vulnerability in Burundi. *Security Dialogue* 41 (5): 515–535.
Sewell, W.H. 2009. From State-Centrism to Neoliberalism: Macro-Historical Contexts of Population Health since World War II. In *Successful Societies: How Institutions and Culture Affect Health*, eds. P.A. Hall and M. Lamont, 254–287. New York: Cambridge University Press.
Simmons, B., and Z. Elkins. 2004. The Globalization of Liberalization: Policy Diffusion in the International Political Economy. *American Political Science Review* 98 (1): 171–189.
Sjostedt, R. 2008. Exploring the Construction of Threats: The Securitization of HIV/AIDS in Russia. *Security Dialogue* 39 (1): 7–29.
Tarschys, D. 1993. The Success of a Failure: Gorbachev's Alcohol Policy, 1985–88. *Europe-Asia Studies* 45 (1): 7–25.
Taylor, B.D. 2014. Police Reform in Russia: The Policy Process in a Hybrid Regime. *Post-Soviet Affairs* 30 (2–3): 226–255.
Taylor, B. D. 2018. *The Code of Putinism*. New York: Oxford University Press.
Taylor, B.D. 2019. Putin's Fourth Term: The Phantom Breakthrough. PONARS Eurasia Policy Memo No. 602.
Twigg, J., ed. 2006. *HIV/AIDS in Russia and Eurasia. Vol. I.* New York: Palgrave Macmillan.
Twigg, J. 2002. Health Care Reform in Russia: Survey of Head Doctors and Insurance Administrators. *Social Science & Medicine* 55 (12): 2253–2265.
Velekhov, L. 2020. Russkaya dusha – stalinistka: Viktor Erofeev v programme Leonida Velekhova. *RFE/RL*, 26 September.
Vieira, M. 2011. Southern Africa's Response(s) to International HIV/AIDS Norms: The Politics of Assimilation. *Review of International Studies* 37 (1): 3–28.
Wang, Y.-T., V. Mechkova, and F. Andersson. 2018. Does Democracy Enhance Health? New Empirical Evidence 1900–2012. *Political Research Quarterly* 72 (3): 554–569.
Way, L. 2015. *Pluralism by Default: Weak Autocrats and the Rise of Competitive Politics*. Baltimore: Johns Hopkins University Press.

Wigley, S., and A. Akkoyunlu-Wigley. 2011. The Impact of Regime Type on Health: Does Redistribution Explain Everything? *World Politics* 63 (4): 647–677.

Young, O. 1994. *International Governance: Protecting the Environment in a Stateless Society*. Ithaca and London: Cornell University Press.

Zhegulev, I. 2016. Pravo na zabvenie Evgeniya Prigozhina. *Meduza.io*, 09 June.

Bibliography

Abbott, K.W., et al. 2016. Two Logics of Indirect Governance: Delegation and Orchestration. *British Journal of Political Science* 46 (4): 719–729.
Abbott, K.W., et al. 2019. The Governor's Dilemma: Competence versus Control. *Regulation & Governance* 14 (4): 619–636.
Abbott, K.W., et al. 2020. Competence–Control Theory: The Challenge of Governing through Intermediaries. In *The Governor's Dilemma: Indirect Governance Beyond Principals and Agents*, ed. K.W. Abbott, et al., 3–36. Oxford: Oxford University Press.
Abbott, K.W., et al. 2021. Beyond Opportunism: Intermediary Loyalty in Regulation and Governance. *Regulation & Governance* 15 (S1): S83–S101.
Aburamoto, M. 2019. An Indispensable Party of Power? United Russia and Putin's Return to the Presidency, 2011–2014. *Russian Politics* 4 (1): 22–41.
Abyzov, M. 2012. Komu i zachem nuzhno otkrytoe pravitel'stvo? *Radiostantsiya Ekho Moskvy*, 27 June.
Acemoglu, D. 2003. Why Not a Political Coase Theorem? Social Conflict, Commitment, and Politics. *Journal of Comparative Economics* 31: 620–652.
Acemoglu, D., and J. Robinson. 2006. Economic Backwardness in Political Perspective. *American Political Science Review* 100 (1): 115–131.
Acemoglu, D., and J. Robinson. 2019. Rents and Economic Development: The Perspective of *Why Nations Fail*. *Public Choice* 181: 13–28.
Agadjanian, A. 2017. Tradition, Morality and Community: Elaborating Orthodox Identity in Putin's Russia. *Religion, State and Society* 45 (1): 39–60.
Aleksandrov, O. 2013a. Roszdravnadzor: shilo na mylo? *The Moscow Post*, 7 March.

Aleksandrov, O. 2013b. Raskol Rospotrebnadzora ili zagovor oligarhov? *The Moscow Post*, 24 October.
Aleksashenko, S. 2019. *Kontrrevolyutsiya: Kak Stroilas' Vertikal' Vlasti v Sovremennoi Rossii i kak eto Vliyaet na Ekonomiku*. Moskva: Al'pina Publisher.
Alekseev, P. 2018. Nasha meditsina perekhodit na kachestvenno inoi uroven. *Meditsinskaya Gazeta* No. 28, 18 July.
Alisova, O. 2013. Gennadii Onishchenko - pobeditel' shprot i Borzhomi. *BBC*, 23 October.
Alyab'eva, E. 2014. VShE o reforme meditsiny: Imitatsiya i pokazukha. *Republic.ru*, 9 April.
Ananyev, M. 2018. Inside the Kremlin: The Presidency and Executive Branch. In *The New Autocracy: Information, Politics, and Policy in Putin's Russia*, ed. Treisman. Washington, D.C.: Brookings Institution.
Andreeva, N. 2019. Letal'naya optimizatsiya: Detskie meduchrezhdeniya zakryvayut, chtoby vypolnit' maiskie ukazy. *Novaya Gazeta* No. 7, 23 January.
Anin, R. 2018. Dvortsy pod okhranoi. *Novaya Gazeta*, 18 November.
Antonova, E. 2018. Zapret na import lekarstv reshili ubrat' iz zakonoproekta o kontrsanktsiyakh. *RBC*, 11 May.
Appel, H., and M.A. Orenstein. 2016. Why did Neoliberalism Triumph and Endure in the Post-Communist World? *Comparative Politics* 48 (3): 313–333.
Appel, H., and M. Orenstein. 2018. *From Triumph to Crisis: Neoliberal Economic Reform in Post-Communist Countries*. Cambridge, UK: Cambridge University Press.
Artyukh, D. 2020. Schetnaya palata vyyavila nevypolnenie porucheniya prezidenta Putina vo Vladimirskoi oblasti. *Zebra-tv.ru*, 2 April.
Aslund, A. 2019. *Russia's Crony Capitalism: The Path from Market Economy to Kleptocracy*. New Haven: Yale University Press.
Auzan, A. 2005. Grazhdanskoe obshchestvo i grazhdanskaya politika. *Polit.ru*, 1 June.
Bækken, H. 2021. Patriotic Disunity: Limits to Popular Support for Militaristic Policy in Russia. *Post-Soviet Affairs* 37 (3): 261–275.
Baev, P. 2017. Tenth Anniversary of Putin's Munich Speech: A Commitment to Failure. *Eurasia Daily Monitor* 14 (17).
Barabanov, I., and N. Morar. 2007. Putin topless. *The New Times*, 27 August.
Barabanov, I., A. Soshnikov, and S. Reiter. 2020. Ona byla tikhayaa-tikhaya: kto takaya Anna Popova. *BBC*, 29 May.
Baranova, O. 2013. Besporyadochnost' spiska. *Farmatsevticheskii Vestnik*, 24 December.
Baringer, L., and S. Heitkamp. 2011. Securitizing Global Health: A View from Maternal Health. *Global Health Governance* 4 (2): 1–21.

Batalova, A., and T. Bateneva. 2019. Nadezhnyi partner udvaivaet sily: Mezhdunarodnye kompanii dali moshchnyi impul's razvitiyu farmotrasli Rossii. *Rossiiskaya Gazeta*, 4 June.
Batalova, E. 2020. Arbidol spaset mir? *Novaya Gazeta*, 20 February.
Baturo, A., and J.A. Elkink. 2016. Dynamics of Regime Personalization and Patron-Client Networks in Russia, 1999–2014. *Post-Soviet Affairs* 32 (1): 75–98.
Beazer, Q.H., and O.J. Reuter. 2021. Do Authoritarian Elections Help the Poor? Evidence from Russian Cities. *The Journal of Politics* 84 (1): 437–454.
Bednyakov, A., and L. Mierin. 2019. Natsional'nye Proekty Rossii: Problemy i Resheniya. *Izvestiya Sankt-Peterburgskogo Gosudarstvennogo Ekonomicheskogo Universiteta* No. 4.
Belton, C. 2020. *Putin's People: How the KGB Took Back Russia and Then Took On the West*. New York: Farrar, Straus and Giroux.
Berdnikova, E. 2019. Dubinki i palochki. *Novaya Gazeta* No. 117, 18 October.
Berestov, A., and N. Kaklyugin. 2008. *Legal'naya Narkoagressiya v Rossii (Khroniki Neobyavlennoi Voiny)*. Moskva: Tsentr Ioanna Kronshtadskogo Moskovskoi Patriarkhii.
Bernhard, M., A.B. Edgell, and S.I. Lindberg. 2020. Institutionalising Electoral Uncertainty and Authoritarian Regime Survival. *European Journal of Political Research* 59: 465–487.
Beshlei, O. 2020. Ne khvataet patologoanatomov i mest pod pokoinikov. *Current Time*, 26 October.
Bindman, E., et al. 2019. NGOs and the Policy-making Process in Russia: The Case of Child Welfare Reform. *Governance* 32 (2): 207–222.
Blackburn, M. 2020. Political Legitimacy in Contemporary Russia 'from Below': 'Pro-Putin' Stances, the Normative Split and Imagining Two Russias. *Russian Politics* 5 (1): 52–80.
Blackburn, M., and B. Petersson. 2021. Parade, Plebiscite, Pandemic: Legitimation Efforts in Putin's Fourth Term. *Post-Soviet Affairs*. https://doi.org/10.1080/1060586X.2021.2020575.
Blank, S. 2008. Ivanov, Chemezov, and State Capture of the Russian Defense Sector. *Problems of Post-Communism* 55 (1): 49–60.
Blyth, M. 2013. *Austerity: The History of a Dangerous Idea*. New York: Oxford University Press.
Bogdanov, B. 2013. Onishchenko prizval Gruziyu zakryt' biolaboratoriyu SShA. *Rossiiskaya Gazeta*, 14 October.
Bogdanov, V. 2017a. MVD: Ukraina stala glavnym tranziterom narkotikov v RF. *Rossiiskaya Gazeta*, 12 April.
Bogdanov, V. 2017b. MVD: Protiv Rossii osushchestvlyaetsya narkoagressiya. *Rossiiskaya Gazeta*, 14 April.
Bogomolov, K. 2021. Pokhishchenie Evropy 2.0. *Novaya Gazeta*, 10 February.

Boiko, V., and E. Fokht. 2017. Pochemu vrachi protiv bol'nitsy, kotoruyu patsienty prosili u Putina. *Russian service BBC*, 30 June.

Boin, A., P. Lagadec, E. Michel-Kerjan, and W. Overdijk. 2003. Critical Infrastructures under Threat: Learning from the Anthrax Scare. *Journal of Contingencies and Crisis Management* 11 (3): 99–104.

Bolkvadze, K. 2016. Hitting the Saturation Point: Unpacking the Politics of Bureaucratic Reforms in Hybrid Regimes. *Democratization* 24 (4): 751–769.

Bransten, J. 2005. Russia: New Public Chamber Criticized as Smokescreen. *RFE/RL*, 17 March.

Bratton, M., and N. van de Walle. 1997. *Democratic Experiments in Africa: Regime Transitions in Comparative Perspective*. New York: Cambridge University Press.

Britskaya, T. 2019. Belye lentochki v belykh khalatakh. *Novaya Gazeta* No. 69, 28 June.

Brown, W. 2015. *Undoing the Demos: Neoliberalism's Stealth Revolution*. New York: Zone Books.

Bucci, E., et al. 2020. Safety and Efficacy of the Russian COVID-19 Vaccine: More Information Needed. *The Lancet* 396 (10256): e53.

Bucci, E., et al. 2021. Data Discrepancies and Substandard Reporting of Interim Data of Sputnik V Phase 3 Trial. *The Lancet* 397 (10288): 1881–1883.

Bueno de Mesquita, B., A. Smith, R.M. Siverson, and J.D. Morrow. 2003. *The Logic of Political Survival*. Cambridge: Cambridge University Press.

Bueno de Mesquita, B., and A. Smith. 2011. *The Dictator's Handbook: Why Bad Behavior is Almost Always Good Politics*. New York: Public Affair.

Burkhardt, F. 2020. Institutionalising Authoritarian Presidencies: Polymorphous Power and Russia's Presidential Administration. *Europe-Asia Studies* 73 (3): 472–504.

Butrin, D. 2018. K natsproektam predyavleny gospretenzii. *Kommersant* No. 214, 21 November.

Buzan, B., O. Weaver, and J. De Wilde. 1997. *Security: A New Framework for Analysis*. Boulder, CO: Lynne Rienner Publishers.

Carnaghan, E. 2007. Do Russians Dislike Democracy? *PS: Political Science & Politics* 40 (1): 61–66.

Cecchine, G. 2006. *Infectious Disease and National Security: Strategic Information Needs*. Santa Monica, CA; Arlington, VA; Pittsburgh, PA: RAND Corporation.

Chaisty, P., and S. Whitefield. 2019. The Political Implications of Popular Support for Presidential Term Limits in Russia. *Post-Soviet Affairs* 35 (4): 323–337.

Chang, E., and M.A. Golden. 2010. Sources of Corruption in Authoritarian Regimes. *Social Science Quarterly* 91: 1–20.

Chazov, E.I. 2014. *Khorovod Smertei. Brezhnev, Andropov, Chernenko.* Mokva: Algoritm.
Chebankova, E. 2012. State-sponsored Civic Associations in Russia: Systemic Integration or the 'War of Position'? *East European Politics* 28 (4): 390–408.
Chehabi, H., and J. Linz. 1998. *Sultanistic Regimes.* Baltimore: Johns Hopkins University Press.
Cherkesov, V. 2004. Moda na KGB? *Komsomol'skaya Pravda*, 29 December.
Chernova, N. 2019. Lyudi v belykh zaplatakh. *Novaya Gazeta* No. 102, 13 September.
Chernykh, A. 2016. Pravitel'stvo ne izyskalo novykh sredstv dlya VICh. *Kommersant* No. 199, 26 October.
Chevtaeva, I. 2015. RF budet unichtozhat' sanktsionnye produkty iz Turtsii i Ukrainy. *Deutsche Welle*, 24 December.
Churakova, O., M. Zholobova, and R. Badanin. 2019. Zhduny. Rasskaz o tom, kak okhranniki Vladimira Putina ne stali slugami naroda. *Proekt.Media*, 20 November.
Connolly, R. 2016. The Empire Strikes Back: Economic Statecraft and the Securitisation of Political Economy in Russia. *Europe-Asia Studies* 68 (4): 750–773.
Cook, L. 2015. *Constraints on Universal Health Care in the Russian Federation.* UNRISD Working Paper 2015-5.
Cook, S. 2007. *Ruling But Not Governing: The Military and Political Development in Egypt, Algeria, and Turkey.* Baltimore: Johns Hopkins University Press.
Croissant, A., and O. Hellmann. 2017. Introduction: State Capacity and Elections in the Study of Authoritarian Regimes. *International Political Science Review* 39 (1): 3–16.
Cronert, A., and A. Hadenius. 2020. Institutional Foundations of Global Well-being: Democracy, State Capacity and Social Protection. *International Political Science Review* 42 (5): 705–724.
Crotty, J., S.M. Hall, and S. Ljubownikow. 2014. Post-Soviet Civil Society Development in the Russian Federation: The Impact of the NGO Law. *Europe-Asia Studies* 66 (8): 1253–1269.
Dawisha, K. 2014. *Putin's Kleptocracy: Who Owns Russia?* New York: Simon & Schuster.
Deryabina, A., and I. Vittel'. 2016. V Rossii stalo men'she deshevykh importnykh zhiznenno vazhnykh lekarstv. *RBC*, 12 February.
Detkova, P., E. Podkolzina, and A. Tkachenko. 2018. Corruption, Centralization and Competition: Evidence from Russian Public Procurement. *International Journal of Public Administration* 41 (5–6): 414–434.
Deutsche Welle. 2019. After 20 Years, is Vladimir Putin's Untouchable Image Crumbling? 8 August.

Dobrovol'skii, T. 2015. Deputaty predlozhili vvesti moratorii na optimizatsiyu zdravookhraneniya. *Vademecum*, 19 November.
Dombrova, E. 2016. Proizvoditel' insulina Gerofarm narastil oborot na 22%. *Delovoi Peterburg*, 14 March.
Dranishnikova, M. 2014. Interv'yu - Aleksei Repik, vladelets i predsedatel' soveta direktorov R-Pharma. *Vedomosti*, 23 September.
Dranishnikova, M. 2017. Lish' odna kompaniya smozhet postavlyat' gosudarstvu katetery i ustroistva dlya perelivaniya krovi. *Vedomosti*, 29 October.
Druzenko, G. 2011. Geopolitics from the Patriarch. *Russian Politics & Law* 49 (1): 65–73.
DSM Group. 2018. Analiticheskii Otchet: Farmatsevticheskii Rynok Rossii: Itogi 2017 g.
DSM Group. 2019. Analiticheskii Otchet: Farmatsevticheskii Rynok Rossii: Itogi 2018 g.
DSM Group. 2020. Analiticheskii Otchet: Farmatsevticheskii Rynok Rossii: Itogi 2019 g.
Duckett, J., and G. Wang. 2017. Why do Authoritarian Regimes Provide Public Goods? Policy Communities, External Shocks and Ideas in China's Rural Social Policy Making. *Europe-Asia Studies* 69 (1): 92–109.
Dzutstsati, A. 2020. Ponimaete, ya do pyatnitsy prosto ne vyzhivu. *Current Time*, 12 November.
Edenborg, E. 2020. Russia's Spectacle of "Traditional Values": Rethinking the Politics of Visibility. *International Feminist Journal of Politics* 22 (1): 106–126.
Egorov, G., and K. Sonin. 2011. Dictators and their Viziers: Endogenizing the Loyalty-Competence Trade-off. *Journal of the European Economic Association* 9 (5): 903–930.
Elbe, S. 2006. Should HIV/AIDS be Securitized? The Ethical Dilemmas of Linking HIV/AIDS and Security. *International Studies Quarterly* 50 (1): 119–144.
Elbe, S. 2010. Haggling Over Viruses: The Downside Risks of Securitizing Infectious Disease. *Health Policy and Planning* 25 (6): 476–485.
Elster, J. 2018. The Resistible Rise of Louis Bonaparte. In *Can It Happen Here? Authoritarianism in America*, ed. C.R. Sunstein, 277–312. New York: Dey St.
Ershov, A., and O. Matveeva. 2022. EpiVakKorona - vrednaya pustyshka, registratsiya kotoroi dolzhna byt' otozvana. *Meduza.io*, 26 January.
Evans, P.B. 1995. *Embedded Autonomy: States and Industrial Transformation*. Princeton: Princeton University Press.
Evropa. 2007. *Prioritetnye Natsional'nye Proekty: Tsifry, Fakty, Dokumenty*. Moskva: Evropa.

Ezrow, N., and E. Frantz. 2011. *Dictators and Dictatorships: Understanding Authoritarian Regimes and Their Leaders*. New York: The Continuum Publishing Group.

Fel'shtinskii, Yu., and V. Popov. 2021. *Ot Krasnogo Terrora k Mafioznomu Gosudarstvu: Spetssluzhby Rossii v Bor'be za Mirovoe Gospodstvo (1917–2036)*. Kyiv: Nash Format.

Filipenok, A. 2017. Yakunin rasskazal o svoem malen'kom shubokhranilishche. *RBC*, 15 June.

Flikke, G. 2018. Conflicting Opportunities or Patronal Politics? Restrictive NGO Legislation in Russia 2012–2015. *Europe-Asia Studies* 70 (4): 564–590.

Flinders, M. 2012. Governance and Patronage. In *The Oxford Handbook of Governance*, ed. D. Levi-Faur. New York: Oxford University Press.

Foa, R.S. 2018. Modernization and Authoritarianism. *Journal of Democracy* 29 (3): 129–140.

Freeze, G. L. 2017. Russian Orthodoxy and Politics in the Putin Era. *Carnegie Endowment for International Peace*, 2 September.

Fukuyama, F. 2013. What is Governance? *Governance* 26 (3): 347–368.

Gaaze, K. 2014. Poker dlya odnogo. *The New Times*, 1 September.

Gaaze, K. 2015. Stsenarii posadok: chem opasno dlya Kremlya delo Gaizera. *Forbes.ru*, 23 September.

Gaaze, K. 2016. Chuzhie zdes' ne khodyat. Igor' Shuvalov i privatizatsiya, kotoroi ne bylo. *Snob.ru*, 11 August.

Gaaze, K. 2017a. Chto oznachaet prigovor Ulyukaevu. *Carnegie.ru*, 15 December.

Gaaze, K. 2017b. Sleduyushchii prezident budet iz dvora Putina. Sobchak ili Dyumin – nevazhno. *Biznes Online*, 23 October.

Gaaze, K. 2018. Kak sdelat' byurokratiyu effektivnoi. *Vedomosti*, 7 March.

Galeotti, M. 2018. *The Vory: Russia's Super Mafia*. New Haven: Yale University Press.

Galieva, D. 2020. Natsproekty perenatselyat na 2030-i: Srok realizatsii obnovlennykh programm prodlevaetsya na shest' let. *Kommersant*, 13 July.

Galimova, N. 2018. Otsenki dlya Kremlya: zachem upravleniya Kirienko vvodyat KPI. *RBC*, 27 November.

Galimova, N. 2021. Gubernator Vladimirskoi oblasti Sipyagin ushel v Gosdumu. *RBC*, 29 September.

Gandhi, J. 2008. *Political Institutions under Dictatorship*. Cambridge: Cambridge University Press.

Geddes, B., J. Wright, and E. Frantz. 2018. *How Dictatorships Work: Power, Personalization, and Collapse*. New York: Cambridge University Press.

Geddes, B. 1994. *Politician's Dilemma: Building State Capacity in Latin America*. Berkeley and Los Angeles: University of California Press.

Gehlbach, S., and P. Keefer. 2011. Investment without Democracy: Ruling-party Institutionalization and Credible Commitment in Autocracies. *Journal of Comparative Economics* 39 (2): 123–139.

Gel'man, V. 2015. The Vicious Circle of Post-Soviet Neopatrimonialism in Russia. *Post-Soviet Affairs* 32 (5): 455–473.

Gel'man, V. 2017. Political Foundations of Bad Governance in Post-soviet Eurasia: Towards a Research Agenda. *East European Politics* 33 (4): 496–516.

Gel'man, V. 2018. Politics versus Policy: Technocratic Traps of Russia's Policy Reforms. *Russian Politics* 3 (2): 282–304.

Gel'man, V. 2019. *Nedostoinoe Pravlenie: Politika v Sovremennoi Rossii*. Sankt-Peterburg: Izdatel'stvo Evropeiskogo Universiteta v Sankt-Peterburge.

Gel'man, V. 2020a. The Politics of Fear: How the Russian Regime Confronts its Opponents. *Russian Social Science Review* 61 (6): 467–482.

Gel'man, V. 2020b. Porazhenie bez Srazheniya: Rossiiskaya Oppozitsiya i Predely Mobilizatsii. In *Novaya (Ne)legitimnost': Kak Prokhodilo i Chto Prineslo Rossii Perepisyvanie Konstitutsii*, ed. K. Rogov, 63–69. Moskva: Fond Liberal'naya Missiya.

Gel'man, V. and A. Starodubtsev. 2016. Opportunities and Constraints of Authoritarian Modernisation: Russian Policy Reforms in the 2000s. *Europe-Asia Studies* 68 (1): 97–117.

George, A., and A. Bennett. 2005. *Case Studies and Theory Development in the Social Sciences*. Cambridge, MA: MIT Press.

Gessen, M. 2013. *The Man Without a Face: The Unlikely Rise of Vladimir Putin*. New York: Riverhead Books.

GMPnews. 2019. ONF podgotovit predlozheniya po peresmotru mekhanizma opredeleniya tsen na zakupki lekarstv, 9 August.

Godovannik, L. 2018. Polivinilkhloridnyi skandal doshel do Peterburga. *Fontanka.ru*, 11 September.

Gogin, S. 2016. Chelovek, kotoryi pereigral Sistemu. *RFL/RL*, 9 October.

Golosov, G.V. 2016. Why and How Electoral Systems Matter in Autocracies. *Australian Journal of Political Science* 51 (3): 367–385.

Gómez, E.J. 2009. The Politics of Receptivity and Resistance: How Brazil, India, China, and Russia Strategically use the International Health Community in Response to HIV/AIDS: A Theory. *Global Health Governance* 3 (1).

Gómez, E.J. 2015. Understanding the BRIC Response to AIDS: Political Institutions, Civil Society, and Historical Policy Backlash in Comparative Perspective. *Commonwealth & Comparative Politics* 53 (3): 315–340.

Gómez, E.J. 2018. *Geopolitics in Health: Confronting Obesity, Aids, and Tuberculosis in the Emerging BRICS Economies*. Baltimore: Johns Hopkins University Press.

Gómez, E.J., and O. Kucheryavenko. 2020. Explaining Russia's Struggle to Eradicate HIV/AIDS: Institutions, Agenda Setting and the Limits to

Multiple-Streams Processes. *Journal of Comparative Policy Analysis: Research and Practice* 23 (3): 372–388.

Goncharova, O., et al. 2017. Kak meditsinskii proekt Viktora Veksel'berga nachal menyat' rynok stentov. *Vademecum*, 6 February.

Gorbachev, M. 1995. *Zhizn' i Reformy*. 2 Vol. Moskva: Novosti.

Gosudarstvennaya Duma. 2011. Materialy Parlamentskikh Slushanii i 'Kruglykh Stolov', Provedennykh Komitetom Gosudarstvennoi Dumy po Okhrane Zdorov'ya v Osennyuyu Sessiyu 2009 Goda, Vesennyuyu i Osennyuyu Sessii 2010 Goda. *Komitet Gosudarstvennoi Dumy po Okhrane Zdorov'ya*, 8 October.

Gosudarstvennaya Duma. 2020a. V GD obsudili zapusk fonda pomoshchi detyam s orfannymi zabolevaniyami. http://duma.gov.ru/news/49134/.

Gosudarstvennaya Duma. 2020b. Viacheslav Volodin: Russia's strength is not oil and gas, but Vladimir Putin. http://duma.gov.ru/en/news/48036/.

Grachev, A. 2001. *Gorbachev: Chelovek, Kotoryi Khotel kak Luchshe*. Moskva: Vagrius.

Greer, S.L., M. Wismar, and J. Figueras, eds. 2016. *Strengthening Health System Governance: Better Policies, Stronger Performance*. Berkshire, England: Open University Press.

Grigoriev, I.S., and A.A. Dekalchuk. 2017. Collective Learning and Regime Dynamics under Uncertainty: Labour Reform and the Way to Autocracy in Russia. *Democratization* 24 (3): 481–497.

Grishankov, M. 2010. Printsipy Dokazatel'noi Meditsiny i Ispol'zovanie Programm Snizheniya Vreda Dlya Profilaktiki VICh-infektsii Sredi Uyazvimykh Grupp. Doklad Ekspertnoi Rabochei Gruppy, 9 April 2009.

Gritsenko, P., and A. Osipov. 2019a. Rodnye i blistery: kak razmenivalis' byudzhetnye milliardy, vydelennye na lekarstvennoe importozameshchenie. *Vademecum*, 3 June.

Gritsenko, P., and A. Osipov. 2019b. Prilipayushchie ugod'ya: kak gluboko vspahali nivu importozameshcheniya tyazhelovesy rossiiskoi farmindustrii. *Vademecum*, 5 June.

Grozovskii, B. 2016. Dryakhleyushchii obshchestvennyi dogovor. *Vedomosti*, 17 January.

Grube, D. 2019. *Megaphone Bureaucracy: Speaking Truth to Power in the Age of the New Normal*. Princeton: Princeton University Press.

Gryzlov, B. 2003. Politicheskii doklad Predsedatelya Vysshego Soveta politicheskoi partii Edinaya Rossiya B. V. Gryzlova pered delegatami III Sezda partii Edinaya Rossiya, 22 September.

Gryzlov, B. 2005. Ot stabilizatsii k razvitiyu: politicheskie prioritety Partii Edinaya Rossiya, VI Sezd Partii Edinaya Rossiya, Krasnoyarsk, 26 November.

Gryzlov, B. 2007. Politicheskie zadachi razvitiya strany. In *Vektor Rossii: Razmyshleniya o Puti Razvitiya Rossii*. SPb: Tsentr sotsial'no-konservativnoi politiki.

Guriev, S., and D. Treisman. 2019. Informational Autocrats. *Journal of Economic Perspectives* 33 (4): 100–127.
Guriev, S., and D. Treisman. 2020. The Popularity of Authoritarian Leaders: A Cross-National Investigation. *World Politics* 72 (4): 601–638.
Gürsoy, Y. 2017. *Between Military Rule and Democracy: Regime Consolidation in Greece, Turkey, and Beyond*. Ann Arbor: University of Michigan Press.
Guzenkova, T., O. Petrovskaya, and I. Nikolaychuk. 2015. *Protivodeistvie Epidemii VICh/SPID: Global'nye Trendy i Natsional'naya Bezopasnost' Rossii*. Moskva: RISI.
Haber, S. 2008. Authoritarian Government. In *The Oxford Handbook of Political Economy*, ed. D.A. Wittman and B.R. Weingast, 693–707. New York: Oxford University Press.
Hale, H.E. 2011. The Myth of Mass Russian Support for Autocracy: The Public Opinion Foundations of a Hybrid Regime. *Europe-Asia Studies* 63 (8): 1357–1375.
Hale, H.E. 2015. *Patronal Politics: Eurasian Regime Dynamics in Comparative Perspective*. New York: Cambridge University Press.
Hale, H.E. 2019. A Surprising Connection between Civilizational Identity and Succession Expectations among Russian Elites. *Post-Soviet Affairs* 35 (5–6): 406–421.
Hale, H.E., and T.J. Colton. 2017. Who Defects? Unpacking a Defection Cascade from Russia's Dominant Party 2008–2012. *American Political Science Review* 111 (2): 322–337.
Han, K. 2020. Autocratic Welfare Programs, Economic Perceptions, and Support for the Dictator: Evidence from African Autocracies. *International Political Science Review* 42 (3): 416–429.
Hanson, E. 2010. *Post-Imperial Democracies: Ideology and Party Formation in Third Republic France, Weimar Germany, and Post-Soviet Russia*. New York: Cambridge University Press.
Hanson, J.K. 2017. State Capacity and the Resilience of Electoral Authoritarianism: Conceptualizing and Measuring the Institutional Underpinnings of Autocratic Power. *International Political Science Review* 39 (1): 17–32.
Hartmann, C. 2022. Authoritarian Origins of Term Limit Trajectories in Africa. *Democratization* 29 (1): 57–73.
Hashim, S.M. 2017. Putin's High-modernism and its Limits—Assessing the Sources of State Incapacity in Russia. *Communist and Post-Communist Studies* 50 (3): 195–205.
Henderson, C. 2011. Civil Society in Russia State-Society Relations in the Post-Yeltsin Era. *Problems of Post-Communism* 58 (3): 11–27.
Herington, J. 2010. Securitization of Infectious Diseases in Vietnam: The Cases of HIV and Avian Influenza. *Health Policy and Planning* 25 (6): 467–475.

Hiskey, J.T., and M.W. Moseley. 2020. *Life in the Political Machine: Dominant-Party Enclaves and the Citizens They Produce*. New York: Oxford University Press.

Homedes, N., and A. Ugalde. 2005. Why Neoliberal Health Reforms Have Failed in Latin America. *Health Policy* 71 (1): 83–96.

Horvath, R. 2016. The Reinvention of 'Traditional Values': Nataliya Narochnitskaya and Russia's Assault on Universal Human Rights. *Europe-Asia Studies* 68 (5): 868–892.

Huang, X. 2020. *Social Protection under Authoritarianism: Health Politics and Policy in China*. New York: Oxford University Press.

Huntington, S.P. 2006. *Political Order in Changing Societies. With a New Foreword by Francis Fukuyama*. New Haven: Yale University Press.

Huskey, E. 2009. The Politics-Administration Nexus in Post-communist Russia. In *Russian Bureaucracy and the State: Officialdom From Alexander III to Vladimir Putin*, ed. D.K. Rowney and E. Huskey, 253–272. New York: Palgrave Macmillan.

Hutcheson, D.S., and B. Petersson. 2016. Shortcut to Legitimacy: Popularity in Putin's Russia. *Europe-Asia Studies* 68 (7): 1107–1126.

Ignatova, O. 2018. Shtraf-menyu: V Rossii khotyat vvesti shtrafy za prodazhu i khranenie sanktsionnykh tovarov. *Rossiiskaya Gazeta* No. 96 (7559), 07 May.

Interfax. 2009. Putin prolechil farmatsevtov, 9 October.

Interfax. 2020. Roshal' predlozhil sobrat' gruppu medekspertov po Naval'nomu, 5 September.

Interfax. 2021. Rospotrebnadzor zayavil o stoprotsentnoi effektivnosti vaktsiny Vektora, 19 January.

Isaacs, R., and S. Whitmore. 2014. The Limited Agency and Life-cycles of Personalized Dominant Parties in the Post-Soviet space: The Cases of United Russia and Nur Otan. *Democratization* 21 (4): 699–721.

Ivanov, M. 2015. Pravitel'stvo eshche podumaet o zaprete goszakupok inostrannykh medmaterialov. *Kommersant*, 20 August.

Ivanov, V. 2009. Direktor FSKN Viktor Ivanov dal interv'yu gazete Kommersant. *Kommersant*, 2 July.

Ivanov, V. 2016. Zapusk sistemy reabilitatsii narkomanov ostanovit epidemiyu VICh. *Ria Novosti*, 23 March.

Izvestiya. 2020. Putin poobeshchal razobrat'sya s obespecheniem lekarstvami ot COVID-19, 17 December.

Jarzyńska, K. 2014. The Russian Orthodox Church as Part of the State and Society. *Russian Politics & Law* 52 (3): 87–97.

Jones, C.W. 2019. Adviser to The King: Experts, Rationalization, and Legitimacy. *World Politics* 71 (1): 1–43.

Jordan, P. 2010. Russia's Managed Democracy and the Civil G8 in 2006. *Journal of Communist Studies and Transition Politics* 26 (1): 101–125.

Kalinovskaya, E. 2015. Delo Arbidola. *Farmatsevticheskii Vestnik*, No. 42.
Kalinovskaya, E. 2017. Slushayu! 62-ya! Konflikt v Moskve vnov' podnyal vopros o tsenakh na lekarstva. *Farmatsevticheskii Vestnik*, 14 February.
Kalinovskaya, E. 2019a. Stress dlya farmy. Otrasl' speshit uznat', kak budet prohodit' pereregistratsiya tsen. *Farmatsevticheskii Vestnik*, 15 October.
Kalinovskaya, E. 2019b. Neuderzhimye. Za chetyre goda s rynka ushla pochti tysyacha lekarstvennykh preparatov. *Farmatsevticheskii Vestnik*, 22 October.
Kalinovskaya E. 2019c. Ekspert: V 2019 g. pri goszakupkah lekarstv nachnut primenyat'sya referentnye tseny. *Farmatsevticheskii Vestnik*, 9 January.
Kandil, H. 2016. *The Power Triangle: Military, Security, and Politics in Regime Change*. New York: Oxford University Press.
Kara-Murza, V. 2011. Spravedlivy li upreki doktora Leonida Roshalya v adres chinovnikov Minzdrava? *RFL/RL*, 20 April.
Kashevarova, A., and A. Lyalyakina. 2013. Rospotrebnadzor mogut rasformirovat' vsled za otstavkoi Onishchenko. *Izvestiya*, 24 October.
Kaye, R. 2006. Regulated (Self-)Regulation: A New Paradigm for Controlling the Professions? *Public Policy and Administration* 21 (3): 105–119.
Keshavjee, S. 2014. *Blind Spot. How Neoliberalism Infiltrated Global Health*. Oakland, California: University of California Press.
Khabriev, R. 2014. Sozdavaya Roszdravnadzor, my sdelali stavku na pravil'nykh lyudei. *Vestnik Roszdravnadzora* No. 5.
Kheifets, V., and K. Dyuryagina. 2020. Al'yans vrachei popytalis' razbit'. *Kommersant*, 3 April.
Khinshtein, A. 2010. *Skazka o Poteryannom Vremeni: Pochemu Brezhnev ne Smog Stat' Putinym*. Moskva: Olma Media Grupp.
Khmelnitskaya, M. 2020. Socio-economic Development and the Politics of Expertise in Putin's Russia: The 'Hollow Paradigm Perspective.' *Europe-Asia Studies* 73 (4): 625–646.
Kiselev, D. 2014. Kogda nichto ne svyato, kogda nichto ne sderzhivaet. *Tetradi Po Konservatizmu* 1 (1): 19–27.
Klein, N. 2007. *The Shock Doctrine: The Rise of Disaster Capitalism*. New York: Metropolitan Books.
Klein, S.H., and F. Vidal Luna. 2017. *Brazil 1964–1985: The Military Regimes of Latin America in the Cold War*. New Haven: Yale University Press.
Kling, A.S. 2016. *Specialization and Trade: A Reintroduction to Economics: An Introduction*. Washington, D.C.: Cato Institute.
Klotz, A., and C. Lynch. 2007. *Strategies for Research in Constructivist International Relations*. Armonk: M.E. Sharpe.
Klyamkin, I., and A. Migranyan. 1989. Nuzhna zheleznaya ruka? *Literaturnaya Gazeta*, 16 August.
Kobernik, O., and O. Baranova. 2020. V Rossii poyavitsya edinyi postavshchik masok dlya LPU i aptek. *Farmatsevticheskii Vestnik*, 23 March.

Kogalovskii, V. 2013. Biocad-ogorod. *Vademecum*, 16 December.
Kolesnikov, A. 2021. Operator buydzhetnykh potokov. Chto pokazal god prem'erstva Mishustina. *Carnegie.ru*, 14 January.
Kolesnikov, A., and D. Volkov. 2019. Pragmatic Paternalism: The Russian Public and the Private Sector. *Carnegie.ru*, 18 January.
Kolesnikov, A., and D. Volkov. 2020. Russians' Growing Appetite for Change. *Carnegie.ru*, 30 January.
Kommersant. 2010. Na modernizatsiyu zdravookhraneniya planiruetsya vydelit' 460 milliardov rublei. *Kommersant-Online*, 23 April.
Kommersant. 2020. Putin peredal Roszdravnadzor v podchinenie Minzdravu, 25 March.
Komrakov, A. 2019. Natsproekty osvoili lish' polovinu deneg. *Nezavisimaya Gazeta*, 7 November.
Kosachev, K. 2006. Diktat nekompetentnosti. *Rossiya v Global'noi Politike* No. 1, January–February.
Kosachev, K. 2007. Rossiya i Zapad: nashi raznoglasiya. *Rossiya v Global'noi Politike* No. 4, July–August.
Kostarnova, N. 2021. Privivai, no proveryai: Populyarizatory dokazatel'noi meditsiny poprosili pravitel'stvo otkryt' dannye o vaktsinatsii. *Kommersant*, 02 Decemebr.
Kostarnova, N., et al. 2021. Ne dumai o vrachebnom svysoka. *Kommersant* No. 72, 23 April.
Kotel'nikov, M. 2010. Tat'yana Golikova proizvela zachistku zdravookhraneniya ot imenitykh opponentov. *Skandaly.ru*, 1 June.
Kotkin, S. 2001. *Armageddon Averted: The Soviet Collapse, 1970–2000: Soviet Collapse Since 1970*. New York: Oxford University Press.
Kotlyar, E. 2020. Morg perepolnen. V skoruyu zvonit' bespolezno. *Current Time*, 29 October.
Kotova, M. 2018. Medizdeliya razbavyat konkurentsiei: ONF otodvigaet Medpolimerprom. *Kommersant*, 19 July.
Kozlov, P., and M. Papchenkova. 2015. Kak Obshcherossiiskii narodnyi front vstroilsya v vertikal' vlasti. *Vedomosti*, 29 November.
Kozlova, D. 2020. Ukol shchedrosti. *Novaya Gazeta*, 27 October.
Kravtsov, V. 2015. *HIV/AIDS and Norm Diffusion in Putin's Russia and Mbeki's South Africa*. Athens: University of Georgia Press.
Kriger, I. 2008. Dura lex: Gosudarstvo posledovatel'no vytesnyaet nekommercheskie organizatsii s pravovogo polya. *Novaya Gazeta*, 24 July.
Krivolapov, A. 2021. Deputaty oppozitsii vystupili s kritikoi optimizatsii zdravookhraneniya Orenburzh'ya. *Orengrad.ru*, 26 January.
Krivoshapko, Yu. 2020. Dvizhenie vverkh: Sem' dostizhenii Federal'noi nalogovoi sluzhby pod rukovodstvom Mikhaila Mishustina. *Rossiiskaya Gazeta* No. 8 (8062), 16 January.

Kruglikova, M. 2015. Natsmedpalata: Fond Zdorov'e provodit fragmentarnyi i tendentsioznyi analiz. *Vademecum*, 30 June.

Kryazhev, D. 2021. Pamyati Eleny Tel'novoi: istoriya odnoi fotografii. *Vademecum*, 29 July.

Kryshtanovskaya, O., and S. White. 2003. Putin's Militocracy. *Post-Soviet Affairs* 19 (4): 289–306.

Kukulin, I., and V. Kurennoi. 2017. Shkola Shchedrovitskogo i ee nasledie. Chast' 1. *Polit.ru*, 31 March.

Kuravskii, P., M. Petrushko, and L. Chizhova. 2011. Minzdrav obidelsya na doktora Roshalya. *RFE/RL*, 19 April.

Kutuzov, R. 2015. Zdorovyi dukh. *Vademecum*, 07 September.

Kuz'menko, A. 2013. Ten' Onishchenko. *RBC*, 25 October.

Kuz'mina, B., and M. Perevoshchikova. 2021. Klubni po interesam: vlasti predlozhili mery po stabilizatsii tsen na borshchevoi nabor. *Izvestiya*, 12 November.

Laband, D.N., and J.P. Sophocleus. 2019. Measuring Rent-Seeking. *Public Choice* 181 (1–2): 49–69.

Labonté, R., and A. Ruckert. 2019. *Health Equity in a Globalizing Era: Past Challenges, Future Prospects*. Oxford, UK: Oxford University Press.

Lake, D.A. 2009. *Hierarchy in International Relations*. Ithaca and London: Cornell University Press.

Lake, D.A., and M.A. Baum. 2001. The Invisible Hand of Democracy: Political Control and the Provision of Public Services. *Comparative Political Studies* 34 (6): 587–621.

Lamberova, N., and K. Sonin. 2018. The Role of Business in Shaping Economic Policy. In *The New Autocracy: Information, Politics, and Policy in Putin's Russia*, ed. D. Treisman, 137–158. Washington, D.C.: Brookings Institution Press.

Lamoreaux, J.W., and L. Flake. 2018. The Russian Orthodox Church, the Kremlin, and Religious (il)liberalism in Russia. *Palgrave Communications* 4 (1): 115.

Laruelle, M. 2015. Patriotic Youth Clubs in Russia. Professional Niches, Cultural Capital and Narratives of Social Engagement. *Europe-Asia Studies* 67 (1): 8–27.

Laruelle, M. 2016. The Izborsky Club, or the New Conservative Avant-Garde in Russia. *The Russian Review* 75 (4): 626–644.

Laruelle, M. 2020. Making Sense of Russia's Illiberalism. *Journal of Democracy* 31 (3): 115–129.

Lassila, J. 2016. The Russian People's Front and Hybrid Governance Dilemma. In *Authoritarian Modernization in Russia: Ideas, Institutions, and Policies*, ed. V. Gel'man, 95–112. London: Routledge.

Latukhina, K. 2017. Golikova rasskazala Putinu o 899 narusheniyakh v sfere goszakupok. *Vedomosti*, 3 March.
Lavrov, S. 2021. O Prave, Pravakh i Pravilakh. *Rossiya v Global'noi Politike* No. 4, 28 June.
Ledeneva, A. 2013. *Can Russia Modernise?: Sistema, Power Networks and Informal Governance*. Cambridge: Cambridge University Press.
Levada-Tsentr. 2017. Religioznost'. *Press-vypusk*, 18 July.
Levada-Tsentr. 2021. Religioznost' v period pandemii. *Press-vypusk*, 14 April.
Levi, M. 1989. *Of Rule and Revenue*. Berkeley and Los Angeles: University of California Press.
Levitsky, S., and L. Way. 2010. *Competitive Authoritarianism: Hybrid Regimes After the Cold War*. New York: Cambridge University Press.
Levitsky, S., and D. Ziblatt. 2018. *How Democracies Die*. New York: Crown Publishing.
Levitsky, S., and J. Loxton. 2013. Populism and Competitive Authoritarianism in the Andes. *Democratization* 20 (1): 107–136.
Levkovich, A. 2018. Zakon o kontrsanktsiyakh vstupil v silu. *Vademecum*, 4 June.
Linz, J. 2000. *Totalitarian and Authoritarian Regimes*. Boulder, CO: Lynne Rienner Publishers.
Linz, J., and A. Stepan. 1996. *Problems of Democratic Transition and Consolidation: Southern Europe, South America, and Post-Communist Europe*. Baltimore: Johns Hopkins University Press.
List, C., and P. Pettit. 2011. *Group Agency: The Possibility, Design, and Status of Corporate Agents*. New York: Oxford University Press.
Ljubownikow, S., and J. Crotty. 2016. Nonprofit Influence on Public Policy: Exploring Nonprofit Advocacy in Russia. *Nonprofit and Voluntary Sector Quarterly* 45 (2): 314–332.
Lo, C.Y. 2015. *HIV/AIDS in China and India: Governing Health Security*. New York: Palgrave Macmillan.
Lo Yuk-ping, C., and N. Thomas. 2010. How is Health a Security Issue? Politics, Responses and Issues. *Health Policy and Planning* 25 (6): 447–453.
Luzhkov, Yu. 2004a. Liberal'noe i sotsial'noe. *Strategiya Rossii* No. 1, January.
Luzhkov, Yu. 2004b. Sotsial'nost' vmesto oligarkhizma. *Strategiya Rossii* No. 10–11, October–November.
Luzhkov, Yu. 2006. My i zapad. *Strategiya Rossii* No. 6, June.
Luzhkov, Yu., and G. Popov, G. 2010. Eshche odno slovo o Gaidare. *Moskovskii Komsomolets*, 21 January.
Lyauv, B., et al. 2018. Gendirektor Rosteca: Novye sanktsii vryad li smogut nas podkosit. *Vedomosti*, 17 December.
Magaloni, B. 2006. *Voting for Autocracy. Hegemonic Party Survival and its Demise in Mexico*. New York: Cambridge University Press.

Makarkina, O., D. Kryazhev, and E. Mihailova. 2014. Pritsepnaya reaktsiya. *Vademecum*, 17 November.
Makarkina, O. 2011a. Nepodemnyi tsennik. Lobbisty v dvuh vitse-prem'erakh uvideli obrazy svoikh zashchitnikov. *Farmatsevticheskii Vestnik*, 13 December.
Makarkina, O. 2011b. Vyrvannyi God. *Farmatsevticheskii Vestnik*, 20 December.
Makarkina, O., and E. Mihailova. 2014. Ironiya subsidii. *Vademecum*, 10 November.
Makarkina, O., et al. 2014. Kartina: korzina, kartonka. *Vademecum*, 10 November.
Makarova, E. 2015. Deputaty razrabotali zakon o zaprete likvidatsii sel'skih bol'nits. *Vademecum*, 16 December.
Makarychev, A., and S. Medvedev. 2015. Biopolitics and Power in Putin's Russia. *Problems of Post-Communism* 62 (1): 45–54.
Malle, S. 2016. The All-Russian National Front – for Russia: A New Actor in the Political and Economic Landscape. *Post-Communist Economies* 28 (2): 199–219.
Malysheva, E. 2016. Meditsina: novaya volna optimizatsii: Finansirovanie rossiiskoi meditsiny vnov' poidet pod nozh. *Gazeta.ru*, 9 January.
Manning, N., and N. Tikhonova. eds. 2009. *Health and Health Care in the New Russia*. Farnham and Burlington: Ashgate Publishing.
Manuilova, A. 2014. Zagranitsu ogranichat v lechenii Rossii. *Kommersant*, 3 September.
Manuilova, A. 2016. Inostrannym lekarstvam ogranichat vkhod. *Kommersant*, 24 November.
Manzetti, L., and C.J. Wilson. 2007. Why Do Corrupt Governments Maintain Public Support? *Comparative Political Studies* 40 (8): 949–970.
Markina, E. 2011. Potrebitelyam ne podstelili aspirinku. *Farmatsevticheskii Vestnik*, 25 January.
Markus, S. 2015. *Property, Predation, and Protection: Piranha Capitalism in Russia and Ukraine*. Cambridge: Cambridge University Press.
Marquez, P.V., et al. 2007. Adult Health in the Russian Federation: More than just a Health Problem. *Health Affairs* 26 (4): 1040–1051.
Martin, A., et al. 2022. Does Process Matter? Experimental Evidence on the Effect of Procedural Fairness on Citizens' Evaluations of Policy Outcomes. *International Political Science Review* 43 (1): 103–117.
Matveev, I. 2020. Benefits or Services? Politics of Welfare Retrenchment in Russia, 2014–2017. *East European Politics* 37 (3): 534–551.
Matveev, I. 2021. State, Capital, and the Transformation of the Neoliberal Policy Paradigm in Putin's Russia. In *The Global Rise of Authoritarianism in the 21st Century: Crisis of Neoliberal Globalization and the Nationalist Response*, ed. B. Berberoglu. New York and Abingdon: Routledge.

Matveev, I., and A. Novkunskaya. 2020. Welfare Restructuring in Russia since 2012: National Trends and Evidence from the Regions. *Europe-Asia Studies* 74 (1): 50–71.

Matvienko, V. 2020. Vstrecha s senatorami Rossiiskoi Federatsii. Kremlin.ru, 23 September. http://www.kremlin.ru/events/president/news/64076.

Mazus, A., and E. Kozhokin. 2005. SPID i demograficheskaya pustynya. *Rossiiskaya Gazeta*, 12 July.

Mazus, A., and E. Kozhokin. 2016. V zashchitu chelovecheskogo zdorov'ya, Freyda i OON. *Nezavisimaya Gazeta*, 17 November.

McCubbins, M.D., and T. Schwartz. 1984. Congressional Oversight Overlooked: Police Patrols versus Fire Alarms. *American Journal of Political Science* 28 (1): 165–179.

McGuire, J. 2020. *Democracy and Population Health* (Elements in the Politics of Development). New York: Cambridge University Press.

McInnes, C., and S. Rushton. 2011. HIV/AIDS and Securitization Theory. *European Journal of International Relations* 19 (1): 115–138.

McInnes, C., and S. Rushton. 2012. HIV/AIDS and Securitization Theory. *European Journal of International Relations* 19 (1): 115–138.

Medvedev, D. 2008. *Natsional'nye Prioritety: Stat'i i Vystupleniya*. Moskva: Evropa.

Medvedev, D. 2009. Rossiya, vpered! *Gazeta.ru*, 10 September.

Medvedev, S. 2004. Juicy Morsels: Putin's Beslan Address and the Construction of the New Russian Identity. PONARS Policy Memo 334.

Medvedeva, I., and T. Shishova. 2000. Demograficheskaya voyna protiv Rossii. *Nezavisimaya Gazeta*, 12 January.

Medvedeva, I., and T. Shishova. 2001. Strana pobedivshego SPIDa. *Pravoslavie.ru*, 25 June.

Melikyan, T. 2014. ONF god spustya: mulyazh partii ili strategicheskii proekt Kremlya? *Moskovskii Komsomolets*, 12 June.

Melville, A., and M. Mironyuk. 2016. Bad Enough Governance: State Capacity and Quality of Institutions in Post-Soviet Autocracies. *Post-Soviet Affairs* 32 (2): 132–151.

Melville, A. 2017. Neo-Conservatism as National Idea for Russia? In *State and Political Discourse in Russia*, ed. P.M. Cucciolla, 147–160. Rome: Reset-Dialogues on Civilizations.

Melville A. 2018. Russian Political Ideology. In *Russia: Strategy, Policy and Administration*, ed. I. Studin, 31–41. London: Palgrave Macmillan.

Meng, A. 2020. *Constraining Dictatorship: From Personalized Rule to Institutionalized Regimes*. Cambridge: Cambridge University Press.

Mereminskaya, E. 2016. Prezident i pravitel'stvo – glavnyi istochnik neprozrachnogo goszakaza. *Vedomosti*, 3 April.

Merzlikin, P. 2019. Ya ne znayu, chem lechit' rebenka. *Meduza.io*, 28 November.

Migranyan, A. 2004. Chto takoe putinizm? *Strategiya Rossii v XXI veke* No. 3.
Mikhalkov, N. 2010. Pravo i Pravda, Manifest Prosveshchennogo Konservatizma. https://polit.ru/article/2010/10/26/manifest/.
Miller, G.J., and A.B. Whitford. 2016. *Above Politics: Bureaucratic Discretion and Credible Commitment*. New York: Cambridge University Press.
Mironov, S. 2007. Sotsial'nyi ideal v sovremennoi politike: O smyslovykh osnovaniyakh spravedlivogo obshchestvennogo ustroistva. *Politicheskii Klass* No. 25, January.
Mishina, V. 2016a. VICh-infektsii otkazali v umerennosti. Eksperty trebuyut perepisat' strategiyu bor'by s epidemiei. *Kommersant*, 13 February.
Mishina, V. 2016b. Minzdrav nadeetsya na soznatel'nost' narkomanov. *Kommersant*, 18 February.
Mishina, V. 2020a. Lekarstvam dlya VICh-infitsirovannykh vredit COVID. *Kommersant*, 17 April.
Mishina, V. 2020b. Bez prezervativov i lubrikantov. Minzdrav podgotovil proekt strategii po bor'be s VICh do 2030 goda. *Kommersant* No. 103, 11 June.
Mishina, V., and A. Manuilova. 2016. SPID ispytyvayut na byudzhetnuyu soprotivlyaemost'. Urezano finansirovanie na zakupku antiretrovirusnykh preparatov. *Kommersant* No. 123, 12 July.
Misnik, L. 2018. Putin rasskazal o sredstvakh, vydelyaemykh na bor'bu s onkologiei. *Gazeta.ru*, 7 June.
Mitrokhin, N. 2004. *Russkaya Pravoslavnaya Tserkov': Sovremennoe Sostoyanie i Aktual'nye Problemy*. Moskva: Novoe Literaturnoe Obozrenie.
Moe, T. 1989. The Politics of Bureaucratic Culture. In *Can the Government Govern?*, ed. J. Chubb and P. Peterson, 267–329. Washington, DC: The Brooking Institution.
Moiseev, I., et al. 2016. Issledovanie RBK: skol'ko Rossiya na samom dele tratit na svoikh grazhdan. *RBC.ru*, 14 December.
Morozov, A. 2016. Epidemiyu VICh obyavili sluchaino. *Gazeta.ru*, 2 November.
Morozov, O. 2014. Osnovnye Polozheniya Sotsial'no-konservativnoi Ideologii. *Tetradi Po Konservatizmu* 1 (1): 9–16.
Morrison, S., and C. Wallander. 2005. Russia and HIV/AIDS: Opportunities for Leadership and Cooperation. *Report of the CSIS Task Force on HIV/AIDS, Joint Brookings-CSIS Delegation to Russia*, 20–26 February. Washington, DC: CSIS.
Moynihan, D. P. 2010. The Promises and Paradoxes of Performance-Based Bureaucracy. In *The Oxford Handbook of American Bureaucracy*, ed. R. F. Durant. New York: Oxford University Press.
Mukhina, A. 2019. Eto ne panika, eto katastrofa. V Saratovskoi oblasti bol'nye ne mogut poluchit' besplatnyi insulin. *Meduza.io*, 03 June.
Muller, J.Z. 2018. *The Tyranny of Metrics*. Princeton and Oxford: Princeton University Press.

Mursalieva, G. 2019. Doktor Aleksei Maschan: Pogibnut tysyachi detei i vzroslykh. *Novaya Gazeta*, 1 November.
Myl'nikov, M. 2018a. Ot lishnikh boevoi i politicheskoi podgotovki. *Vademecum*, 11 January.
Myl'nikov, M. 2018b. Edinstvennyi postavshchik medizdelii iz PVH vyigral 90% konkursov, v kotorykh uchastvoval. *Vademecum*, 18 July.
Myl'nikov, M. 2018c. Pravitel'stvo lishilo monopol'nogo statusa postavshchikov medizdelii iz PVH. *Vademecum*, 24 December.
Myl'nikov, M. 2018d. ONF prizval pravitel'stvo rasshirit' reestr postavshchikov medizdelii iz PVH. *Vademecum*, 18 July.
Myl'nikov, M. 2020. Gendirektor Medpolimerproma Aleksei Borisov priznal vinu v dache vzyatki po delu pomoshchnitsy Dvorkovicha. *Vademecum*, 16 December.
Myl'nikov, M. 2021. Minpromtorg nameren uzhestochit' parametry lokalizatsii medtekhniki. *Vademecum*, 14 May.
Myl'nikov. M. 2019a. Liga stavlennikov: Komu iz igrokov rynka medizdelii chashche vezet na rynke goszakaza. *Vademecum*, 2 January.
Myl'nikov, M. 2019b. Minzdrav propisal kriterii nezavisimoi ekspertizy kachestva medpomoshchi. *Vademecum*, 21 January.
Nagornykh, I., I. Safronov, and N. Korchenkova. 2012. Spetssluzhba personala. *Kommersant*, 3 October.
Nagornykh, I. 2018. Vernut' doverie narodnykh mass: Kreml' zadumalsya nad programmoi na 2019 god. *RTVi*, 13 November.
Nazarova, K. 2019. Vo mnogikh regionakh nachalis' pereboi s insulinom. Bol'nym navyazyvayut novyi otechestvennyi preparat. *Otkrytye media*, 11 January.
Nikishina, M. 2021. Farmproizvoditeli vyrazili opaseniya iz-za vvedeniya pravila vtoroi lishnii. *Vademecum*, 14 April.
Nikolaeva, D., I. Parfent'eva, and P. Netreba. 2010. Roszdrav ostalsya bez nadzora: Opponenty zakona o lekarstvakh sdayut posty. *Kommersant* No. 21/P (4321), 8 February.
Nikolskaya, A., and M. Dmitriev. 2020. The End of the Crimean Consensus: How Sustainable are the New Trends in Russian Public Opinion? *Russian Politics* 5 (3): 354–374.
North, D.C. 1990. *Institutions, Institutional Change and Economic Performance*. Cambridge: Cambridge University Press.
North, D.C., J.J. Wallis, and B.R. Weingast. 2009. *Violence and Social Orders: A Conceptual Framework for Interpreting Recorded Human History*. New York: Cambridge University Press.
Novaya Gazeta. 2016. Zoloto partitury, 3 April.
Novaya Gazeta. 2021. Lyubov' k otecheskim grosham, 23 February.

Nunes, J. 2020. Critical Security Studies and Global Health. In *Oxford Handbook of Global Health Politics*, ed. C. McInnes, K. Lee, and J. Youde, 161–177. Oxford, UK: Oxford University Press.
Obshchetsvennaya Palata. 2011. Profilaktika VICh-Infektsii v Rossii: Problemy i Perspektivy, 24 March.
Olevskii, T. 2019. Sposob, kotoryi primenyaetsya pri voinakh i epidemiyakh. *Curent Time*, 5 December.
Olimpieva, I., and O. Pachenkov. 2013. Corrupt Intermediaries in Post-Socialist Russia: Mutations of Economic Institutions. *Europe-Asia Studies* 65 (7): 1364–1376.
ONF. 2019a. Farmatsevticheskim proizvoditelyam nado predostavlyat' spetsial'nye vozmozhnosti dlya proizvodstva novykh preparatov, 20 September.
ONF. 2019b. ONF i Natsional'naya meditsinskaya palata rabotayut v tesnom kontakte po resheniyu problem v sfere zdravookhraneniya, 10 October.
ONF. 2019c. V penzenskoi oblasti posle sryva srokov stroitel'stva vozveden pervyi fel'dshersko-akusherskii punkt, 1 November.
ONF. 2019d. Blagodarya ONF v Kirovskoi oblasti bolee 70 patsientov s nachala 2019 goda poluchili zhiznenno neobkhodimye lekarstva, 5 December.
Oreshkin, D. 2019. *Dzhugafiliya i Sovetskii Statisticheskii Epos*. Moskva: Mysl'.
Osei, A., et al. 2020. Presidential Term Limits and Regime Types: When Do Leaders Respect Constitutional Norms? *Africa Spectrum* 55 (3): 251–271.
Osipov, A., and N. Kostarnova. 2021. Immunoglobulinovyi krizis perekhodit v kollaps. *Kommersant* No. 197, 28 October.
Osokina, E. 2021. *Stalin's Quest for Gold. The Torgsin Hard-Currency Shops and Soviet Industrialization*. Ithaca: Cornell University Press.
Ostbo, J. 2017. Securitizing "Spiritual-moral Values" in Russia. *Post-Soviet Affairs* 33 (3): 200–216.
Ostergard, R. 2002. Politics in the Hot Zone: AIDS and National Security in Africa. *Third World Quarterly* 23 (2): 333–350.
Owen, C., and E. Bindman. 2019. Civic Participation in a Hybrid Regime: Limited Pluralism in Policymaking and Delivery in Contemporary Russia. *Government and Opposition* 54 (1): 98–120.
O'Manique, C. 2004. *Neoliberalism and AIDS Crisis in Sub-Saharan Africa: Globalization's Pandemic*. Houndmills, Basingtoke: Palgrave Macmillan.
Paget, D. 2020. Again, Making Tanzania Great: Magufuli's Restorationist Developmental Nationalism. *Democratization* 27 (7): 1240–1260.
Pan, J. 2020. *Welfare for Autocrats: How Social Assistance in China Cares for its Rulers*. New York: Oxford University Press.
Paneyakh, E. 2014. Faking Performance Together: Systems of Performance Evaluation in Russian Enforcement Agencies and Production of Bias and Privilege. *Post-Soviet Affairs* 30 (2–3): 115–136.
Pape, U. 2014. *The Politics of HIV/AIDS in Russia*. London: Routledge.

Pape, U. 2018. Framing the Epidemic: NGOs and the Fight Against HIV/AIDS in Russia. *Russian Politics* 3 (4): 486–512.
Papkova, I. 2011. Russian Orthodox Concordat? Church and State under Medvedev. *Nationalities Papers* 39 (5): 667–683.
Parsons, C. 2007. *How to Map Arguments in Political Science*. New York: Oxford University Press.
Patriarchia.ru. 2000. Osnovy Sotsial'noi Kontseptsii Russkoi Pravoslavnoi Tserkvi. http://www.patriarchia.ru/db/text/419128.html.
Patterson, A. ed. 2005. *The African State and the AIDS Crisis*. Farnham and Burlington: Ashgate Publishing.
Patterson, A. 2018. *Africa and Global Health Governance: Domestic Politics and International Structures*. Baltimore: Johns Hopkins University Press.
Pavlovsky, G. 2012. *Genial'naya Vlast'! Slovar' Abstrakcii Kremlya*. Moskva: Evropa.
Pavlovsky, G. 2016. Ekspertogoniya. Memuar o Grazhdanskom forume—2001. *Gefter.ru*, 18 November. http://gefter.ru/archive/20078.
Pakhomov, A. 2019. ONF: goszakupki lekarstv sryvayutsya iz-za novykh pravil formirovaniya nachal'noi tseny kontrakta, *Vademcum*, 4 February.
Pelevin, V. 1999. *Generation P*. Moskva: Vagrius.
Pertsev, A. 2015. Privet iz GDR: Kak Kreml' primenit Narodnyi front. *Carnegie.ru*, 9 December.
Pertsev, A. 2017. Volodin vs. Kiriyenko: The Battle for Influence in Russia's Power Vertical. *Carnegie.ru*, 16 June.
Pertsev, A. 2020. Edinaya Rossiya pomenyaet nazvanie i obedinitsya s Narodnym frontom. *Meduza.io*, 25 February.
Petroshai, A. 2015. Parenaya skrepa. *Vademecum*, 7 September.
Petrov, I. 2015. FSKN: Spaysy mogut ispol'zovat' dlya organizatsii tsvetnykh revolyutsii. *Rossiiskaya Gazeta*, 21 April.
Petrov, N., M. Lipman, and H. Hale. 2014. Three Dilemmas of Hybrid Regime Governance: Russia from Putin to Putin. *Post-Soviet Affairs* 30 (1): 1–26.
Petrov, N., and M. Rochlitz. 2019. Control Over the Security Services in Periods of Political Uncertainty: A Comparative Study of Russia and China. *Russian Politics* 4 (4): 546–573.
Piketty, T. 2020. *Capital and Ideology*. Cambridge and London: Belknap Press: An Imprint of Harvard University Press.
Pisano, J. 2014. Pokazukha and Cardiologist Khrenov. In *Historical Legacies of Communism in Russia and Eastern Europe*, eds. M. Beissinger and S. Kotkin, 222–242. New York: Cambridge University Press.
Pis'mennaya, E. 2013. *Sistema Kudrina. Istoriya Klyuchevogo Ekonomista Putinskoi Rossii*. Moskva: Mann, Ivanov i Farber.
Poku, N., and J. Sundewall. 2018. Political Responsibility and Global Health. *Third World Quarterly* 39 (3): 471–486.

Polozhenie o Pravitel'stvennoi Komissii po Voprosam Profilaktiki, Diagnostiki i Lecheniya Zabolevaniya, Vyzyvaemogo Virusom Immunodefitsita Cheloveka (VICh-Infektsii) No. 608, 9 October 2006.

Pomerantsev, P. 2014. The Hidden Author of Putinism: How Vladislav Surkov Invented the New Russia. *The Atlantic*, 7 November.

Pomeranz, W. E., and K. Smith. 2016. Commentary: Putin's Domestic Strategy: Counting the Trees, Missing the Forest. *Reuters*, 20 May.

Ponomareva, V. 2021. Tsena platsebo. Afera s EpiVak mozhet stoit' zhizni tysyacham lyudey. *The Insider*, 09 July.

Primakov, E. 2014a. 2013. Hard Problems of Russia: Why Neoliberal Policy Cannot Be Accepted Today. *Nezavisimaya Gazeta*, 14 January.

Primakov, E. 2014b. Russia's Problems: Why Neoliberal Policy is Unacceptable Today. Valdai Discussion Club, 27 January. https://valdaiclub.com/a/highlights/russia_s_problems_why_neoliberal_policy_is_unacceptable_today/.

Prosina, E. 2018. V Apatitakh pokhoronili Dar'yu Starikovu. *Kommersant*, 24 May.

Prozorov, S. 2005. Russian Conservatism in the Putin Presidency: The Dispersion of a Hegemonic Discourse. *Journal of Political Ideologies* 10 (2): 121–143.

Pryanikov, P. 2016. Metodologi - eto totalitarnyi tekhnokratizm. *Tolkovatel*, 6 October.

Pugachev, A. 2020. V bol'nitse v Kamenske-Ural'skom iz-za koronavirusa ostalas' tret' medpersonala. *Current Time*, 30 October.

Pushkarskaya, A. 2020. Nesmenyaemee Putina. *Zhurnal Kholod*, 13 November.

Putin, V. 2000. Pervoe Poslanie Federal'nomu Sobraniyu Rossiiskoi Federatsii, 8 July. [Published in Pavlovskii, G.O. 2007. *Plan Prezidenta Putina. Rukovodstvo dlya Budushchikh Prezidentov Rossii. Sbornik*. Moskva: Evropa, pp. 31–55].

Putin, V. 2002. Tret'e Poslanie Federal'nomu Sobraniyu Rossiiskoi Federatsii, 18 April. [Published in Pavlovskii G.O. 2007. *Plan Prezidenta Putina. Rukovodstvo dlya Budushchikh Prezidentov Rossii. Sbornik*. Moskva: Evropa, pp. 97–125].

Putin, V. 2006. Vstupitel'noe slovo na zasedanii prezidiuma Gosudarstvennogo soveta "O Neotlozhnykh Merakh po Bor'be s Rasprostraneniem VICh-infektsii v Rossiiskoi Federatsii", 21 April. http://kremlin.ru/events/president/transcripts/23547.

Putin, V. 2007. Stenogramma pryamogo tele- i radioefira ("Pryamaya liniya s Prezidentom Rossii"), 18 October. http://kremlin.ru/events/president/transcripts/24604.

Putin, V. 2008. Bol'shaya press-konferentsiya Vladimira Putina. Otvety prezidenta RF Vladimira Putina na voprosy zhurnalistov. *Lenta.ru*, 14 February.

Putin, V. 2009a. V.V. Putin provel v Zelenograde soveshchanie "O strategii razvitiya farmatsevticheskoi promyshlennosti", 9 October. http://archive.government.ru/docs/7859/.
Putin, V. 2009b. Pochemu trudno uvolit' cheloveka. *Russkii Pioner*, 22 August. http://ruspioner.ru/ptu/single/1195/.
Putin, V. 2010. Razgovor s Vladimirom Putinym. Prodolzhenie. Polnyi tekst programmy, 16 December. https://www.vesti.ru/article/2072038.
Putin, V. 2012. Press-konferentsiya Vladimira Putina, 20 December. http://kremlin.ru/events/president/news/17173.
Putin, V. 2013a. Konferentsiya Obshcherossiiskogo narodnogo fronta. Vladimir Putin prinyal uchastie v konferentsii Obshcherossiiskogo narodnogo fronta "Forum deistvii", 5 December. http://kremlin.ru/events/president/news/19787.
Putin, V. 2013b. Prezidentu predstavleny plany raboty ministerstv po ispolneniyu maiskikh ukazov, 7 June. http://www.kremlin.ru/news/18277.
Putin, V. 2015. Vstupitel'noe slovo na plenarnom zasedanii Foruma Obshcherossiiskogo narodnogo fronta "Za kachestvennuyu i dostupnuyu meditsinu!" 7 September. http://kremlin.ru/events/president/news/50249.
Putin, V. 2017. Bol'shaya press-konferentsiya Vladimira Putina, 14 December. http://kremlin.ru/events/president/news/56378.
Putin, V. 2018a. Poslanie Prezidenta Federal'nomu Sobraniyu, 1 March. http://kremlin.ru/events/president/transcripts/56957.
Putin, V. 2018b. Soveshchanie po voprosam povysheniya effektivnosti sistemy lekarstvennogo obespecheniya, 16 November. http://special.kremlin.ru/events/president/transcripts/59143.
Putin, V. 2018c. The plenary session of the 15th anniversary meeting of the Valdai International Discussion Club, 18 October. http://en.kremlin.ru/events/president/news/58848.
Putin, V. 2019a. Pryamaya liniya s Vladimirom Putinym, 20 June. http://www.kremlin.ru/events/president/news/page/91.
Putin, V. 2019b. Zasedanie Soveta po razvitiyu grazhdanskogo obshchestva i pravam cheloveka, 10 December. http://kremlin.ru/events/president/news/62285.
Putin, V. 2020. Vystuplenie na final'noi sessii diskussionnogo kluba Valdai, 22 October. http://kremlin.ru/events/president/news/64261.
Rahat, G., and O. Kenig. 2018. *From Party Politics to Personalized Politics? Party Change and Political Personalization in Democracies*. New York, Oxford University Press.
Raskin, A., and O. Makarkina. 2013. Otsvechivai i ne sidi. *Vademecum*, 17 June.
Ratigan, K. 2022. Riding the Tiger of Performance Legitimacy? Chinese Villagers' Satisfaction with State Healthcare Provision. *International Political Science Review* 3 (2): 259–278.

RBC. 2007. V Rossii poyavitsya megaregulyator potrebrynka, 9 February.
RBC. 2010a. Sotrudnikov Minzdrava privlekut k otvetstvennosti za zakupki tomografov, 13 August.
RBC. 2010b. Sud vydal sanktsiyu na arest eks-zamglavy Minzdrava RF, 29 November.
RBC. 2012. Chinovnikov Minzdrava ulichili v rastrate VICh-millionov, 13 November.
RBC. 2014. Na gostabletkakh: Kakie farmkompanii zavisyat ot byudzhetnykh deneg, 07 October.
RBC. 2015. Putin potreboval vyyasnit' prichiny uskorennogo rosta tsen na lekarstva, 07 September.
Reiter, S., and M. Zholobova. 2021. Pishite podobree, oni delayut takoe khoroshee delo. *Meduza.io*, 19 December.
Remington, T. 2008. Patronage and the Party of Power: President-Parliament Relations Under Vladimir Putin. *Europe-Asia Studies* 60 (6): 959–987.
Remington, T.F. 2019. Institutional Change in Authoritarian Regimes: Pension Reform in Russia and China. *Problems of Post-Communism* 66 (5): 301–314.
Remizov, D. 2019. Pochemu vrachi ne vyderzhali? *RBC*, 31 October.
Renz, B. 2006. Putin's Militocracy? An Alternative Interpretation of Siloviki in Contemporary Russian Politics. *Europe-Asia Studies* 58 (6): 903–924.
Reprintseva, Yu. 2016. Pochemu gosudarstvo obyavlyaet bortsov s VICh inoagentami. *Novaya Gazeta*, 9 August.
Reuter, O.J., and T.F. Remington. 2009. Dominant Party Regimes and the Commitment Problem: The Case of United Russia. *Comparative Political Studies* 42 (4): 501–526.
Rhodes, T., et al. 2010. Policy Resistance to Harm Reduction for Drug Users and Potential Effect of Change. *British Medical Journal* 341: c3439.
Richter, J. 2009. Putin and the Public Chamber. *Post-Soviet Affairs* 25 (1): 39–65.
Rivera, D.W., and S.W. Rivera. 2018. The Militarization of the Russian Elite under Putin. *Problems of Post-Communism* 65 (4): 221–232.
Rivera, S.W., and D.W. Rivera. 2006. The Russian Elite under Putin: Militocratic or Bourgeois? *Post-Soviet Affairs* 22 (2): 125–144.
Roberts, D. 2010. *Global Governance and Biopolitics: Regulating Human Security*. London, New York: Zed Books.
Robinson, N. 2017. Russian Neo-patrimonialism and Putin's Cultural Turn. *Europe-Asia Studies* 69 (2): 348–366.
Robinson, N. 2020. Putin and the Incompleteness of Putinism. *Russian Politics* 5 (3): 283–300.
Rodionova, A., and K. Sedov. 2013. Ustav ot edineniya. *Vademecum*, 1 July.
Rodionova, A. 2013. Prokuratura vyyavila 46,000 narushenii pri realizatsii natsproekta Zdorovie v 2012 godu. *Vademecum*, 26 February.

Rodionova, A. 2014. Vavilonskaya basnya. *Vademecum*, 31 March.
Rodrick, D. 2010. The Myth of Authoritarian Growth. *Project Syndicate*, 9 August.
Roemer-Mahler, A., and S. Elbe. 2016. The Race for Ebola Drugs: Pharmaceuticals, Security and Global Health Governance. *Third World Quarterly* 37 (3): 487–506.
Romanova, I. 2016. Onishchenko: Na mirovoi arene tol'ko Rossiya sposobna effektivno protivodeystvovat' narashchivaniyu voenno-biologicheskogo potentsiala. *Rossiiskaya Gazeta*, 20 May.
Rosenau, J.N. 2003. *Distant Proximities: Dynamics beyond Globalization*. Princeton and Oxford: Princeton University Press.
Roshal, L. 2011. Zachem nuzhno samoregulirovanie? *Medportal.ru*, 13 April.
Rousselet, K. 2015. The Church in the Service of the Fatherland. *Europe-Asia Studies* 67 (1): 49–67.
Rowden, R. 2009. *The Deadly Ideas of Neoliberalism: How the IMF has Undermined Public Health and the Fight against AIDS*. New York: Zed Books.
Rutland, P. 2013. Neoliberalism and the Russian Transition. *Review of International Political Economy* 20 (2): 332–362.
Ryakin, S. 2019. Chtoby men'she provalivalos'. *Farmatsevticheskii Vestnik*, 26 November.
Rybina, L. 2010. Nikolai Yurgel' rasskazyvaet. *Novaya Gazeta*, 10 February.
Rykovtseva, E. 2020. Kholuistvo ne trebuet soglasovanii. *RFE/RL*, 24 September.
Sagdiev, R. 2011. Chempion po goszakupkam. *Vedomosti*, 30 May.
Saikkonen, I. 2021. Coordinating the Machine: Subnational Political Context and the Effectiveness of Machine Politics. *Acta Politica* 56 (4): 658–676.
Satter, D. 2016. *The Less You Know, the Better You Sleep: Russia's Road to Terror and Dictatorship under Yeltsin and Putin*. New Haven and London: Yale University Press.
Savina, E. 2010. Prezident otsovetoval natsproekty. *Gazeta.ru*, 28 September.
Schatzberg, M.G. 1988. *The Dialectics of Oppression in Zaïre*. Bloomington: Indiana University Press.
Schedler, A. 2013. *The Politics of Uncertainty: Sustaining and Subverting Electoral Authoritarianism*. New York: Oxford University Press.
Schrecker, T. 2020. The State and Global Health. In *Oxford Handbook of Global Health Politics*, ed. C. McInnes, K. Lee, and J. Youde, 281–299. Oxford, UK: Oxford University Press.
Schrecker, T., and C. Bambra. 2015. *How Politics Makes Us Sick: Neoliberal Epidemics* Houndmills, Basingstoke: Palgrave Macmillan UK.
Scott, J.C. 1998. *Seeing Like a State: How Certain Schemes to Improve the Human Condition Have Failed*. New Haven and London: Yale University Press.

Seckinelgin, H., J. Bigirumwami, and J. Morris. 2010. Securitization of HIV/AIDS in Context: Gendered Vulnerability in Burundi. *Security Dialogue* 41 (5): 515–535.
Sedakov, P. 2015. Zhizn' posle Arbidola: Kak Viktor Kharitonin zavoeval rynok farmy. *Forbes*, 12 May.
Sedov, K. 2011. Navalnyi vglyadelsya v monitoring. *Farmatsevticheskii Vestnik* No. 33, 20 October.
Sedov, K. 2014. Britvy titanov. *Vademecum*, 14 January.
Seeberg, M.B. 2014. State Capacity and the Paradox of Authoritarian Elections. *Democratization* 21 (7): 1265–1285.
Serkov, D., M. Alekhina, and P. Zvezdina. 2018. Minzdrav preduprezhdayut: v SKR poyavyatsya otdely po vrachebnym oshibkam. *RBC*, 29 November.
Sewell, W.H. 2009. From State-Centrism to Neoliberalism: Macro-Historical Contexts of Population Health since World War II. In *Successful Societies: How Institutions and Culture Affect Health*, eds. P. Hall and M. Lamont, 254–287. New York: Cambridge University Press.
Sharafutdinova, G. 2014. The Pussy Riot Affair and Putin's Démarche from Sovereign Democracy to Sovereign Morality. *Nationalities Papers* 42 (4): 615–621.
Sharafutdinova, G. 2020. *The Red Mirror: Putin's Leadership and Russia's Insecure Identity*. New York: Oxford University Press.
Shevtsova, L. 2015. Itogi goda. 2014 god—konets illyuziona? *Ezhednevnyi Zhurnal*, 1 January.
Shishkin, S.V., et al. 2018. *Zdravookhranenie: Neobkhodimye Otvety na Vyzovy Vremeni*. Moskva: Tsentr Strategicheskikh Razrabotok.
Shpil'kin, S. 2021. Vybory po nakatannoi kolee. *Troitskii variant—Nauka*, 5 October.
Shubina, D., and M. Myl'nikov. 2018. Kak o stenty gorokh: Na chem spotykaetsya edinstvennyi meditsinskii proekt Viktora Veksel'berga. *Vademecum*, 16 April.
Shubina, D., M. Sidorova, and E. Rechkin. 2017. Chego boyatsya ispolniteli goskontraktov na postavku meditsinskikh izdelii. *Vademecum*, 8 August.
Shubina, D. 2017. Natsmedpalata poluchila prezidentskii grant na zashchitu medikov ot SMI. *Vademecum*, 2 August.
Shubina, D. 2018. Medpolimerpromu ne khvataet deneg na stroitel'stvo zavoda izdelii iz PVH. *Vademecum*, 13 July.
Shubina, D., and E. Rechkin. 2017. Pochemu ne rabotaet importozameshchenie na rynke medizdelii. *Vademecum*, 9 August.
Simmons, B., and Z. Elkins. 2004. The Globalization of Liberalization: Policy Diffusion in the International Political Economy. *American Political Science Review* 98 (1): 171–189.

Sjostedt, R. 2008. Exploring the Construction of Threats: The Securitization of HIV/AIDS in Russia. *Security Dialogue* 39 (1): 7–29.
Skokova, Y., et al. 2018. The Non-profit Sector in Today's Russia: Between Confrontation and Co-optation. *Europe-Asia Studies* 70 (4): 531–563.
Skorobogat'ko, T. 2004. Klinicheskii sluchai. *Moskovskie Novosti*, 25 March.
Skvortsova, V. 2016. Epidemiyu VICh v Rossii nikto ne obyavlyal. *TASS*, 1 December.
Smith, B. 2005. Life of the Party: The Origins of Regime Breakdown and Persistence under Single-Party Rule. *World Politics* 57 (3): 421–451.
Smyth, R. 2012. Thief or Savior? Contesting Personalism in Russia's Rallies and Protests. PONARS Eurasia Policy Memo No. 215.
Snyder, T. 2018. *The Road to Unfreedom: Russia, Europe*. America. New York: Tim Duggan Books.
Sokolova, E. 2016. *State Response to the HIV/AIDS Epidemic in Russia: Institutional Factors*. PhD diss.: Temple University.
Soldatov, A., and I. Borogan. 2011. *The New Nobility: The Restoration of Russia's Security State and the Enduring Legacy of the KGB*. New York: Public Affairs.
Soldatov, A., and M. Rochlitz. 2018. The Siloviki in Russian Politics. In *The New Autocracy: Information, Politics, and Policy in Putin's Russia*, ed. D. Treisman, 83–108. Washington, D.C.: Brookings Institution.
Solodun E., and M. Nikishina. 2020. Nemetskie mediki otkazalis' sotrudnichat' s Natsmedpalatoi po delu Naval'nogo. *Vademecum*, 8 September.
Solopov, M. 2015. Pravitel'stvo zadumalos' o sozdanii megaregulyatora na potrebrynke. *RBC*, 08 September.
Solov'eva, O. 2019. Effekta ot natsproektov tri goda zhdut. *Nezavisimaya Gazeta*, 13 November.
Sperling, V. 2014. *Sex, Politics, and Putin: Political Legitimacy in Russia*. New York: Oxford University Press.
Stanovaya, T. 2015. Biznes i vlast': K novoi modeli otnoshenii. *Politcom.ru*, 28 December.
Stanovaya, T. 2019. Grudges Before Politics: Arrests in Russia Are Increasingly Random. *Carnegie Moscow Center*, 5 April.
Stanovaya, T. 2020. The Taming of the Elite: Putin's Referendum. *Carnegie Moscow Center*, 1 July.
Starkov, M. 2019. Rukotvornyi defitsit. V Rossii mozhet propast' geparin. *Farmatsevticheskii Vestnik*, 29 October.
Stenin, A. 2004. Veterinaram otpustili grekhi. *Rossiiskaya Gazeta*, 25 September.
Stepanova, E. 2015. The Spiritual and Moral Foundation of Civilization in Every Nation for Thousands of Years: The Traditional Values Discourse in Russia. *Politics, Religion & Ideology* 16 (2–3): 119–136.
Stoeckl, K. 2016. The Russian Orthodox Church as Moral Norm Entrepreneur. *Religion, State and Society* 44 (2): 132–151.

Stoeckl, K. 2020. The Rise of the Russian Christian Right: The Case of the World Congress of Families. *Religion, State and Society* 48 (4): 223–238.

Stromseth, J.R., E.J. Malesky, and D.D. Gueorguiev, eds. 2017. *China's Governance Puzzle: Enabling Transparency and Participation in a Single-Party State.* New York: Cambridge University Press.

Sulakshin, S. (ed.) 2007. *Natsional'naya Identichnost' Rossii i Demograficheskii Krizis.* Moskva: Nauchnyi Ekspert.

Surkov, V. 2005. My real'no schitaem, chto davat' vlast' liberal'nym druz'yam opasno i vredno dlya strany. Vystuplenie na zakrytom zasedanii General'nogo soveta obedineniya Delovoi Rossii, 17 May. *Polit.ru*, 12 July. https://polit.ru/article/2005/07/12/surk/.

Surkov, V. 2007. Russkaya politicheskaya kul'tura. *Strategiya Rossii* No. 7, July.

Surkov, V. 2019. Dolgoe gosudarstvo Putina. *Nezavisimaya Gazeta*, 2 November.

Svolik, M. 2012. *The Politics of Authoritarian Rule.* New York: Cambridge University Press.

Tagaeva, L. 2013. Pochemu Putin sdal Onishchenko. *Republic.ru*, 25 October.

Talleh Nkobou, A., and A. Ainslie. 2021. Developmental Nationalism? Political Trust and the Politics of Large-Scale Land Investment in Magufuli's Tanzania. *Journal of Eastern African Studies* 15 (3): 378–399.

Tarschys, D. 1993. The Success of a Failure: Gorbachev's Alcohol Policy, 1985–88. *Europe-Asia Studies* 45 (1): 7–25.

TASS. 2019. Istoriya natsproektov v Rossii, 11 February.

Taylor, B.D. 2007. *Russia's Power Ministries: Coercion and Commerce.* Syracuse: Institute for National Security and Counterterrorism, Syracuse University.

Taylor, B.D. 2011. *State Building in Putin's Russia: Policing and Coercion after Communism.* New York: Cambridge University Press.

Taylor, B.D. 2014. Police Reform in Russia: The Policy Process in a Hybrid Regime. *Post-Soviet Affairs* 30 (2–3): 226–255.

Taylor, B.D. 2017. The Russian Siloviki and Political Change. *Daedalus* 146 (2): 53–63.

Taylor, B.D. 2018. *The Code of Putinism.* New York: Oxford University Press.

Taylor, B.D. 2019. Putin's Fourth Term: The Phantom Breakthrough. PONARS Eurasia Policy Memo No. 602.

Teague, E. 2020. Russia's Constitutional Reforms of 2020. *Russian Politics* 5 (3): 301–328.

The Federal Law 'On the sanitary-and-epidemiological well-being of the population' No. 52-FZ, March 30, 1999.

The Insider. 2021. Na PMEF podpisali soglashenie ob eksporte EpiVakKorony v Braziliyu i Venesuelu, 7 June.

Thomson, H. 2019. *Food and Power: Regime Type, Agricultural Policy, and Political Stability.* Cambridge and New York: Cambridge University Press.

Ting, M. 2003. A Strategic Theory of Bureaucratic Redundancy. *American Journal of Political Science* 47 (2): 274–292.
Titov, S. 2011. U narkopolitseyskikh okazalos' slishkom mnogo del. *Kommersant-Online*, 6 October.
Tkachenko, K., and E. Gubernatorov. 2019. Eks-glavu Komi Gaizera prigovorili k 11 godam kolonii. *RBC*, 10 June.
Transparency International. 2017. Kak gosmonopoliya Nacimbio zarabotala na vaktsinakh i kto ot etogo vyigral: Rassledovanie peterburgskogo otdeleniya Transparency International - Rossiya, 16 October. https://transparency.org.ru/special/natsimbio/.
Treisman, D. 2011. Presidential Popularity in a Hybrid Regime: Russia under Yeltsin and Putin. *American Journal of Political Science* 55 (3): 590–609.
Treisman, D. 2018. Introduction: Rethinking Putin's Political Order. In *The New Autocracy: Information, Politics, and Policy in Putin's Russia*, ed. D. Treisman, 1–28. Washington, D.C.: Brookings Institution.
Trifonova, A. 2018. Vrachebnym oshibkam podbirayut tsenu. *Kommersant*, 25 July.
Truex, R. 2017. Consultative Authoritarianism and its Limits. *Comparative Political Studies* 50 (3): 329–361.
Tsygankov, A. 2016. Crafting the State-Civilization Vladimir Putin's Turn to Distinct Values. *Problems of Post-Communism* 63 (3): 146–158.
Tumakova, I. 2021a. Operatsiya "E": My vam rasskazhem, chto poluchaet s EpiVakKoronoi chelovek, chto - krolik, a chto - razrabotchiki vaktsiny. *Novaya Gazeta* No. 60, 04 June.
Tumakova, I. 2021b. EpiVakAfera: V privivochnykh kabinetakh nachali zamenyat' vaktsinu Sputnik preparatom EpiVakKorona, ne preduprezhdaya patsientov. *Novaya Gazeta* No. 67, 23 June.
Twigg, J., ed. 2006. *HIV/AIDS in Russia and Eurasia. Vol I.* New York: Palgrave Macmillan.
Twigg, J. 2002. Health Care Reform in Russia: Survey of Head Doctors and Insurance Administrators. *Social Science & Medicine* 55 (12): 2253–2265.
UNICEF. 2010. *Blame and Banishment: The Underground HIV Epidemic Affecting Children in Eastern Europe and Central Asia.* Geneva, Switzerland: UNICEF.
Vahabi, M. 2016. A Positive Theory of the Predatory State. *Public Choice* 168 (3): 153–175.
Vahabi, M. 2020. Introduction: A Symposium on the Predatory State. *Public Choice* 182: 233–242.
Vedomosti. 2017. V vine iz Chernogorii nashli pestitsidy. *Vedomosti*, 31 May.
Vedomosti. 2019. Lokalizuite eto: Kak vernut' inostrannykh investorov v proizvodstvo lekarstv v Rossii. *Vedomosti*, 30 October.

Velekhov, L. 2020. Russkaya dusha – stalinistka: Viktor Erofeev v programme Leonida Velekhova. *RFE/RL*, 26 September.

Vieira, M. 2011. Southern Africa's Response(s) to International HIV/AIDS Norms: The Politics of Assimilation. *Review of International Studies* 37 (1): 3–28.

Vinnik, S. 2015. Tabletki s igloi. *Rossiiskaya Gazeta*, 15 October.

Vinokurov, A., et al. 2019. Vitse-gubernatora prizvali na front: Mikhail Kuznetsov mozhet reanimirovat' ONF. *Kommersant*, 12 September.

Vinokurova, E. 2016. Putin poprosil ne otkryvat' okhotu na elitu. *Znak.ru*, 25 January.

Vinokurova, E. 2018. ONF snova v poiske sebya. *Znak.ru*, 14 June.

Visloguzov, V., D. Nikolaeva, and D. Butrin. 2010. Bol'she gippokratii, bol'she sotsializma. *Kommersant*, 21 April.

Vladykin, O. 2016. Polchishcha boevykh virusov podgotovleny dlya nastupleniya. *Nezavisimoe Voennoe Obozrenie*, 25 March.

VSP. 2021. Aktual'nye Problemy Rossiiskogo Zdravookhraneniya v 2020 godu v otsenkakh patsientov i patsientskikh NKO. *Vserossiiskii soyuz patsientov*, 26 April. https://vspru.ru/senter/issledovaniia-analitika-mneniia/issledovaniia.

Wallander, C. 2006. Russian Politics and HIV/AIDS: The Institutional and Leadership Sources of an Inadequate Policy. In *HIV/AIDS in Russia and Eurasia*, vol. I, ed. J. Twigg, 33–56. New York: Palgrave Macmillan.

Waller, J. 2021. Elites and Institutions in the Russian Thermidor: Regime Instrumentalism, Entrepreneurial Signaling, and Inherent Illiberalism. *Journal of Illiberalism Studies* 1 (1): 1–23.

Wang, E.H., and Y. Xu. 2018. Awakening Leviathan: The Effect of Democracy on State Capacity. *Research & Politics* 5 (2): 1–7.

Wang, Y.-T., V. Mechkova, and F. Andersson. 2018. Does Democracy Enhance Health? New Empirical Evidence 1900–2012. *Political Research Quarterly* 72 (3): 554–569.

Way, L. 2008. The Real Causes of the Color Revolutions. *Journal of Democracy* 19 (3): 55–69.

Way, L. 2015. *Pluralism by Default: Weak Autocrats and the Rise of Competitive Politics*. Baltimore: Johns Hopkins University Press.

Wendt, A. 1999. *Social Theory of International Politics*. Cambridge: Cambridge University Press.

Wengle, S., and M. Rasell. 2008. The Monetisation of *L'goty*: Changing Patterns of Welfare Politics and Provision in Russia. *Europe-Asia Studies* 60 (5): 739–756.

White, D. 2011. Dominant Party Systems: A Framework for Conceptualizing Opposition Strategies in Russia. *Democratization* 18 (3): 655–681.

White, D. 2017. State Capacity and Regime Resilience in Putin's Russia. *International Political Science Review* 39 (1): 130–143.

Whitmore, S. 2010. Parliamentary Oversight in Putin's Neo-patrimonial State. Watchdogs or Show-dogs? *Europe-Asia Studies* 62 (6): 999–1025.
Wigley, S., and A. Akkoyunlu-Wigley. 2011. The Impact of Regime Type on Health: Does Redistribution Explain Everything? *World Politics* 63 (4): 647–677.
Wilkinson, C. 2014. Putting "Traditional Values" Into Practice: The Rise and Contestation of Anti-Homopropaganda Laws in Russia. *Journal of Human Rights* 13 (3): 363–379.
Wintrobe, R. 1998. *The Political Economy of Dictatorship*. Cambridge, UK: Cambridge University Press.
Wood, D. B. 2010. Agency Theory and the Bureaucracy. In *The Oxford Handbook of American Bureaucracy*, ed. R. F. Durant. New York: Oxford University Press.
Yakoreva, A., and A. Ershov. 2020. Tol'ko odna chastnaya kompaniya v Rossii mozhet prodavat' testy na koronavirus. *Meduza.io*, 28 March.
Yakovlev, A., and A. Aisin. 2019. Friends or Foes? The Effect of Governor-Siloviki Interaction on Economic Growth in Russian Regions. *Russian Politics* 4 (4): 520–545.
Yasakova, E. 2021. Syr'e moe: novyi mekhanizm goszakupok mozhet privesti k defitsitu lekarstv. *Izvestiya*, 14 April.
Yasuda, J. 2017. *On Feeding the Masses: An Anatomy of Regulatory Failure in China*. Cambridge: Cambridge University Press.
Yildirim, T.M., et al. 2022. Agenda Dynamics and Policy Priorities in Military Regimes. *International Political Science Review* 43 (3): 418–432.
Young, O. 1994. *International Governance: Protecting the Environment in a Stateless Society*. Ithaca and London: Cornell University Press.
Yurchak, A. 2006. *Everything Was Forever, Until It Was No More: The Last Soviet Generation*. Princeton: Princeton University Press.
Yurgel, N. 2014. Roszdravnadzor—odin iz kraeugol'nykh kamnei v sisteme natsional'noi biobezopasnosti Rossii. *Vestnik Roszdravnadzora*, No. 5.
Yushkov, I. 2019. Vankomytsin dlya prezidenta. *Daily Storm*, 19 February.
Zavadskaya, M., and L. Shilov. 2021. Providing Goods and Votes? Federal Elections and the Quality of Local Governance in Russia. *Europe-Asia Studies* 73 (6): 1037–1059.
Zhegulev, I. 2016. Pravo na zabvenie Evgeniya Prigozhina. *Meduza.io*, 09 June.
Zhegulev, I. 2017. Importozamestitel': Kak sozdannaya v 2016 godu kompaniya stala edinstvennym postavshchikom meditsinskogo plastika dlya rossiiskikh bol'nits. *Meduza.io*, 30 November.
Zvezdina, P., and A. Mogilevskaya. 2017. Veksel'bergu otkazali v monopolii. *RBC*, 16 February.
Zvezdina, P. 2014a. Bez posrednikov. *Farmatsevticheskii Vestnik* No. 32, 14 October.

Zvezdina, P. 2014b. Svyashchennaya vacca. *Farmatsevticheskii Vestnik* No. 18, May.

Zvezdina, P. 2016a. Boginya zachistki. *Farmatsevticheskii Vestnik* No. 19, 6 June.

Zvezdina. P. 2016b. Shpionskii most. *Farmatsevticheskii Vestnik* No. 13, 11 April.

Zvezdina, P. 2017. Eksperty predskazali sokrashchenie chisla bol'nits do urovnya 1913 goda. *RBC*, 7 April.

Zvezdina, P. 2018. Roszdravnadzor poimal 56 aptek na prodazhe zapreshchennykh lekarstv. *RBC*, 22 February.

Index

A
Abyzov, Mikhail, 17, 128
Accounts Chamber, 58, 64, 69, 135
  and All-Russian Popular Front, 22, 127
  and National Priority Projects in Health, 48, 162
Active pharmaceutical ingredients (APIs). *See* Import Substitution
Advisory Council of the Ministry of Health on HIV/AIDS, 103
Agents
  and bureaucratic gaming, 26, 72, 207
  and competence, 19, 49, 81, 84, 208
  and mission drifts, 25, 165
  and professional ethos, 13, 26, 101, 165
  as clients, 17
  as Mandarins, 24
  as Opportunists, 24, 25, 101
  as Vassals, 24, 43
  as Zealots, 24, 47, 101, 108

Akunin, Boris, 71
Alexy II, 164
Alliance of Doctors. *See* Fire alarms
All-Russian Popular Front (ONF)
  and Anisimov, Alexey, 131
  and external oversight, 22, 127, 131, 144
  and Govorukhin, Stanislav, 130
  and political control, 12, 205
  and social work, 176
  as governance intermediary, 15, 29, 109, 126, 127
Andrey Ryl'kov's Foundation, 168
Anisimov, Alexey. *See* All-Russian Popular Front (ONF)
Anti-Westernism. *See* Ideology
Arbidol, 67, 90, 96
Artemiev, Igor, 116
Authoritarianism, 3, 5, 8, 12, 14, 26, 27, 29, 43, 65, 84, 87, 117, 119, 123, 126, 140, 155, 190, 203, 209, 212, 214

© The Editor(s) (if applicable) and The Author(s), under exclusive license to Springer Nature Switzerland AG 2022
V. Kravtsov, *Autocracy and Health Governance in Russia*,
https://doi.org/10.1007/978-3-031-05789-2

B

Basic natural states. *See* States
Bekmambetov, Timur, 59
Belousov, Andrey, 204
Belozertsev, Ivan, 17
Belton, Catherine, 8, 9, 18, 158, 198, 210
Belyaninov, Andrey, 17
Belykh, Nikita, 83
Berdyaev, Nikolay, 157
Biotec. *See* Russian medical companies
Bogomolov, Konstantin, 159
Bolotnaya protests. *See* Legitimacy
Borzova, Olga, 106
Bryun, Evgeny, 172
Bureaucracy
  and personalized appointments, 83
  and state quality, 91
  and vulnerability, 144, 162
  Weberian bureaucracy, 13, 17
Bureaucratic mandates. *See* Mandates

C

Chaplin, Vsevolod, 177
Chazov, Evgeny, 137
Chemezov, Sergey, 9, 54, 86, 99, 100. *See also* Nacimbio; Rostec
Chereshnikov, Valery, 105
Cherkesov, Viktor, 167
Chilingarov, Artur, 105
Circle of Kindness, 70. *See also* Orphan diseases
Civic Forum, 127. *See also* Pavlovsky, Gleb
Coercion. *See* Regime
Color revolutions. *See* Regime
Competence-control theory. *See* Indirect governance
Constructivism, 165, 206
contractual state. *See* States
Copenhagen School. *See* Securitization

Corporate identity. *See* Personalization
Corporate vulnerability. *See* Personalization
Council for Strategic Development and Priority Projects, 62, 65, 84
COVID-19, 4, 15, 30, 66, 92, 93, 96, 124, 140, 142, 195, 211
Credible commitments. *See* Putin, Vladimir
Cystic fibrosis, 53. *See also* Public procurement

D

Davisha, Karen, 200. *See also* Kleptocracy
Decommodification of medicines. *See* Price controls
Delrus. *See* Russian medical companies
Developmentalism. *See* States
Direct Line with President Putin. *See* Putin, Vladimir
Dmitriev, Viktor, 50
Dominant coalition. *See* Regime
Dvorkovitch, Arkady, 98

E

Electoral authoritarianism. *See* Personalism
Electoral manipulation, 14, 157
Elites. *See* Regime
EpiVacCorona. *See* Vaccines
Erofeev, Viktor, 212
Essential Life Saving Medicines (ELSMs), 30, 31, 43, 50, 134, 194
  and import substitution, 42, 59, 134
  and shortages, 31

F

Federal AIDS Center, 171

Federal Antimonopoly Services (FAS), 51
Federal Drug Control Service (FSKN)
  and conflicts, 162–164
  and HIV/AIDS, 103
  and ROC, 165
Federal Taxation Services, 16, 200
Fire alarms
  and Alliance of Doctors, 126, 141, 142
  and failures, 21, 116, 129, 130
  and Golikova, Tayana, 96
  and nonstate actors, 103, 105, 129, 140, 165, 166, 182
  definition, 126
Furgal, Sergey, 83

G
Gaizer, Vyacheslav, 17
Gaming strategies
  and ideological adaptations, 25, 164
  in health outcomes, 193, 199
  in import substitution, 204
Gel'man, Vladimir, 5, 8, 106, 162, 198, 200, 214
Generics, 53, 55, 56, 97
Generium. *See* Import substitution
Gerasimova, Nadezhda, 105
Geropharm. *See* Russian medical companies
Getta, Anton, 134. *See also* All-Russian Popular Front (ONF)
Glazunov, Ilya, 196
Golikova, Tatyana
  and Arbidol, 90, 96
  and external health oversight, 32
  and internal health surveillance, 32, 145
  and NMC, 136–138
  and regulation, 121, 136
  and Russian medical companies, 122

See also Ministry of Health
Gorbachev, Mikhail, 207, 212
Governance
  and kleptocracy, 32, 184, 192, 197–199, 201
  bad governance, 4, 27, 88, 100, 108, 130, 190, 191, 193, 209, 213
  definition, 190
  goal convergence, 25
  good governance, 2, 4, 20, 26, 29, 31, 130, 191, 197, 212, 213
Governmental commission for the protection of public health, 103
Govorin, Nikolay. *See* All-Russian Popular Front (ONF)
Govorukhin, Stanislav. *See* All-Russian Popular Front (ONF)
Gref, German, 86, 146
Grishankov, Mikhail, 105–107
Gryzlov, Boris, 106, 128, 204
Gumilyov, Lev, 157

H
Harm reduction, 105, 166, 168, 173, 181
Heparin. *See* Shortages
HIV/AIDS, 30, 32, 90, 101, 102, 104–107, 122, 126, 153–155, 160, 161, 163–166, 168, 170–174, 176–178, 180–182, 195, 206–209

I
Ideological adaptations. *See* Gaming strategies
Ideology
  and anti-Westernism, 157
  and illiberalism, 156, 159
  and Izborsky Club, 159
  and militarism, 159

and Notebooks on Conservatism, 159
and traditional values, 159
its functions, 128
Ilyin, Ivan, 157
Import substitution
  and active pharmaceutical ingredients (APIs), 54
  and bureaucratic gaming, 26, 72, 208, 212
  and corruption, 83, 133
  and eculizumab, 58
  and Generium, 58
  and its outcomes, 42, 58, 60, 61
  and Manturov, Denis, 57, 58
  and medical devices, 43, 54–56, 59, 63, 66, 132, 133, 203
  and Minpromtorg, 55, 58, 59
  and monopolization, 54, 134
  and odd one out, 56
  and regulation, 43, 46, 51
  its political significance, 153
Incentive schemes
  and patron-client relationships, 20, 80
  and punishments, 17, 18, 72, 83, 88, 93, 108
  and Putin's governance, 42, 172
  and rewards for loyalty, 17, 19, 24, 25
Indirect governance
  and competence-control theory, 14, 20, 129
  and competence-control tradeoffs, 25
  and coopting intermediaries, 32, 145
  and delegation, 70
  and inversion of authority, 19, 87, 95
  and principal-agent theory, 16, 25, 85
  and trusteeship, 20, 129
Inducements
  and coercion, 6
  and ideology, 9
  material, 7, 11, 13, 14, 16, 24, 43, 46, 160
  non-material, 45
Informational autocracy. *See* Legitimacy
Institutional constraints. *See* Personalism
Insulin. *See* Shortages
Intermediaries
  and cooptation process, 22, 127, 131, 140, 145
  nonstate, 32, 126, 140
  quasi-state, 21, 127, 130, 146
International Treatment Preparedness Coalition (ITPC), 30, 142–144
Inversion of authority. *See* Indirect governance
Investigative Committee of the Russian Federation (SKR), 139
Ivanov, Sergey, 9
Ivanov, viktor, 165, 167

K
KGB, 9, 99
Khabriev, Ramil, 120
Kharitonin, Viktor, 96, 121. *See also* Pharmstandard
Khristenko, Viktor, 54
Kirill I, 175, 176
Kiriyenko, Sergey, 85, 89, 128, 131
Kiseleva, Alevtina, 68. *See also* Optimization
Kleptocracy, 32, 184, 192, 197–199, 201
Kozhokin, Evgeny, 173
Kudrin, Alexey, 16, 64

L

Lavrov, Sergey, 176
Legitimacy
  and acquiescence, 46
  and Bolotnaya protests, 157, 160
  and informational autocracy, 15, 158
  and social promises, 14, 49, 214
  definition and types, 44
  in personalistic regimes, 4, 11, 43, 117, 214
  performance-based legitimacy, 44, 49, 200
  rational-legal legitimacy, 14
Levi, Margaret, 15, 190, 199
Longin (Korchagin), 179
Losev, Aleksey, 157
Loyalty. *See* Putin, Vladimir
Lung ventilation devices, 57

M

Magnetic resonance imaging (MRI), 193
Magufuli, John, 11, 161
Mandarins. *See* Agents
Mandates
  and implementation, 13, 24, 63, 69, 70, 86, 101
  contradictory, 46, 47, 89
  definition and types, 47
  lopsided, 46, 47, 203
  microscale, 43, 47, 49, 68–70
  narrow, 13, 19, 84
Manturov, Denis, 57, 58. *See also* Import substitution; Minpromtorg
Manual control. *See* Putin, Vladimir
Matvienko, Valentina, 154
Mazus, Alexei, 172, 173
Medical oxygen. *See* Shortages
Medpolimerprom. *See* Russian medical companies

Medvedeva, Irina, 178
Medvedev, Dmitry, 15, 24, 54, 61, 82, 83, 97, 98, 104, 133, 168, 204
  and HIV/AIDS, 104
  as Vassal, 24
Medvedev, Sergey, 156
Mendelevich, Vladimir, 104, 171
Mezhregional'naya Deputatskaya Gruppa (MDG), 105, 106
Migranyan, Andranik, 2
Mikhailov, Alexey, 143
Mikhalkov, Nikita, 159
Milov, Vladimir, 212
Ministry of Culture, 159
Ministry of Health
  and bureaucratic gaming, 208
  and ELSMs, 50
  and Golikova, Tatyana, 90, 120
  and HIV/AIDS, 90, 103, 107, 161, 170
  and internal oversight, 120
  and international organizations, 174
  and regulation of medicines, 92
  and Skvortsova, Veronika, 63, 89
Minpromtorg, 50, 58, 59. *See also* Import substitution
Mishustin, Mikhail, 16, 200
Mission drifts. *See* Agents
Monopolies. *See* Russian medical companies
Murakhovsky, Alexander, 92
Murashko, Mikhail, 89, 116, 120, 122, 143

N

Nabiullina, Elvira, 16
Nacimbio. *See* Russian medical companies
National Medical Chamber (NMC)
  and ONF, 138

and SKR, 139
as governance intermediary, 137
National Priority Projects in Health
 and inefficiencies, 64, 88, 140, 194, 200
 and Medvedev, Dmitry, 61, 104
 and political agenda, 61, 62
 and Putin, Vladimir, 61, 65
 as pockets of efficiency, 60
 its outcomes, 48, 65, 84
Natural states. *See* States
Navalny, Alexey, 22, 52, 83, 92, 93, 117, 137, 138, 141, 142, 198, 212
Neoliberalism, 193, 194, 197, 201, 203, 205
Non-elites. *See* Regime
North, Douglas, 3

O

Odd-one out. *See* Import Substitution
Onishchenko, Gennady, 122, 123
Opportunists. *See* Agents
Optimization
 and its consequences, 3, 48
 and its implementation, 13
 and revenue-maximization, 64
 and rural outpatient clinics, 65
 and social protest, 108
 in Apatity (Murmansk oblast), 68
 in Strunino (Vladimir oblast), 69
Optimizing responses. *See* Personalism
Orlova, Svetlana. *See* Optimization
Orphan diseases, 55, 70, 96, 200
 and Circle of Kindness, 70
 and Zolgensma, 70
Orphan drugs, 55, 70

P

Patron-client relationship
 and bureaucratic competence, 16
 and codependence, 19, 81
 and regime survival, 43
 and rent-making, 56
 and rent-seeking, 17, 87
 and single-power pyramid, 82, 86
Pavlovsky, Gleb, 84, 94, 127
Pelevin, Viktor, 67
Performance-based indicators, 19
Performance-based legitimacy. *See* Legitimacy
Personalism
 and bad governance, 209
 and decision-making, 100, 190
 and electoral authoritarianism, 3, 5, 12, 14, 87, 190, 203
 and institutional constraints, 27, 212
 and negative equilibrium, 26
 and optimizing strategies, 130
 and social contracts, 14
 and weak institutionalization, 18, 95
 definition, 6
 personalized exchanges, 4, 10, 22, 24, 27, 82, 83, 86, 88, 117, 146, 156, 195
 tolerating bureaucratic gaming, 208
Personalization
 and corporate identity, 22, 117
 and corporate vulnerability, 165
 and intermediaries, 13, 19, 22–24, 26, 29, 92, 129, 130, 145, 146, 161, 190, 196
 definition and types, 6
Pharmstandard. *See* Russian medical companies
Piketty, Thomas, 198, 205
Pluralism by default, 213
Pokrovsky, Vadim, 106, 144, 171
Pokrovsky, Valentin, 171
Police patrols

and internal health surveillance
  organs, 118
and Popova, Anna, 123
and Rospotrebnadzor, 123
definition, 20
Polyvinyl chloride plastics (PVCs), 97
Popova, Anna, 123–125
Predatory state. *See* States
Presidential administration, 21–23,
  66, 70, 85, 118, 128–131, 134,
  138, 145
Price controls
  and decommodification of
    medicines, 15, 42
  and food items, 46
  and pharmaceuticals, 43, 49, 54,
    55, 57
Prigozhin, Yevgeny, 198
Primakov, Yevgeny, 203, 204
Principal, 8, 12, 13, 15–18, 20, 22,
  23, 25, 26, 31, 46, 48, 49, 58,
  59, 71, 72, 81, 85, 87–89, 91,
  94, 100, 101, 108, 109, 116,
  118, 122, 125, 126, 131, 135,
  136, 140, 145, 155, 162, 164,
  165, 169, 181, 190, 195, 196,
  198, 202, 208, 210
Principal-agent dilemma. *See* Indirect
  governance
Principal-agent theory. *See* Indirect
  governance
Public Chamber, 107, 127, 128, 136
Public goods, 2, 4, 25, 26, 42–44,
  85, 87, 95, 190, 193, 205
Public procurement
  and corruption, 132
  and cystic fibrosis, 52, 53
  and failed tenders, 52, 53
  and influvac, 52
  and law, 56
  and regulation, 51, 52
Pussy Riot, 157

Putin, Vladimir
  and commitment deficits, 15, 21,
    146
  and Direct Line with President
    Putin, 67
  and G-8, 101, 102
  and HIV/AIDS, 32, 90, 101–103,
    106, 122, 160, 163, 166, 170,
    181, 208
  and import substitution, 19, 42,
    46, 54–58, 62, 134, 212
  and loyalty, 19, 23, 24, 32, 49, 62,
    82, 91, 92, 126, 129, 183,
    196, 197, 214
  and manual control, 18, 31, 86, 94,
    95
  and May Decrees, 45, 132, 212
  and ONF, 56, 130–134, 146, 196
  and popularity, 7, 15, 19, 22, 65,
    67, 83, 86, 108, 130, 136,
    204, 214
  and Ukraine, 46, 123, 158, 169
  his ideological posturing, 24
  his mentality, 210

R
Rationalism, 28, 165
Regime
  and coercion, 6, 9, 14, 27, 214
  and color revolutions, 6, 83
  and dominant coalition, 7, 16, 80,
    91, 100
  and elites, 6, 7, 9–11, 17, 23–27,
    32
  and non-elites, 6, 7, 10, 11, 20, 21,
    26, 45, 117, 118, 159–161,
    208
  and revenue-maximization, 64, 68
  and siloviki, 9, 12, 23
  and subservience, 12, 27, 191, 196
  definition and types, 2, 4, 5, 193

Rent-making. *See* Patron-client relationship
Rent-Seeking. *See* Patron-client relationship
Repik, Alexey, 96, 97. *See also* R-Pharm
Revenue-maximization, 64, 66. *See also* Regime
and optimization, 64
Revolution of Dignity. *See* Ukraine
Roldugin, Sergey, 198
Romanov, Vladimir, 105, 169
Roshal, Leonid
and Navalny's poisoning, 92, 138
and NMC, 136–139
his critique of health governance, 90
Rospil, 137
Rospotrebnadzor, 105, 119, 120, 122–125
Rostec, 54, 94, 99
Roszdrav, 119, 120
Roszdravnadzor, 119–122
R-Pharm. *See* Russian medical companies
Russian Institute of Strategic Studies (RISI), 172
Russian medical companies
and corruption, 93, 121, 125, 133, 137
and monopolies, 86, 87, 94, 95, 97, 99
Biotec, 121
Delrus, 94
Geropharm, 94
Medpolimerprom, 94, 97, 98
Nacimbio, 60, 99
Pharmstandard, 96, 121
R-Pharm, 97
Stentex, 97, 98
Russian Orthodox Church (ROC)
and HIV/AIDS, 161, 165

and rechurching, 176
and traditional values, 154

S
Sechin, Igor, 9, 86
Securitization
and bureaucratic gaming, 208
and FSKN, 161, 162, 164–166, 180, 207
and ideology, 156, 164
and Ministry of Health, 155, 161, 162, 164, 166, 170, 175, 180–182, 207
and ROC, 165
Copenhagen School, 206
securitization theory, 206
Shchedrovitsky, Georgy, 85
Shevchenko, Yury, 90
Shishova, Tatyana, 178, 179
Shortages
and ELSMs, 31, 134, 194
of antiretrovirals, 170, 199
of heparin, 52
of hospital beds, 42, 195, 203
of insulin, 52
of medical oxygen, 67, 142, 194
of personnel, 66
Shpigel, Boris. *See* Biotec
Siloviki. *See* Regime
Single-power pyramid. *See* Patron-client relationships
Sipyagin, Vladimir. *See* Optimization
Skvortsova, Veronika, 63, 69, 89, 90, 107, 137. *See also* Ministry of Health
Snyder, Timothy, 5, 157, 158
Social contract. *See* Personalism
Stanovaya, Tatyana, 17, 82
Starikova, Darya. *See* Optimization
State Council, 63, 92, 101, 178
State Duma, 2, 12, 30, 58, 69, 105, 106, 116, 121, 163

States
   basic natural states, 7, 21, 117
   contractual state, 27
   developmentalism, 10
   natural states, 7, 21, 117
   predatory state, 15, 64
   state autonomy, 2
   state capacity, 4, 19, 42, 44, 67, 95, 128, 145, 194, 195
   state quality, 91, 145
Stebenkova, Lyudmila, 172
Stentex. *See* Russian medical companies
Storchak, Sergey, 17
street-level bureaucrats, 21, 27, 93, 122, 163
Surkov, Vladislav, 10, 130, 156, 157

T
Tel'nova, Elena, 120, 121
Tikhon (Shevkunov), 179
Traditional values. *See* Ideology
Trusteeship. *See* Indirect governance
Tsargrad-TV, 159
Tsvetkov, Nikolay, 178
Tsyb, Sergey, 58

U
Ukraine
   and narcotics, 166, 168
   and Yanukovich, Viktor, 169
   Revolution of Dignity, 169
Ulyukaev, Alexey, 17
United Russia, 7, 8, 12, 43, 82, 131, 137, 157, 176

V
Vaccines
   and corruption, 93
   and Putin, 42
   EpiVacCorona, 125
   Sputnik-V, 42
Valdai Club, 203
Vancomycin, 67
Vasilyeva, Anastasiya, 142. *See also* Alliance of Doctors
Vassals. *See* Agents
VECTOR (State Research Center of Virology and Biotechnology), 124
Vekselberg, Viktor, 98. *See also* Stentex
Volodin, Vyacheslav, 2, 128, 130, 131, 191
Voronkova, Eva, 53

W
Weak institutionalization. *See* Personalism
Weberian bureaucracy. *See* Bureaucracy

Y
Yakovleva, Tatyana, 172
Yakunin, Vladimir, 80, 179
Yanukovich, Viktor. *See* Ukraine
Yeltsin, Boris, 9, 23
Yurgel, Nikolay, 120, 121

Z
Zealots. *See* Agents
Zolgensma, 70
Zubov, Valery, 105
Zurabov, Mikhail, 90, 163

Printed by Printforce, the Netherlands